THE B-2 BOMBER

Air Power for the 21st Century

Edited by
Keith Payne
and
John J. Kohout, III

University Press of America, Inc.
Lanham • New York • London

and the

National Institute for
Public Policy

Copyright © 1995 by
National Institute for Public Policy

University Press of America®, Inc.
4720 Boston Way
Lanham, Maryland 20706

3 Henrietta Street
London WC2E 8LU England

All rights reserved
Printed in the United States of America
British Cataloging in Publication Information Available

Copublished by arrangement with
the National Institute for Public Policy

Library of Congress Cataloging-in-Publication Data

The B-2 bomber: strategic utility for the twenty-first century / Keith
    B. Payne [et al.]. p. cm.
    Includes bibliographical references.
    1. B-2 bomber. 2. Air power—United States 3. United
    States—Military policy. I. Payne, Keith B.
UG1242.B6B24   94-30902
358.4'283—dc20   CIP

ISBN 0-8191-9736-X (cloth: alk paper)
ISBN 0-8191-9737-8 (pbk.: alk paper)

Printed in the United States of America

⊖™ The paper used in this publication meets the minimum
requirements of American National Standard for Information
Sciences—Permanence of Paper for Printed Library Materials,
ANSI Z39.48–1984.

Contents

Introduction: The B-2 Bomber: A Study in Future Strategic Utility vii

Chapter 1: Modern Long-Range, Land-Based Bombers in the New Security
    Environment 1
    Colin S. Gray and John J. Kohout III
    The Pieces of the Puzzle 1
    The New Security Environment 3
    U.S. Roles in the New Security Environment 7
    Conditions that Generate Demand for Modern Long-Range, Land-Based
    Bomber Forces 8
    Regional Aggression 12
    Local Disorder 12
    Transnational, Non-Traditional "Security" Threats 13
    International Emergencies 13

Chapter 2: America's Option: The Long-Range, Land-Based Bomber 15
    Steven J. Lambakis
    Early Developments 15
    World War II 16
    The Bomber and the Beginning of the Cold War 21
    The Korean War 22
    The Vietnam War 24
    Crises and Deterrence Missions 28
    The 1991 Gulf War and Subsequent U.S. Policy 32
    Conclusion 36

Chapter 3: Defense Planning and the Modern Long-Range Bomber 39
    Colin S. Gray and John J. Kohout III
    Principles for Successful Defense Planning 39
    U.S. Forces Should Be... 41
    Long-range Bomber Missions and the Threats of the 1990's 50
    Modern Long-Range, Land-Based Bombers and National Security Policy . 55

Chapter 4: Access, Basing and the Reach of U.S. Combat Power 57
    John J. Kohout III
    Central America/Caribbean 61
    South America 64
    North Africa 69
    Sub-Saharan Africa 73
    Middle East 77
    The Levant 82
    Central Asia 85

Chapter 4: (cont'd)
    Eastern Europe 87
    Southeast Asia 89
    East Asia 92
    South Asia 95
    Global Commons 98
    Conclusions 100

Chapter 5: The B-2 and the U.S. Domestic Politics 103
    Bernard C. Victory
    The B-2 in the Executive Branch 103
    The B-2 in the Congress 104
    Party Positions on B-2 106
    Congressional Leadership and the B-2 109
    Clinton Administration Perspectives 113
    Bomber Issues in 1994–1995 115
    Conclusions 120

Chapter 6: The B-2 and the U.S. Defense-Industrial Base 123
    Bernard C. Victory and John J. Kohout III

Chapter 7: Stealth in Context 135
    John J. Kohout III
    The Nature of "Stealth" 136
    The Submarine Precedent 137
    Options for Reducing Detectability 138
    The Operational Potential of Stealth 144

Chapter 8: The Cost-Effectiveness of the B-2 Bomber 161
    Steven J. Lambakis and John J. Kohout III
    Key Attributes of the B-2 162
    Potential Applications of the B-2 173
    B-2 Versus Aircraft Carrier Cost-Effectiveness 182
    B-2 Production Cost-Effectiveness 184

Chapter 9: Conclusion: The Question of Numbers 189
    Reopen the B-2 Production Issue? 190
    How Many B-2s Should the United States Produce? 197

Endnotes 203

About the Authors 233

Tables and Figures

Figure 1: The Structure of the Problem 2
Figure 2: Sources of Demand for U.S. Long-Range Bomber Employment .. 11
Figure 3: Military Power in Support of U.S. Foreign Policy 40
Figure 4: Regional Conflict Locations 58
Figure 5: Air Force Power Projection Aircraft Comparative Unrefueled Combat Radii 60
Figure 6: The Value of Stealth 112
Figure 7: U.S. Long-Range Bomber Forces, 1946 to 1999 116
Figure 8: B-2 Worldwide Power Projection 156
Figure 9: B-2 Range and Responsiveness 167
Figure 10: Contribution to GPS-Aided Attack Made Possible by B-2 Avionics 172

Table 1: Gulf War Aerial Refueling 79
Table 2: Regional Basing Summary 102
Table 3: B-2 Conventional Weapons 164
Table 4: Radar Cross Sections 166
Table 5: Conventional Firepower of the Future U.S. Bomber Force 180

Introduction

The B-2 Bomber:
A Study in Future Strategic Utility

This monograph undertakes a systematic review of the future strategic utility of an existing force structure element, the B-2 Advanced Technology Bomber, and the capability it represents. It is intended to serve as a case study of the type of analysis that should precede, trigger, and sustain force structure decisions in this period of great change in the international security environment.

The B-2 possesses potential utility across a wide range of conflict levels; has evident utility in operations focused on land, sea, or in the atmosphere; does not find its utility jeopardized by withdrawal of foreign support to U.S. operations; is not already approaching the end of its service life; and is seen by the American public and government as embodying an acceptable and appropriate form of military capability. In and of themselves, these criteria say nothing about the relative utility of the one force element and technology selected for review versus any other, but they do combine to highlight a weapon system that should remain in active consideration throughout any near-term review of future U.S. force structure and exercise fully the analysis presented here.

The B-2 bomber is the most advanced of an entire class of weapons systems—long-range, land-based strike aircraft—which are uniquely suited to strategic geography that the United States cannot change and future strategic challenges that the United States must answer. Such weapons have been employed in raids, regional conflicts, major conventional wars and superpower confrontation. The long-range bomber has a long history of contributing to land campaigns, naval operations and offensive counter-air operations. It is global in its ability to influence an enemy and relatively insensitive to the location of enemy assets or the availability of forward basing. Furthermore the B-2 is well differentiated from other systems in the same class in terms of future relevance. The B-52 has been phasing out for over 28 years [1]. The B-1, procured as an interim system, relies on high speed and an extremely low altitude penetration tactic that unavoidably stresses aircraft structure and tends to render service life extension beyond the system's designed life time problematical. Thus the long-range bomber in general, and the B-2 in particular, is well suited as a vehicle for exploring the rationale and criteria for the future strategic utility of today's weapons systems.

This monograph proposes to address weapon system utility in terms tailored to the defense and policy environments likely to pertain through the 1990's and beyond. It emphasizes the policy demand that the United States is likely to place on its military forces in the new security environment and how that demand meshes with the characteristics of particular weapons systems. This analysis undertakes the development of eight areas, each the focus of one chapter, from broad observations about the international security environment and domestic attitudes to more detailed aspects of defense decision-making and the specific formulation of defense program initiatives.

(1) The utility of a specific defense capability, long-range attack aviation in the form of the B-2 in this case, is developed in terms of U.S. policy and strategy needs of the 1990's and beyond. Aspects of this discussion address features of the new environment, levels of conflict likely to be encountered, the international role or roles the United States is likely to choose for itself over the coming decades, and conditions likely to trigger decisions to use its military power.

(2) Debate over alternative defense options takes place in a historically conditioned setting consisting of popular attitudes about suitable ways to prepare for and deter war. This chapter assembles the history of cases where the United States chose to employ bomber forces and develops and assesses the reasons for the bomber's status as a favored weapon system. These arguments emphasize perceptions about geography, geostrategy and larger moral and policy issues faced by the American democracy in confronting external dangers, and devising appropriate, effective, and broadly acceptable approaches to going to war and shaping a war-winning strategy.

(3) Enduring lessons from contemporary and historical military experience are presented here in the form of thirteen principles for successful defense planning. These principles illuminate the characteristics of long-range bomber forces across the full range of military operational and force planning and help to probe the B-2's potential for contributing to success in war or deterrence.

(4) It is uncertain where specific conflicts engaging U.S. interests will occur. Thus it is important to develop a concise characterization of the global

access and basing challenges the coming decades hold for U.S. forces. This provides a context for judgments about the relative significance of a force element's ability to operate globally without dependence on forward basing or extensive, in-theater support infrastructure.

(5) Pressures for rationalizing the U.S. defense establishment and a shifting of priorities toward domestic programs following the fall of the Berlin Wall have stimulated probing reviews by Congressional leaders and defense decision-makers. While only beginning the formulation of new concepts for deriving the U.S. requirement for military capabilities and force structure, defense leaders in the Congress and uniformed military already have gone far toward setting the terms of the debate and creating the language in which the debate is engaged. Key themes elaborated by Congressional leaders have particular relevance to decisions concerning the B-2 and the future roles the nation chooses to assign to its weapons systems. These are assembled to help frame a policy-relevant understanding of the strategic utility of modern bomber forces.

(6) As the nation draws down its defense investment, decisions about what forces it buys and how it buys them become more important. The availability of alternative military technologies reflect the relative efficiency with which U.S. technological leadership and economic strength can be converted into military power. This chapter helps to address investment strategies for the maintenance of required military power as both spending and force structure are reduced. By addressing the efficiency with which national treasure can be converted to alternative military force structures that serve strategically effective missions, it sheds light on one important aspect of deciding among qualitative alternatives.

(7) The exploration of specific technological bases for tactical advantage and strategic utility is the next dimension of this study. "Stealth," the technological key to our B-2 example, will be considered less as an absolute attribute of weapon systems than as one attribute among many that interact and must be weighed together in estimating both current combat effectiveness and the length of anticipated service life. This aspect of the analysis explores the significance of specific technological advantages, in this case low observable characteristics.

(8) The dollar costs of the B-2 and how they compare with the costs of alternative systems must be addressed directly. Understanding the economics of the B-2 has become a prerequisite for informed decisions on further B-2 production. Regardless of the strategic utility sought from a larger fleet of B-2s, a strong argument must made that production beyond the original twenty can be undertaken with high confidence in both quality and predictability of unit cost.

(9) The monograph concludes with a summation of the findings of each chapter. The conclusion is inescapable: Some level of continued B-2 production, which the American people can afford, is critical to ensuring that the United States has the military reach and striking power in the future to protect its global interests.

Chapter 1
Modern Long-Range, Land-Based Bombers in the New Security Environment

COLIN S. GRAY AND JOHN J. KOHOUT III

This analysis explores the role and strategic utility of modern long-range, land-based bomber forces as an instrument of U.S. policy, grand strategy, and military strategy in the new security environment of the 1990's. Domestic and international change (political, economic, social, military) is assumed; the issue is one of finding and applying a defense policy and approach that are robust in the face of uncertainty. In brief, the challenge is to identify the role of bomber forces in the new security environment: *given* what we know about bomber forces; *given* the enduring nature of American political and strategic culture; and *given* recurring patterns of conflict, domestic and international.

The Pieces of the Puzzle

Arguably, the problem in the 1990's is less to divine the shape and workings of the emerging security environment than to determine what role or roles the United States will want to play in it. That is the proper context for analysing future demand for the services of any military force element. Frequently, advocates and detractors of contending force alternatives describe the capabilities in question, characterize the shape of the security world to be, but fail to connect the two in any intelligible way. For the puzzle to be assembled so as to constitute a coherent picture, none of the principal pieces must be neglected. Figure 1 illustrates this line of thinking.

Figure 1: The Structure of the Problem

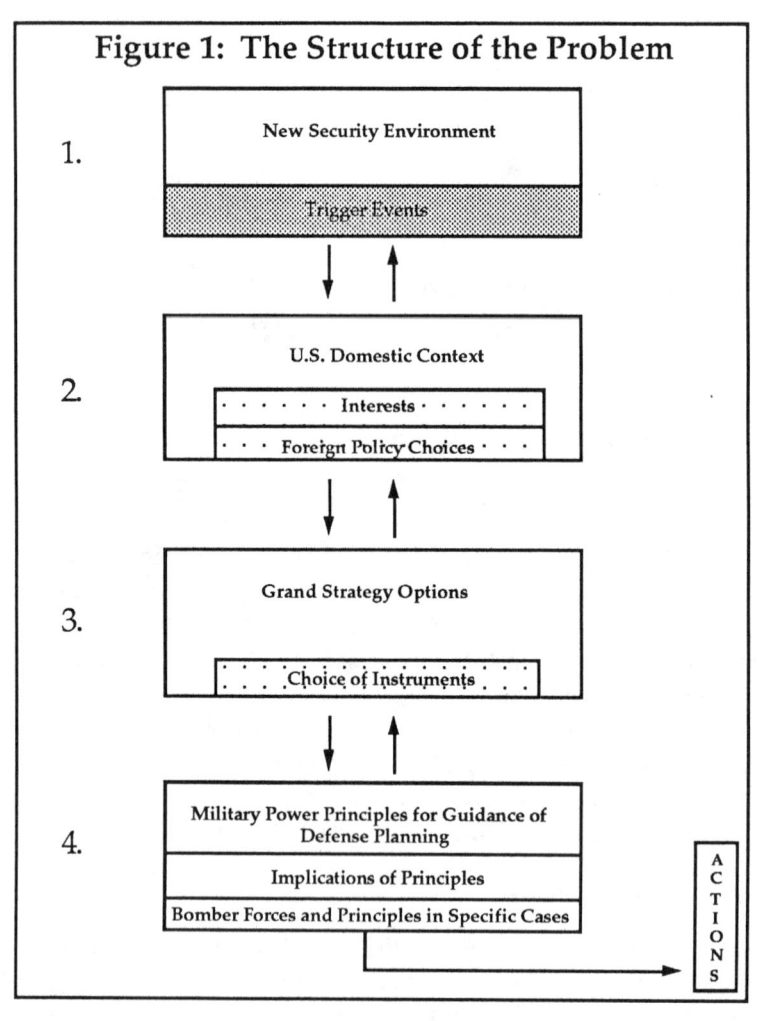

1. New Security Environment
   Trigger Events

2. U.S. Domestic Context
   Interests
   Foreign Policy Choices

3. Grand Strategy Options
   Choice of Instruments

4. Military Power Principles for Guidance of Defense Planning
   Implications of Principles
   Bomber Forces and Principles in Specific Cases

ACTIONS

In and of themselves, the new security environment, the changing U.S. domestic context, and the evolving capabilities of U.S. military power (including modern bombers), each will lack a more general meaning. For example, to observe the former Yugoslavia in a condition of complex civil/international war is not to identify the relevant strand in U.S. foreign policy. Similarly, to note what U.S. military power could do in a specific case is not synonymous with high-policy choice. Naturally, capability influences decisions on behavior, just as foreign misbehavior influences foreign policy choices. But, still, a critical filter is absent. That traditionally is called the national interest.

It is commonplace to find assertions that national interests are at risk; it is much less commonplace to find consensus over how important they are and how much they are at risk and, as a consequence, what ought to be done about it. Statements on the subject of preferred action should also be related to the belief that suitable instruments of grand strategy are available to be used. The pieces of the puzzle addressed here can be expressed in the form of these questions:

- What is happening in the world (new security environment)?
- How much does the United States care about a particular development or event (national interest analysis)?
- Shall the United States act—and to accomplish what? (foreign policy choice)?
- What instrument or instruments of policy shall be used (grand strategy)?
- If the military instrument is used, what role, if any, should modern long-range bomber forces play, and why (military power and its desirable characteristics--particularly the characteristics and capabilities of B-2-class bombers)?

The array of uncertainties is formidable indeed. Those uncertainties appear as problems or as opportunities. Specifically, there are uncertainties about the still very dynamic new security environment, U.S. foreign policy (in detail), and the resources that the United States will allocate for defense. It is quite apparent, however, that today's defense planner knows a great deal about the world outside the United States, about his own country, and about the strengths and limitations of military power in general and bomber force structure in particular.

The New Security Environment

It is important to begin this analysis with frank recognition of a key unknown, even unknowable, quality to this era. Namely, are the 1990's a post-war or an inter-war, and hence pre-war period? In 1919, Great Britain adopted the assumption that it would not be involved in a major war for ten years; this Ten Year Rule enjoyed official blessing until 1932 [2]. Today, it is no exaggeration to say that there is a broad consensus in the United States for such a Ten Year Rule, while many people probably would be willing to sign-on for twenty- or even thirty-year variants, and a few nurture the conviction that major war truly is obsolescent, if not obsolete. It may be of interest to note that several times in American history an extravagantly optimistic view of a peaceful future for the nation has been popular. The 1870's and 1920's provide leading examples of the recurring popularity of this belief. Nothing in the past actually proves anything about the future, since the course of history is unique and deeply contingent. Nonetheless, an awareness of history at least should encourage some humility and caution in the face of the temptation to predict a radically different future.

Popular democracies perennially have great difficulty keeping their swords sharp in a long period of peace. There are several examples in American history of the U.S. armed forces descending from the first rank in quantity and quality to near impotence in a handful of years. The 1990's may well be different, but the willingness of a democracy to reduce its ready military prowess in the absence of a clear and present danger should never be underestimated. If more and more people, quite possibly for apparently good reasons, slip into the column of endorsing a Ten-Year Rule, the U.S. armed forces increasingly will reflect the fact.

If the utility of modern U.S. bomber forces in the new security environment must flow from responses to the demands placed by high policy, what are the more important features of that still-emerging environment?

1. Continuity in goals and methods of statecraft. Without denying the fact of massive cumulative change in the structure of the international system, there is no evidence to suggest that the basic character of international politics is in transition to some new order. Time after time in international history, old "orders" have gone and new "orders" have come. The teaming arrangements may be different in the 1990's from the Cold War era, but there is every reason to believe that the "game" of security politics will continue along lines, for goals, and by methods that are long familiar. Above all else, the use or threat of force and the value of alliance, as contrasted with genuinely collective (universal) security guarantees, are not in general decline. If anything, military force may well be deemed more useful as a tool of statecraft in this post-Cold War era than was the case from 1945-90, given the reduced likelihood that recourse to force will escalate to strategic nuclear war.

Implications for modern long-range, land-based bomber forces: While the possibility of a global war involving high-intensity conflict appears to have evaporated, there are significant prospects for U.S. participation in mid- and lower-intensity conflicts for which bomber forces remain useful.

2. Superpower and great power political-military rivalry is absent. This is a historically unique condition. It is unprecedented in modern times for there to be effectively no political-military antagonism among the great powers. Realistically viewed, the great powers of the 1990's—forgetting formal membership on the U.N. Security Council—are the United States, Russia, China, Germany, and Japan. With the minor exceptions of some border controversies between China and Russia, and Japan and Russia, there are no very meaningful strategic relations among these polities, let alone political-military antagonisms. The ongoing Russian revolution has caused the international security system familiar for nearly half a century to unravel. Many plausible possibilities exist for the return of balance-of-power security politics, but at this time of writing the pattern of future rivalry is not predictable in detail. The capabilities for provocative behavior, however, along with political motive and historical opportunity, will be present in abundance in Europe and Asia.

Implications for modern long-range, land-based bomber forces: The absence of super or even great-power rivals to the United States in these early 1990's should mean that the deterrence role for bomber forces will change, with the traditional nuclear delivery function being supplanted, though not superceded entirely, by conventional capabilities.

    3. United States as the solitary superpower. There is a sense in which the United States always was the only multi-dimensional, "full-service" superpower. With the Cold War interred and the principal adversary of yesteryear consigned to history, there is a non-trivial possibility that the United States inadvertently may contribute to the losing of the peace, notwithstanding having just won the (cold) war. Far from succumbing to some alleged "imperial temptation" [3], it is much more likely that in the absence of a clear and present great-power danger the United States will behave as if a permanent peace has been founded. Americans have an admirable track record in undertaking and succeeding with great enterprises, but their performance of tasks that call for finesse and subtlety has been less assured [4]. The United States has become used to enjoying hegemonic security relationships; first in the Americas, then globally. The idea of exercising a rather subtle cooperative, consensual guardianship over an international system struggling to settle upon new patterns of security is not an idea that sits well with American taxpayers. It is one thing to organize, lead, arm and partially bankroll a global alliance against the "evil empire" of the U.S.S.R. It is quite something else to play the role of helpful guardian to economic rivals (*inter alia*) who are striving, in part, to liberate themselves from their condition of being dependent on the U.S. superpower!

Implications for modern long-range, land-based bomber forces: Since U.S. foreign and defense policy lack a dominant functional or regional focus, the capabilities of U.S. air power must be global. Given the versatility, readiness, flexibility, and particularly range of modern bomber forces, the fact of a disparate array of actual or potential duties adds to the potential value of these forces. The domestic constraints upon U.S. military operations will similarly add value to the flexibility of modern bomber forces.

4. **Increase in regional and local instability.** The ending of the Cold War in so rapid and thoroughgoing a manner inevitably has transformed Europe from geopolitically the most stable continent to one of the least stable. Indeed, even the basic geopolitical terms of forty-five years no longer apply. In the Middle East, as in Europe, the good news—that Soviet/Russian policy is no longer contributing to regional instability—is offset to some degree by the bad news that the former bloc alliances are no longer restraining regional clients. At the present time such trend as there has been towards democracy in formerly Soviet Europe, in Africa, and Central and South America, looks distinctly patchy, fragile, and generally reversible.

Implications for modern long-range, land-based bomber forces: The facts of, and trends in, disorder and instability are undeniable; regional and local instability is rising rather than declining. U.S. bomber forces offer the potential of conducting potent military activity according to the geography and logistical constraints of the region without actually stationing forces in the region, or putting sailors or ground forces at risk. For example, air operations have been repeatedly suggested as an appropriate response by those who seek a wider role in the on-going Balkan Wars.

5. **Proliferation of high-technology weaponry, including weapons of mass destruction (nuclear, biological, and chemical or NBC weapons).** Proliferation threatens to undermine stability in regions where the United States has interests and place at risk deployed U.S. forces or those of our allies. In the immediate aftermath of the Cold War there is a global surplus of high-technology weapons and weapon-making industrial capacity. The plain facts are that the world is well stocked with weapons suppliers eager to sell, regional and local powers eager to purchase, and unscrupulous middlemen of all kinds [5].

Implications for modern long-range, land-based bomber forces: Long-range bomber operations have long been actions of choice against enemy weapons and productive capacity. Destruction of these targets was the major objective of the World War II Combined Bomber Offensive and the bombing campaign against Japan. In a more contemporary example, Iraq's missile and NBC weapons capabilities were targeted in a series of air operations. The Israeli Air Force mounted a uniquely focussed attack on Iraq's embryonic nuclear capability with its June 7, 1981 raid on the Osirak reactor. A decade later in the course of the Persian Gulf War, major objectives of the Coalition bombing campaign included the destruction of NBC production and storage facilities.

6. **America "comes home."** It is undeniable that the 1990's are witnessing a greater concentration of American political energy on domestic than

on foreign matters. The "come home" theme is in good measure both inevitable and highly desirable in the wake of success in the Cold War and changing economic relationships. As noted already, the pace and breadth of U.S. national security adjustment to the ending of the Cold War, closing of bases overseas, and return of forces to the United States, have been as responsibly deliberate as anyone could ask.

Implications for modern long-range, land-based bomber forces: The process of American military reconcentration at home, in the context of cumulatively large force-level reductions, should have the effect of enhancing the relative strategic utility of modern bomber forces. Modern bombers are flexible in employment, capable of penetrating likely enemy defenses, and designed to deliver great fire power rapidly over long distances. The fact that U.S. general purpose forces will be less readily available for employment in large numbers on quite short notice around the periphery of Eurasia suggests that the requirements for the capabilities inherent in modern bomber forces will increase.

U.S. Roles in the New Security Environment

At this juncture it is necessary to proceed beyond trend identification and specify the following: first, the U.S. role in the world of the 1990's; second, the global insecurity conditions likely to generate U.S. policy and strategy demand for military action in the form of long-range bomber operations; and third, classes of plausible "trigger" events that might lead to U.S. employment of modern bomber forces.

Some critics of recent U.S. foreign policy have lamented what they discern to be a gaping hole at its center. Their error lies in misunderstanding the most fundamental, yet still relevant, level of policy determination. Specifically, the Cold War policy of "Containment" was only a derivative instrumental concept and doctrine for policy guidance. Why was the Soviet Union to be contained? Because that state, with its aggressive designs, brutal regime, and malign ideology, threatened to dominate much of Europe and Asia. Viewed in this way the end of the Cold War does not leave the United States floundering in the absence of an organizing principle. The organizing principle still holds sway, as it always has: to prevent, oppose, or correct imbalances of power likely to imperil U.S. security. At the present time, the Soviet Union has not been succeeded in U.S. threat estimation by a foe of anything approaching similar capabilities.

The United States, by virtue of its size, power potential, and recent history, is the principal guardian of the democratic, free-trade vision of world order. Key to the structure of this order is a basic network of power relationships that favors the United States. In the medium term, the leading menace to this still early post-Cold War order will be the emergence or reemergence of centers of power able to present clear and present dangers of regional hegemony. As many people have noticed recently, the United States is seen internationally as the guardian against regional aggression.

Different Americans, and possibly different American political parties, may phrase the argument presented here in distinctive ways. The argument will remain the same, however, virtually regardless of who wins presidential and congressional elections through this decade. The core of the argument is as follows:

- The defining concept of the U.S. role in the world in this decade is that of chief guardian of a global democratic, free market order.
- The principal menace to that global order will be the actual or potential rise of new, or revived centers of power, which will threaten regional imbalances of power.
- As the only possible guardian of last, and often even of first, resort the United States will need to play a vigilant multi-regional role.
- America's reputation as a just and reliable protector will be critical for her "creditworthiness" in support of regional security and stability.
- Because of the U.S. global security role as guardian of "order," individual Americans and their assets will have merit as hostages and targets in the eyes of some of the envious, the angry, and the ambitious. In principle, Americans and American assets are worth imperiling precisely because the United States is a country whose policy is worth influencing.

Conditions that Generate Demand for Modern Long-Range, Land-Based Bomber Forces

Although the United States has been bequeathed by historical accident the leading guardianship role for international order and civilized values and a geographic setting that contributes to the utility of long-range combat aircraft, she is not the world's policeman. The external conditions of actual or predicted disorder that might lead to licensed American bomber activity have to be conditions that positively engage three decision rules which tend to drive U.S. decisions to employ force. First, does a potentially menacing imbalance of power loom as a distinct possibility? Second, is U.S. reputation involved in the matter at issue? Third, are Americans or American assets directly at risk?

Illustrative "trigger" events that could produce bomber operations are suggested below. What matters at this juncture in the discussion is to make sense of the emerging new security environment with reference to setting the parameters for detailed argument and suggestions. What follows are not predictions of due events to come. Rather, this is a terse synthesis of historical evidence, current features, and apparent trends. The purpose is to identify the conditions in the 1990's and beyond under which modern U.S. bomber forces should seem to policymakers and defense planners to provide useful answers.

1. Regional Aggression. Even in the absence of a superpower rivalry, regional disorder may have wide implications. Few cases of regional aggression will be as manifestly licensing of U.S. military action as was Saddam Hussein's bid for glory in 1990-91; but that case should serve as a wake-up call to those who saw the future and found it to be peaceful: There are many possible regional, even local, crises that predictably would engage U.S. national interests intensely.

Regional disorder in the Caribbean and Central America, for example, are close to home for the United States, and are regions characterized by long traditional American guardianship. Or consider the Arab-Israeli dispute. Standard national-interest analysis does not function in this case. Were Israel's existence threatened, the United States would likely fight to protect her. More to the point for the limited purpose of this discussion, the United States is engaged in the Middle East in the linked and tension-ridden roles of honest-broker-peacemaker and last-ditch guarantor of Israel. For America's support of the "peace process" to be effective, it must repose upon a far more substantial manifestation of U.S. power than artful and energetic diplomacy and the granting of economic assistance. The military arm of U.S. power is crucial, particularly the potential for applying force quickly without extensive preliminary deployments to the region.

Regional disorder must engage U.S. national interests. The reason is often not so much because of the immediate stakes in the conflicts at issue, but rather because of the potential effect of regional, or local, crises upon possible great power antagonisms and upon the terms of conflict more broadly. Specifically, when aggression goes unrestrained, let alone unpunished, that visible fact must encourage provocation elsewhere. (Given the changing borders of the former Soviet Union and the other irredenta that litter the map of Central, Eastern and Southern Europe, the importance of this topic would be difficult to exaggerate). Also, the use of weapons of mass destruction in a regional conflict must help erode the norms against employing such weapons.

2. **Local disorder.** The regional problems that can have global ramifications always have local roots. Local disorder, however, can manifest itself in the seizure of American hostages or property, can attract predatory neighbors, and may engage world attention on moral grounds. The issue for the remainder of the 1990's is not whether there will be conditions of local disorder from Bosnia to Peru, but whether those local conditions are likely to generate a policy response by the United States that includes bomber operations. No coherent detailed answer can possibly be provided here (or anywhere else), but it is safe to argue that single-country, local disorder is likely to generate demand for a response including bomber operations only when much broader issues are at stake.

3. **Transnational, non-traditional "security" threats.** This third category of conditions in the 1990's likely to generate demand for the employment of U.S. military action that may involve bombardment operations refers to such problems as drugs, international/transnational organized crime, terrorism of all kinds, and even economic "warfare." The importance of these security threats is relative to what else is threatening the country. Compared with categories one and two above, this third class of problems fades rapidly in significance. Nonetheless, it does present a set of challenges to which some modern bomber force qualities are uniquely (among military agents) suited. The leading role in each of the non-traditional issue-areas cited here plainly has to be taken by police forces, U.S. and foreign. When such threats are state-sponsored, however, more conventional force employment is implied, and raiding operations by long-range, land-based bombers become a distinctly valuable alternative. The 1986 air strike campaign on Libya is a clear historical example. Conventional military capabilities will increasingly be needed in the 1990's as a complement to traditional police and military methods chosen to address these threats. Intervention at such a level will not be required very often to solve problems created by drug lords or terrorists, but when that policy requirement comes down, there is likely to be no acceptable substitute for bomber operations.

4. **International Emergencies.** Emergencies come in different sizes, but they have the common characteristic of erupting with little or no warning. Many kinds of military organizations could be useful in national human-political emergencies, but bomber forces enjoy the obvious advantages of range, flexibility, rapidity of response, and massive fire power likely to impose the desired effect. The point is not to claim that bomber forces are uniquely useful in emergency conditions, which would not be true. It is to claim that for *many* international emergencies, the existence of long-range, land-based bomber assets provides a "high end" alternative that has both existential and operational utility.

Further, it is safe to claim that politically and naturally created emergencies will occur throughout the 1990's. In this post-Cold War era, there will be fewer inhibitions both upon those in need calling the United States, and upon the United States being willing to respond without fear of adverse regional or global consequences.

What events plausibly could trigger decisions by the United States to employ her modern long-range, land-based bomber forces? The structure of this question is outlined in Figure 2.

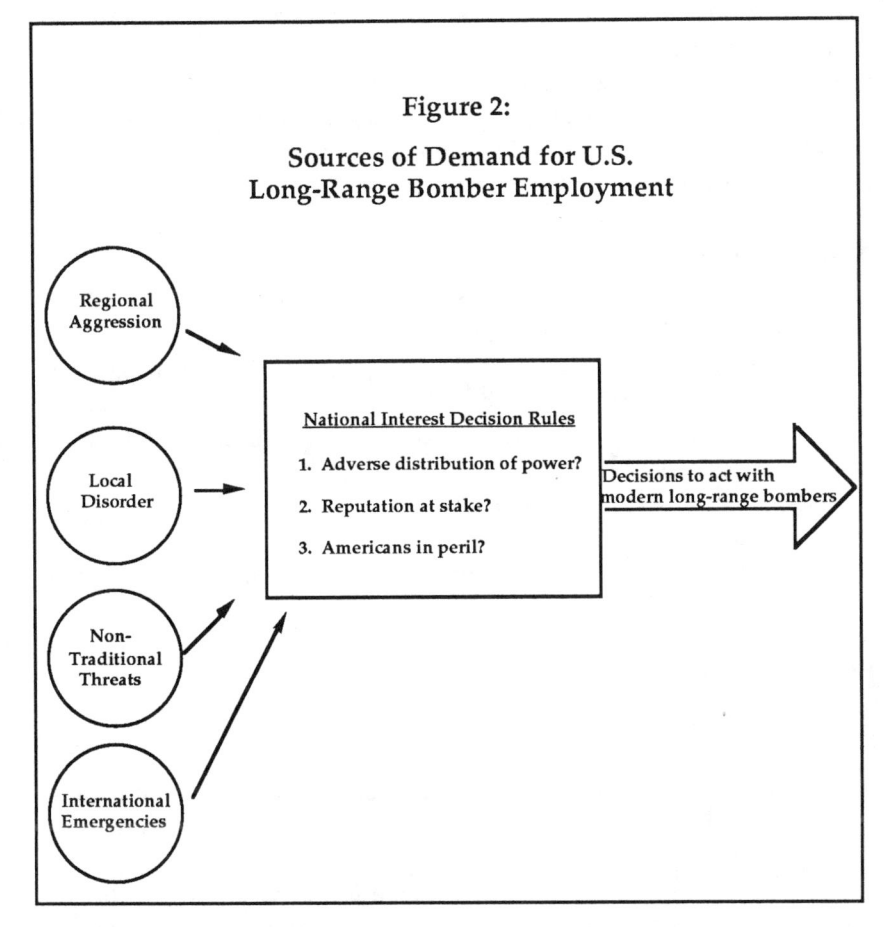

Figure 2:

Sources of Demand for U.S. Long-Range Bomber Employment

- Regional Aggression
- Local Disorder
- Non-Traditional Threats
- International Emergencies

National Interest Decision Rules

1. Adverse distribution of power?
2. Reputation at stake?
3. Americans in peril?

Decisions to act with modern long-range bombers

Illustrative "triggers" for bomber force employment by and large must be "triggers" for the use of other instruments of grand strategy. The existence of modern bomber forces should be viewed as integral to a wide range of U.S. military threats and actions in conflicts of all levels of intensity.

It follows from the argument immediately above that modern long-range, land-based bomber forces and operations have operational relevance virtually across the board of U.S. political-military behavior. Far from comprising exotic capabilities and actions to be employed rarely as a "silver bullet" triggered by some desperate necessity, modern bomber forces are now a regular and traditional instrument of U.S. grand strategy and component in theater war plans. Of course there will always be the possibility of the policy demand for a bomber-heavy "silver bullet" operation. Indeed, the ability of extraordinarily effective aircraft to penetrate hostile territory and perform a mission of the greatest strategic significance does and should inspire the strategic concept that legitimizes and explains why modern long-range, land-based bombers are so important to the United States. The following illustrative "trigger events" serve to illustrate the categories presented here:

Regional Aggression

- An Iranian bid for influence or even imperium over the formerly Soviet Islamic Republics of Central Asia.
- An Iranian bid for revenge, prestige, and greater territorial holdings at the expense of a still weak Iraq.
- Another Balkan war, with its center of territorial gravity in Macedonia and Kosovo.
- Another Indo-Pakistani conflict.
- Another Korean war.
- Any of half-a-dozen conflagrations within the periphery of the former U.S.S.R.

Local Disorder

- Chaos in Russia (and several other former Soviet Republics).
- Chaos in China.
- Civil war in Lebanon, the former Yugoslavia, Slovakia (Hungarian minority), Rumania, Egypt, Iraq, Iran, Panama, Nicaragua, and so on and so forth.
- Political disturbances and incipient civil war in countries important to the United States on criteria critical to the kind of national interest analysis outlined above. How "local" is local disorder? What, if any, are the regional implications of a particular local disorder, and how

much does the United States care? By way of the clearest possible illustration of this argument, compare and contrast U.S. policy towards events in Grenada in 1983, with policy towards Haiti ten years later.

Transnational, Non-traditional "Security" Threats

- Transnational drug trafficking that has the consequences of both turning America's inner cities into war zones and of ruining the lives of many of America's young people.
- An illegal drug industry so profitable that it comes to shape the political, economic, and social destiny of particular countries of interest to the United States.
- The functioning of partially pariah-state-sponsored transnational terrorist organizations that have the power to destabilize countries or whole regions.
- Acts of terroristic violence that kill, damage, or otherwise menace American citizens.
- Transnational criminal syndicates, including drug traffickers that, albeit only for financial profit, can influence the course and quality of local or regional political and social development.
- A climate of economic competition among states and trading coalitions so intense that industrial/scientific espionage and tariff (trade-law) evasion assume a significance relevant to the prosperity of the United States.

International Emergencies

By their very nature, emergencies are not routine events. But, emergency calls for assistance of a kind that can be provided readily by U.S. military forces have become generically routine. Bomber forces provide the distant but rapidly reacting firepower "cover" for a U.S. humanitarian presence suddenly threatened by unanticipated violence.

- Natural disasters almost anywhere on earth. If the pessimists are even partially correct, military missions providing emergency humanitarian aid will become increasingly common.
- Man-made disasters, such as those in Iraq, Somalia, and the former Yugoslavia.

The extensive discussion in this section of the report does not amount to advocacy of a particular view of the utility of modern, U.S. long-range, land-based bomber forces. The discussion above has been restricted to: (1) description of the most likely U.S. role in the world through the remainder of this decade; (2) identification of the conditions of national and international security liable to generate U.S. policy responses that could include bomber operations; and (3) discussion of possible "trigger" events or trends for U.S. deployment and employment of military forces with emphasis on modern long-range, land-based bomber forces.

Chapter 2
America's Option: The Long-Range, Land-Based Bomber

STEVEN J. LAMBAKIS

The bomber became a favored vehicle for the projection of U.S. military power across vast ocean frontiers long before the state of bomber and munitions technology could reliably assure the performance of strategically useful missions. The American people have characteristically welcomed the promise of what bombers could do for them, even when the complete fulfillment of that promise remained somewhere in the technological future. Washington has consistently turned to its bomber forces in moments of crisis and national peril to defeat, punish, or deter an enemy with an enthusiasm not often accorded other military options. This chapter surveys the reasons for the bomber's status as a weapon system favored in the eyes of the American people and their political leaders.

Early Developments

Far from being decisive, World War I air power was to be described more as an experimental or marginal adjunct to terrestrial forces [6]. Yet, there were clearly those in the U.S. Government and armed forces who recognized air power's potential to contribute to victory. In July 1917, the Congress showed its clear support for American military aviation by voting to grant combat flyers a pay that was fifty percent more than that paid ground officers of the same rank. Congress defied official military advice and maintained the flying bonuses throughout the war [7].

The Great War spawned aviation visionaries. Brigadier General William "Billy" Mitchell, the father of American air power, who believed that "an airplane is an offensive and not a defensive weapon," began a long campaign to influence military leaders and their political superiors. Others, at home and abroad, who shared his optimistic views of the airplane, saw the promise of behind-the-lines aerial bombardment [8]. The brief, tentative air experience from that war was enough to sustain these enthusiasts' message that military aviation, once developed, could deliver potentially decisive action against strategic targets as well as air supremacy. These ideas sparked steady progress in military aviation in the United States in the post-war years. By the time the United States found itself confronted by another war to liberate Europe some two decades hence, the Army Air Forces had on hand aircraft capable of long-range bombing missions and the beginnings of air warfare doctrine.

Yet, the real aviation breakthrough from World War I to Pearl Harbor occurred in the minds of the American people. The airplane had caught the nation's imagination. The "barn-storming" exploits of returned World War I pilots, the first air mail service, embryonic airlines, record flights across the oceans and continents, and the famous air races of the thirties made aviation a mass mania. The unique aspect of this "air mindedness" was that it riveted popular American awareness on the future potential of air power, rather than on what had been demonstrated in the past. In a significant sense the American people had become infected with some of the same visionary strain of air mindedness that had claimed air power's "prophets." This development was not lost on political leaders of the day.

While the Army and Navy of the late thirties saw the airplane as a source of support for land and sea forces, air power enthusiasts advocated air power's potential for engaging in independent bombardment operations to destroy the enemy's will to fight. General Frank M. Andrews, in a January 1938 memo to the Secretary of War, summed up these thoughts when he argued that air power that included bombardment aviation as its basic element "is as vital a requirement to the military efficiency of a great nation as land power and sea power, and there is no hope for victory in war for a nation in which it is lacking" [9].

World War II

In the course of the 1930s U.S. air forces progressed technically and doctrinally. However, they remained small, and never escaped organizational and doctrinal tension over how and to what ends they were to be employed. Early episodes of aerial bombardment, in World War I and later in Nicaragua's Sandino War [10], had some resonance in U.S. political and military circles. They provided demonstrations that air power had military effectiveness and could strike lethally over great distances. From the 1920s until the present day, these qualities of the bomber would constitute the essential rationale and attraction for those in responsible positions who would decide to employ similar successor systems.

During these years Congress did allocate funds to design and build aircraft sufficiently modern to equip a capable bomber force. This national effort resulted in the construction of the B-17, a medium-range bomber, that, in its day, was capable of outrunning the fastest fighters [11]. It was not until the early 1940's, though, after world developments had turned grim, that the United States recognized the strategic mission for bomber forces. It was only then that the magnitude of that mission could be seen to require harnessing the full potential of the technical advances in aerial bombardment made since the end of World War I [12].

From August 9 to August 12, 1941, President Franklin Roosevelt, Prime Minister Winston Churchill, and key military staff representatives met aboard the *Prince of Wales* in Placentia Bay, Newfoundland. In the course of military staff discussions at this Atlantic Conference, General Henry H. "Hap" Arnold first became aware of the degree to which the British were depending on air power in their planning for the war and on U.S. productive capacity to provide that air power. Air Chief Marshall Freeman was seeking an RAF fighting strength of 10,000 combat aircraft including 4,000 heavy bombers [13].

At the same time in the Munitions Building in Washington, DC, officers of the Air War Plans Division were assembling the first plan that would state how the United States would use U.S. air power. At the core of this plan was a massive, sustained strategic bombing offensive to defeat the Axis powers. Those in the Air War Plans Division believed that "if the air offensive is successful, a land offensive may not be necessary" [14]. This plan, AWPD-1, spelled out a requirement for a force of 21,813 combat aircraft, including 13,038 bombers, not including attrition replacements [15]. That these numbers could be briefed successfully and stand as accepted planning factors through the final months before the entry of the United States into the war testify to the degree to which the concept of long-range aerial bombardment had captured the minds of decision-makers by the beginning of the war.

In late December 1941 at the ARCADIA Conference it was determined that: 1) U.S. strategy would focus on Germany first, rather than Japan; and 2) the centerpiece of the war plan would be strategic bombing. The "round-the-clock" combined bomber offensive was reaffirmed one year later at Casablanca as a fundamental part of Allied strategy. Roosevelt believed strongly that air power could quickly bring unconditional surrender with minimum loss of American lives. The bomber had earned its first strategic mission.

Following these decisions, heavy bombardment units of the Army Air Force (AAF) were sent overseas to fly missions out of bases in eastern England. In concert with this Anglo-American strategy for prosecuting the war, the Victory Program was adopted to reach the goal of producing 50,000 aircraft per year. This program eventually resulted in a margin of Allied production superiority of 4-to-1 in 1943 and 3-to-1 in 1944 [16].

The rationale behind the choice of the bomber was two-fold. Fundamentally, it was viewed as a militarily effective instrument for knocking Germany out of the war, or at least weakening it, and it was to be an important component of the operations against Japan.

Secondly, and perhaps more significantly, the Combined Bomber Offensive was the only offensive military operation that could be readily implemented early in the war. The bomber offered a political solution for the maintenance of popular support for the war against Germany. The Roosevelt Administration had to do something to justify subordination of the war in the Pacific to that in Europe. And despite popular demands for a second front in Europe, the main amphibious assault would not materialize for another two years. Thus, offensive action on some front was required sooner rather than later, especially in light of the coming congressional elections, if national and Allied morale was to be sustained [17].

On the eve of World War II and during its early months, political leaders gave eloquent voice to the sentiments that turned the United States so readily toward an unproven course of military action. Some of the strongest supporters of developing a long-range bombing capability were members of Congress. New York Congressman Alfred Beiter criticized the armed forces on December 30, 1941 for having focused primarily on land and sea preparations. "We know that wars today are won or lost in the air," he said to the House. The Japanese had demonstrated the ability of air power to strike from long distances, and the Congressman deplored the inordinate attention given to acquiring overseas air bases rather than focusing on the development of the long-range airplane. He argued that

> because we do not have the range to fight from the air over the Philippines the Japanese have been able to bomb Manila and invade a part, if not all, of those Pacific islands. Had the money poured into the outlying air bases been spent on development of long-range fighting planes, we would not now be worrying about our national defense; we would be in a position to carry the offensive to the enemy and retaliate in kind for its treachery [18].

A ten-year supporter of air power, Congressman Jennings Randolph of West Virginia also argued early on that the "paramount theater of war is in the air." "Air supremacy will win this war," he declared to his home town in December 1941. He observed that the Army and Navy only reluctantly were coming around to this point of view, but that they were "beginning to plan the conflict against the Axis Powers with an eye trained on the effectiveness of bombers" [19].

Congressman John E. Rankin of Mississippi, also a strong supporter of air power, made similar arguments as early as May 1941. He argued that the air force was "the first line of defense," and that air power also harnessed tremendous offensive capability. To support his remarks he pointed to the sinking of the battleship *Bismarck* by British air strike forces and recommended to his Congressional audience an article by Major Alexander P. de Seversky on the rise of air power in modern warfare [20]. Congressman Randolph would cite another de Seversky article in July 1942 to buttress his point that "air power has been, and will continue to be, the deciding factor in defeat or victory." In that article, de Seversky concluded that

> when the new long-range air power is available, it will, of course, serve also as the knock-out weapon against Germany. In considering the strategy and tactics of eliminating Germany by means of aerial assault, this should be remembered: Air strategists normally consider it impossible to hold an advance base when it is closer to the enemy than it is to its own primary base [21].

During the war, other U.S. politicians testified to their faith in the power of the bomber. Congressman John Cochran of Missouri told the House in February 1942 that he was called out to the Virginia Capes to witness the bombing of what was called, because it had many airtight compartments, an "unsinkable" battleship. The pilots, he said, had orders to drop their bombs alongside of the ship (which was supposed to spring the plates) rather than make a direct hit. The bombers delivered their bombs as instructed, making for the Congressman "one of the most dramatic scenes" he had ever witnessed. "That great 40,000-ton piece of steel went below the water in 19 1/2 minutes..."[22].

Senator Harry Flood Byrd of Virginia offered in May 1943 to the Senate a "most authoritative" article by Francis Vivian Drake about bombing Germany out of the war. The Senator endorsed this article, which claimed that German industry could be paralyzed by the end of 1943 if enough emphasis was given to the bombing mission. It is both cheaper and quicker, stated Drake, to "eradicate the enemy by going after his heart with bombs than after his feet with gunfire."

Enormous damage can be inflicted by a handful of men—"fewer than participated in the [1942] Dieppe commando raid." The article concluded by stressing that the use of bombers is the great alternative to the "heartache of great land offensives" [23]. A significant effort was made to publicize these claims. The Speaker of the House, Sam Rayburn, in order to "clarify" the Representatives' "impressions of the ability of bombing aircraft to inflict damage on the enemy," arranged a special exhibit displaying RAF photographs of bombed out German cities [24].

Vice President Henry Wallace also made headlines by claiming that air power was needed to both win the war and keep the peace once the war was won. He also spoke out strongly in favor of a bomber force that could be used to project power overseas. "The possibility of enforcing peace upon the world by air power," he said in December 1942, "consists of adequate numbers of planes and strategically located bases." This "will make the task an easier one than might be possible otherwise" [25].

The capability of the bomber also captured the hearts and minds of the American populace. *The Cleveland News* led a campaign in that city to rally factory workers, labor organizations, employers and men, women and children from all walks of life to give funds to "purchase a bomber for MacArthur." Cleveland's bomber was described by Ohio Congressman George Bender as "a symbol of the real unity of our Nation" [26].

The end of the war in Europe further advanced American willingness to count on its air power in the form of long-range bomber forces. The Combined Bomber Offensive had not by itself brought about the defeat of Nazi Germany. Yet, the performance of Allied air power, long the only offensive capability able to reach German soil, had vindicated the faith of air power enthusiasts, even if it had not matched their vaunted projections of alone being able to defeat Hitler.

In the Pacific, strategic bombardment had an even greater role in defeating Japan. At the outset a naval war, the U.S. effort against the Japanese empire turned into a series of campaigns aimed at tightening a noose of air bases close enough to the Japanese homeland to subject the Japanese to relentless bombardment. Telegraphed by the brilliant "grandstand play" of the Doolittle Raid, aimed as much at bolstering morale at home as damaging enemy targets, the shift toward a concerted air war met the challenge of avoiding a ground invasion of Japan that could have cost a million lives. Most desired that the defeat of Japan come in a matter of months, not years. Bombers, mainly B-29s, were directed in 1944 and 1945 against enemy airfields, ports, supply depots, and communications centers. But even the force of B-29's which could accomplish the fire-bombing of Tokyo that killed up to 90,000 people still did not bring a halt to Japan's war industries and the national war effort. However, two B-29's, *Enola Gay* and *Bock's Car* did provide the *coup de grace*. The impact of long-range bombers in both theaters, coupled with the new atomic bomb, gave strategic air power an aura in the summer of 1945 that placed long-range bomber forces even higher in the estimation of the American people and supported the 1947 decision to create an independent United States Air Force [27].

The Bomber and the Beginning of the Cold War

From 1947 to 1953, the United States began to recognize the Soviet Union as a new threat of global dimensions, an adversary that intended to and could match or overmatch the United States, not only in conventional power, but more threateningly in nuclear capability. The range of actions undertaken by the United States to reconstruct its military capability from the "ashes" of post-World War II demobilization, and then reorient it into an effective nuclear deterrent, was heavily focused on long-range air power. No period relevant to the history of U.S. air power more clearly illustrates the degree to which the American people and their political leaders accept air power and are willing to turn to it than did this period of "reconstitution." (For detailed examples, see chapter 3.) It was characteristic of the long-range bomber focus of the Cold-War build-up that the Strategic Air Command was established on March 21, 1946, to orchestrate the creation and operation of a global nuclear force structure capable of deterring Soviet aggression. SAC was founded over a year before the birth of the U.S. Air Force itself.

Strategic air power advocates recognized the role of public opinion in supporting a nuclear-armed, air power-based, long-range strike force structure. New capabilities were willingly demonstrated for domestic and foreign audiences. On March 2, 1949, a B-50 bomber named *Lucky Lady II* completed the first non-stop around the world flight. Congressman Francis Case of South Dakota called it "an epochal event," a clear message to the rest of the world "what the American people can do in the event of a war." He went on to say, about this flight, which lasted 94 hours and included four in-flight refuelings, that

> this demonstrated ability to fly anywhere, anytime, and carry a pay load to the ends of the earth, is a more effective deterrent for any world aggressor than all the conferences that have been held. This flight can mean more for peace and more to secure human freedom in the world than all the millions of words that have been spoken and all the billions of dollars that are being spent to secure bases and to win friends.

He finished by paraphrasing former President Theodore Roosevelt: "Let us speak softly and temperately while we carry the big stick." Congressman Carl Hinshaw added the next day that "it is comforting to know that we have the ability to make such a flight" [28].

Congressional confidence in the deterrent effect of the bomber continued to grow. Arkansas Congressman W. F. Norrell reminded the House that the start of the "the Second World War found us with only one long-range bomber," the B-17, and he deplored the tendency in Congress to permit the Air Force to "slip back into its prewar condition with a starvation diet." Congressman Matthew Neely of West Virginia cited approvingly an article by de Seversky, which stated that the strategy of air power was "uniquely suited to American genius and capacity." Congressman Styles Bridges of New Hampshire also welcomed an air strike fleet as a balance to rising Soviet air power and as a foundation for "a permanent peace" [29].

The Korean War

On June 25, 1950 the Soviet-backed forces of North Korea crossed the 38th parallel into independent South Korea and moved quickly to take the capital, Seoul. After persuading United Nations members to assist the United States in obtaining the withdrawal of the North Korean forces, President Truman gave orders to General Douglas MacArthur, who had under his command the Far East Air Forces (FEAF), to provide the besieged country air and naval support. He initially was instructed not to conduct operations north of the 38th parallel, although later in the war this limitation was removed to permit the bombing of North Korean military targets [30].

As part of the first significant military action taken by U.S. forces in response to the aggression, B-29s of the 19th Bombardment Group, which immediately had been moved nearer to the Korean Peninsula from Guam to Kadena Air Base in Okinawa, and B-26s of the Fifth Air Force were thrown into action against North Korean troop concentrations, tanks, guns, and supplies. While the initial June 28 bomb runs were somewhat disappointing in their results, the American Embassy in Seoul was heartened by the strikes and suggested that the FEAF direct its attacks against targets near the capital. The embassy stated that it believed that a constant display of American air power was "fundamental" to the morale of ROK troops assigned to hold the ground around Seoul [31].

Some Congressional members also were strong advocates for the use of bombers as a major part of the U.S. counteroffensive. Senator Owen Brewster of Maine sought to press Truman to allow MacArthur to use the atomic bomb at his discretion against the invaders. "We are not spending billions for bombs out of scientific curiosity," he argued. "Presumably, they are designed to save the lives of American boys." Then-congressman Lloyd Bentsen of Texas suggested the President should advise the North Koreans either to withdraw or to "use that week to evacuate a named list of principal cities which would be subject to atomic attack by our air force" [32].

President Truman decided that the war to free the Republic of Korea would be an Army-Navy-Air Force effort. The United States, as the executive agent for the United Nations, pledged to apply force from the air discriminately. Thus, when Truman authorized bombing missions in North Korea, he stressed that the targets would be "purely military," and that great effort would be taken to spare the civilian populace. The Joint Chiefs of Staff, guided by Truman's request that the bombers strike with discrimination, generally disapproved of massive bombing attacks if they could be interpreted as attacks against civilians [33].

Most believed that unless nodes of logistical support for the North Koreans and associated industries in the north were targeted, the invasion would not be repulsed. It was not until nearly the end of July that the first strategic bombing mission was authorized. Once the sustained strategic campaign was under way, the B-29s attacked major industrial centers, rail centers, oil refining facilities, chemical and metallurgical plants, iron foundries, and hydroelectric plants. By September 15, officials could claim that practically all of the major industrial targets in the north had been neutralized, in time for the amphibious landing at Inchon.

Subsequent ground operations allowed penetrations of the North Korean lines and UN forces advanced northward above the 38th parallel. By October 27, 1950, believing that victory was near, FEAF Bomber Command was disbanded and two wings returned to the United States [34]. One month later, however, UN troops were surprised by a massive Chinese ground assault and beaten back to positions south of the 38th parallel.

Once the UN advance was repulsed by Chinese troops, Truman was reluctant to widen the war by striking trans-Yalu river bases in the Chinese homeland. He considered using atomic weapons to help rescue the UN forces (a prospect quite frightening to American allies), and B-29s practiced an atomic bomb attack against Pyongyang [35]. The attacks never were authorized. Some members of Congress, however, believed that Truman's policy did not go far enough and thought that a second front against the Chinese mainland should be undertaken to counter the Chinese and North Korean aggression. Senator Styles Bridges announced that he would oppose the war effort unless Truman went so far as to authorize bombing attacks against Red China's bases [36].

Despite the political opposition, which was not broadly based, plans for a more limited campaign against targets in North Korea were drawn up. Some officials proposed using the B-29 as a political weapon by hitting Pyongyang with a massive air strike after warning the population, believing that this action would force the North Koreans to come to terms with the UN more easily. This was denied by Washington. Thus, UN (U.S.) air power continued to be used primarily in a tactical role [37].

During the Korean war, Congressman Leroy Johnson of California brought to the attention of the House an article written by Democratic Congressman W. J. Bryan Dorn (South Carolina) and Republican Congressman O.K. Armstrong (Missouri). This article, said Johnson, was a "lessons-learned" look at the war, and one of the conclusions he stressed was that air power had become "the predominant destructive force against ground troops in the field." The Congressmen-authors concluded that American policy makers were "more dependent upon air power than they themselves realize." The reason for this was the growing belief that the Communists should be stopped with the least possible cost to American lives. The bomber gives policy makers a capability to destroy enemy troops, and the authors expected that this would lead to a great air power build up within the country. "The doughboy," they wrote, "is delighted that airpower is capable of such destructive force; he just wants to get the job done, he doesn't care how, and get back home" [38]. The Korean conflict was curtailed by an armistice in 1953. Historians speculate that the possibility of atomic bombing by the United States was one factor that led the North Koreans and Chinese to come to terms. After the war, the Eisenhower Administration adopted a declared policy of "massive retaliation" against aggression. This policy led to significant growth in the U.S. Air Force in the 1950's.

The Vietnam War

Air power became the favored tool of the civilian and military leadership throughout the next major war fought by the United States, in Vietnam. Indeed, roughly half the funds allocated to the Vietnam war effort went to support aerial operations, and U.S. and allied air forces dropped twice the bomb tonnage used during World War II [39].

While U.S. bombing in North Vietnam did not begin until August 1964, in March of that year, President Johnson's team and the Joint Chiefs of Staff drew up contingency plans for a bombing program. The objectives of the campaign were three-fold: 1) to signal Hanoi of U.S. resolve to defend South Vietnam; 2) to boost the morale of the South Vietnamese government; and 3) to impose increasing costs and strains on Hanoi for its support of communist subversion and aggression [40]. The U.S. ambassador to South Vietnam, Henry Cabot Lodge, clearly seconded these plans, for he too favored a "selective bombing campaign" against North Vietnamese military targets to bolster the morale of Saigon [41]. In May 1964, Senator Barry Goldwater urged the bombing of bridges, roads and railroads used to bring supplies into South Vietnam. "I think the first decision is that we are going to win," he said [42]. The bomber had become the chief tool of American policy when it called for the application of overwhelming force overseas.

The question became not *whether* to use the bomber to project U.S. military might, but rather *how* and *when* to employ it. So certain were those in the highest government offices of the bomber's role in this Southeast Asian crisis. While the JCS argued for a decisive bombing campaign, most in Johnson's coterie argued for a measured and gradual approach that would rise and fall in intensity according to the behavior of North Vietnam's leaders. The "carrot and stick" tactic would symbolize the Johnson Administration's approach to war fighting in Vietnam, an approach that many would blame for the failure of air power to deliver victory.

The initial bombing plan had been put aside when, on August 4, 1964, two North Vietnamese torpedo boats attacked two U.S destroyers in the Gulf of Tonkin, an event that triggered the stepped-up U.S. involvement in Vietnam. Following this action, Johnson ordered bombing strikes (carried out by carrier-based fighter aircraft) against selected targets in retaliation. Johnson's action received general approval. Congress passed a joint-resolution in support of the military actions. Republican Richard Nixon also backed the measures, as did Ambassador Lodge, who said he was happy with the U.S. decision to meet force with force [43].

Subsequent to the initial air strikes, General Maxwell Taylor argued that a forceful, "carefully orchestrated" bombing campaign against North Vietnam's military targets and infiltration routes was necessary. Consideration of these limited reprisal strikes led to a consensus within the administration in September that a sustained bombing campaign probably would have to begin in early 1965 [44]. Johnson authorized only limited air strikes in December and again in early February (Operation Flaming Dart) until he ordered in mid-February 1965 to begin Operation Rolling Thunder.

The regular and sustained air operations of Rolling Thunder lasted from March 1965 until October 1968. The Johnson administration clearly viewed the bomber as a potent and manageable instrument of war. The bombing campaign was tightly controlled by Washington and very limited in scope. On average three attacks per week against such selected targets as trucks, barracks, bridges, and ammunition dumps took place. Usually a dozen F-105s, which had the equivalent payload of two B-29s, conducted these strikes [45]. During this time, the administration was in nearly continuous contact with the North Vietnamese leadership in anticipation of peace negotiations. Bombing was halted often in the hope that concessions would be forthcoming, a tactic that seemed only to give the enemy forces the opportunity for a stepped-up campaign to resupply subversives in the South.

In the months ahead bombing operations were widened to include attacks on bridges, air fields, railroad yards, oil storage facilities and power plants, and eventually encompassed targets around Hanoi and Haiphong. The intensification of the air campaign was attractive to Johnson in light of the alternative: sending large numbers of American soldiers to fight in the jungles of Vietnam. At any rate, he understood that both Congress and the public had to believe that air power had been applied to the fullest and was not working before he could commit American ground troops [46].

In 1965, opposition in Congress to the bombing was on the rise [47]. Public disfavor also rose. Many believed it to be an impediment to peace negotiations. Moreover, military effectiveness did not compensate for the domestic and international political costs. By early 1967, it had become evident that the bombing, for various reasons, was falling well short of debilitating North Vietnam's economic and military sectors and cutting off the flow of supplies to the Viet Cong subversives. The failure of the administration's overly restrictive bombing strategy prompted the JCS to argue against the restrained bombing program in August 1967 and in favor of a more forceful use of air power, a position strongly supported by Mississippi Senator John Stennis and his Preparedness Subcommittee [48]. Military officials still believed that effective bombing could shorten the war and save American lives.

The peace negotiations progressed in April 1968 when Hanoi announced its readiness to meet with U.S. representatives, an event that could not be linked directly to Johnson's bombing strategy. Months later a compromise was worked out. The United States had agreed to cease bombing, which it did on October 31, 1968. Rolling Thunder rumbled to a halt, but North Vietnam continued to violate the promises it made to Washington when it persisted in infiltrating South Vietnam's borders and shelling South Vietnamese cities. These developments ultimately sabotaged the peace negotiations, making the U.S. decision to halt the bombing in effect a unilateral concession.

Richard Nixon was elected to the presidency in November 1968, in part because he promised to withdraw U.S. forces from Vietnam. Nixon believed that making the South Vietnamese armed forces self-sufficient, in conjunction with the use of air strikes to interdict supplies, would accomplish this aim. By 1972 it was clear that North Vietnam was preparing for a large-scale conventional offensive across the demilitarized zone. In February, B-52s were deployed to Guam to increase the monthly sortie rate. The first B-52 strikes took place in April and, according to Nixon's National Security Advisor, were "a warning that things might get out of hand if the offensive did not stop" [49]. The B-52s played a significant role in blunting the March-to-June offensive [50].

In May President Nixon elected to start "Linebacker" operations, using B-52s to bomb targets throughout North Vietnam (except for those in a 25 mile buffer zone near the Chinese border) and help mine Haiphong and other ports. This full-scale bombing offensive remained politically unpopular but was run with greater tactical flexibility than Rolling Thunder. The offensive was directed against war-related resources and supply routes into the South. The seven month campaign often included targets around Hanoi and Haiphong and was intended to reduce the assistance North Vietnam received from abroad. Of important note, new precision munitions, including laser- and TV-guided bombs, increased the accuracy and effectiveness of American bombing strikes [51].

The bombing jarred awake the long-stalled Paris peace talks. Nixon met compromises by Hanoi over the composition of the South Vietnamese government with a suspension of bombing in October 1972. Kissinger announced that peace was at hand, a statement made premature by new problems and a decision by Hanoi to abandon the talks in November. Nixon began a new round of bombing on December 19 (Linebacker II) in order to coerce the North Vietnamese into returning to the negotiations. Transportation, power, and transmitter targets were hit along with air fields, railroad yards, shipyards, and docks. Once the B-52 bombing had started, Nixon stressed to JCS Chairman Admiral Moorer that the North Vietnamese must be hit hard, and he told him that this was his chance "to use military power effectively to win this war." He called the decision to use the B-52s a "clear cut and necessary" one [52].

The twelve-day campaign caused extensive damage in North Vietnam. By the end of December, Hanoi had agreed to resume negotiations, and the heavy bombing was stopped on December 30. A cease-fire agreement was prepared in January 1973, and the United States agreed to remove all of its remaining forces within sixty days. Hanoi agreed to remove its forces from South Vietnam. Admiral Moorer was convinced that Linebacker II "served as a catalyst for the negotiations" and that air power, "given its day in court after almost a decade of frustration, confirmed its effectiveness as an instrument of national power—in just 9 1/2 flying days" [53]. According to Henry Kissinger:

Faced with the prospect of an open-ended war and continued bitter divisions [at home], considering that the weather made the usual bombing ineffective, Nixon chose the only weapon he had available [SAC's B-52s]. His decision speeded the end of the war; even in retrospect I can think of no other measure that would have [54].

Nixon continued to turn to the B-52s once the Paris peace accords were abrogated by North Vietnam in the ensuing months. The Washington Special Actions Group also argued that, in view of Hanoi's violations, "the best military option appear[ed] to be a resumption of bombing" [55]. Despite Hanoi's subsequent compromises, usually in response to American air strikes, the peace agreement continued to unravel. In a couple of years, exploiting a weakened U.S. presidency, North Vietnam would overrun the South and claim victory. When he knew that all had been lost, Kissinger remarked to a concurring Nixon in April 1973 that "if we didn't have this damn domestic situation [the Watergate scandal], a week of bombing would put this Agreement in force" [56].

Crises and Deterrence Missions

On a number of occasions since its establishment in 1946, the U.S. Air Force was called upon to flex its air power muscles to signal U.S. resolve in a crisis or to bolster the credibility of the deterrent forces. The chief messenger during these critical moments to American and allied national security was long-range, attack aviation. The following cases demonstrate the perceived utility of the bomber to U.S. policy makers in those instances when the United States stood on the brink of war.

Berlin Blockade. On June 22, 1948, Soviet forces stepped up pressure on Berlin by occupying the rail routes into the city and forbidding passage to allied traffic, thereby threatening to starve the city's two million inhabitants. The United States, in consultation with its allies, made the decision to begin the Berlin Airlift, which brought food, fuel, and other necessities over the Soviet blockades into the city. To discourage any thoughts of shooting down vulnerable allied transport aircraft, the United States sent a wing of SAC's B-29s to bases in England. After eleven months, the Soviet authorities conceded defeat and ended the blockade without major incident.

Crisis in Lebanon. The 1958 crisis in Lebanon also triggered bold moves by President Eisenhower, who sought to maintain stability both in the Middle East and in the U.S.-Soviet relationship. Between April and July 1958, there was a series of border crossings from Syria into Lebanon and insurrections around the country. Most, including Eisenhower, believed that the newly established United Arab Republic under Egyptian Colonel Gamal Abdal Nasser had inspired these subversive activities in order to extend its influence further in the region. Eisenhower also believed that the Soviet Union was partly responsible for these provocations.

Events reached a boiling point on July 14 when pro-Nasser elements in the Iraqi armed forces overthrew the Hashemite monarchy, an event that had repercussions throughout the region and threatened to set the Middle East ablaze. The coup in Baghdad renewed unrest in Lebanon, and Eisenhower began to worry for western interests in the region as well as the safety of Americans living in Lebanon. Lebanese President Camille Chamoun requested that the United States and Britain land forces in his country immediately to provide his regime protection.

The following day Eisenhower deployed U.S. soldiers and Marines without resistance in Lebanon around Beirut and the airport. Foremost in Eisenhower's mind was the Soviet reaction to his moves. Eisenhower's Secretary of State John Foster Dulles believed that the Soviets respected U.S. power too much— especially the "overwhelming" U.S. bomber capability—to risk a confrontation. Eisenhower agreed and, following recommendations from the JCS, ordered Air Force tankers to take up forward positions and placed SAC's bomber forces on an increased level of alert. Eisenhower wrote that the message sent to the Soviet Union "would be desirable, as showing readiness and determination without implying any threat of aggression"[57]. The situation in Lebanon was stabilized by August 1958, and withdrawal of U.S. forces was completed by October.

The Cuban Missile Crisis. The primary reaction of the United States to the October 14, 1962 discovery that the Soviet Union was deploying ballistic missiles to Cuba was the presidential decision on October 22 to place the Strategic Air Command on full scale nuclear alert. All day-to-day operations ceased, all aircraft and missiles were placed on ground nuclear alert except for the aircraft supporting 24-hour-a-day airborne alert operations, and some alert aircraft were moved to dispersal bases. This posture was maintained until November 20, 1962 when the Soviets agreed to remove their missiles from Cuba [58].

The 1973 October War. Dissatisfied with the Israeli occupation of Arab lands seized during the 1967 war, a coalition of Arab countries, led by Egypt, attacked Israeli positions on October 6 in the Sinai Peninsula and on the Golan front. Following initial Arab battlefield successes, the Israeli armed forces inflicted a series of reversals, retaking seized territories before a cease-fire was announced on October 24.

The United States, a long-time supporter of Israel, feared that the war, while not directed by the Soviets, could have led to greater Soviet influence in this vital region. Fearing an Israeli collapse, the United began to supply Israel by air beginning October 13, supplementing supply operations begun earlier by Israeli aircraft. The Soviet Union also had begun its own airlift to Egypt and Syria. President Nixon hoped the Soviets would not become directly involved, possibly sparking a direct confrontation with the United States [59]. Following the cease-fire, Nixon vetoed an idea of Egypt's leader Anwar Sadat to permit the introduction of American and Soviet troops into the region to enforce the peace, a move that Nixon believed may have been a veiled threat of Soviet intervention.

Nixon believed that swift action was required, "even the shock of a military alert" [60]. On October 25, the United States placed its nuclear forces, including its strategic bombers, on alert. The DefCon (Defensive Condition) at Strategic Air Command reportedly was changed from IV to III to signal increased U.S. readiness to the Soviets, an alert level that did not indicate that war was imminent but that war was a possibility. B-52s were moved from Guam to the United States to "give the Soviets another indication that we were assembling our forces for a showdown" [61]. Nixon also ordered the 82nd Airborne on alert and an aircraft carrier to the eastern Mediterranean. These actions, generally supported by Congress and the media, were intended to signal U.S. determination to act militarily to counter Soviet intervention [62]. The crisis abated after a conciliatory gesture by Soviet leader Brezhnev on October 26 and the completion of an agreeable United Nations peacekeeping accord on October 27.

The 1986 Raid on Libya. Following the revelation that Libya's leader Muammar Qaddafi was responsible for the April 5, 1986 bombing of a night club in West Berlin, which killed and injured U.S. servicemen, the United States drew up plans to deliver "a focused response" to terrorism. President Ronald Reagan, after deciding that there was "no alternative but a military response," asked the JCS for ideas on "sending Qaddafi a signal without harming innocent people" [63]. White House and DoD officials planned to strike from the air various Libyan targets associated with terrorism, including training grounds, headquarters, airfields, and aircraft.

The bombing raid involved over 100 aircraft, including 33 Air Force F-111 fighter-bombers and A-6 carrier-based strike planes. The United States received cooperation from Great Britain, which allowed American planes to take off from England, but was denied access to French air space (despite the fact that French President Mitterand wanted American planes to hit Qaddafi hard), a decision that added considerably to the length of time it would take to complete the mission [64]. U.S. aircraft struck just after midnight (local time) on April 15 and were largely successful in destroying the intended targets, with one stray bomb hitting an apartment complex near the French embassy. American bombs even had managed to come close to Qaddafi himself, an unexpected but not unwelcome outcome. The success of the mission permitted Reagan to underscore to the nation his message that "it must be the core of western policy that there be no sanctuary for terror" [65].

Despite complaints on Capitol Hill that the President failed to consult them properly before undertaking the air strike, most legislators in both parties expressed their support. Senator Bob Dole stated that he believed that "the president did what people want him to do—a proportionate response to an act of terrorism." Senator Richard Lugar called it "the logical next step" to the bombing in Berlin. House Speaker Thomas P. O'Neill, Jr. and Democratic Senator Edward Kennedy also expressed their support.

Representative Dan Coats argued that "in launching these air attacks against Libya, President Reagan has chosen to speak the only language terrorists understand, the language of force." Senator William Proxmire brought to his colleagues' attention Libya's possible interest in nuclear weapons and, after praising Reagan's decision, said that "there may have to be more such strikes." He emphasized that the United States had to "make the price of terroristic actions so high that states directing terrorism will recognize they are in a losing game." A number of other legislators registered in the *Congressional Record* their strong support of the bombing of Libya. Comparisons were made on the Hill to Thomas Jefferson's harsh retaliation against the Barbary pirates in the early 1800s. The American people also generally supported the bombing out of fear that international terrorism would increase without the use of air power to retaliate [66].

The 1986 air raid on Libya elicited strong support from those who argued that there was a growing need to respond to terrorism by striking at the source, to fight effectively in what Republican House leader Robert Michel called "a new kind of war." An important element of an effective response-package in this new kind of war is the ability to strike and destroy distant targets without endangering scores or even hundreds of American lives and to do so quickly and surely. The capability to hit hard and precisely from the air would allow the country to overcome its growing sense of impotence vis-á-vis the terrorist.

This series of crises clearly mark the progression of U.S. public and political willingness to employ air power, with long-range, land-based bombers as an instrument of choice. In those few cases where serious opposition to bombing was raised, it reflected more opposition to the war itself than to the classes of weaponry being used.

The 1991 Gulf War and Subsequent U.S. Policy

On August 2, 1990, Iraqi leader Saddam Hussein launched an invasion of the neighboring principality of Kuwait. Having vastly outmanned and outgunned this small oil-rich state, he achieved his objectives within hours. Determined that Saddam Hussein's aggression not be rewarded by U.S. and international acquiescence, President Bush set about trying first to persuade Arab countries to accept American help in the region and later to muster the support of U.S. allies and other countries for the defense of Saudi Arabia and possibly the ouster of Iraqi forces from Kuwait. The advice he received from Chairman of the JCS General Colin L. Powell (who had learned the bitter lessons of "gradualism" in the Vietnam war) was that if force was to be used, it must be used "decisively from the beginning" [67].

On August 6 President Bush, strongly supported by Capitol Hill, ordered the first American troops and squadrons to Saudi Arabia to defend the kingdom. That same month, the United States began deploying B-52s to Diego Garcia and sent F-111s, F-117s, and F-15E fighter-bombers to Saudi Arabia. During the ensuing months, while Saddam stubbornly continued to dig in Kuwait, the anti-Iraq coalition continued to take shape and the United States proceeded with its build-up of air, land, and sea power in the Gulf region as part of Operation Desert Shield. By November 1990, it had become clear that the coalition was gearing up for a full-scale counteroffensive.

Months prior to the start of the war, all indications were that, in the event of war, the coalition would depend upon a furious and extensive bombing campaign to destroy Iraq's ability to undertake effective military operations. Air Force Chief of Staff General Michael Dugan, revealing part of U.S. strategy, announced in September that a massive bombing campaign against Baghdad and Iraq's war-making capabilities was "the only answer available to our country." Dugan believed that the open desert would facilitate the effectiveness of air strikes relative to the U.S. experience in Vietnam [68].

In joint hearings before the Senate Armed Services Committee, begun on November 27, arguments were heard regarding the military mission of the United States and the effectiveness of UN sanctions. The hearings also highlighted a general consensus in the United States that, in the interest of both saving American lives and achieving high levels of military effectiveness, air strikes should take the lead in the war effort. In the event of war, U.S. forces should undertake "an intensive air campaign," testified Admiral William Crowe, which "would deal Saddam Hussein a crushing political and military blow." Chairman Sam Nunn stated that he always thought that "the air threat was the best U.S.

strength," a statement which Henry Kissinger seconded by saying that "the preferable strategy would be to rely on our air and naval power." Analyst Edward Luttwak argued that "an air offensive lasting at least several days," initially using "long range means," would help the United States avoid the enormous human cost of executing ground warfare. Senator John McCain largely agreed with Luttwak. Lieutenant General William Odom, USA (Ret.) summed up a general consensus that bombing would reduce Iraq's military capabilities much faster than could economic sanctions [69].

Following the passage of UN Resolution 678, which authorized the use of "all necessary means" to liberate Kuwait, and a joint Congressional resolution in support of the military option, the U.S.-led coalition forces began the air war on January 17, 1991. Once Operation Desert Storm had begun, B-52s were launched from Barksdale AFB in Louisiana flying 14,000 miles to launch points for conventionally armed cruise missiles and then returning to Barksdale. Throughout the war, these heavy bombers were used tactically along with allied fighter-bombers and strike aircraft in a 43-day air bombardment of Iraqi military, economic, and political targets. The intensive air campaign prepared the way for a four-day allied ground campaign that routed the beleaguered Iraqi forces at a cost of very few Coalition casualties and led the way to the signing of a cease-fire agreement on March 3.

Desert Storm stands as the most vivid historical example of a growing U.S. reliance on an air strike capability to accomplish policy objectives. It also demonstrated that this reliance is now matched by the technical ability of air power to meet popular expectations. This war came closest to vindicating the vision of early air power visionaries that strike aircraft could defeat an enemy by leaping over his defensive lines and striking his economic, military, and political centers.

Subsequent to the end of Desert Storm, U.S. policy makers and commentators have voiced an evolving advocacy for resorting to air strikes to help quell or control crises abroad. The promise of strike aircraft to deliver a quick, precise, and forceful military response, of Gulf War precision, leads the list of reasons for the wide support for such missions. Postwar developments in Iraq and the war in the Balkans are two representative cases.

Postwar developments in Iraq. Following the end of the Gulf War, the ability to strike Iraqi targets gave the United States and the United Nations a tool for enforcing the cease-fire agreement and UN Resolution 687 and protecting subsequent humanitarian and military operations in northern and southern Iraq. Resolution 687 lays the basis for the destruction of Iraq's weapons of mass destruction. The sharpest confrontations between the United States and Iraq have been over Saddam Hussein's refusal to cooperate with UN inspection teams assigned to inspect and destroy Iraq's declared and hidden nuclear, chemical, and biological arsenals and ballistic missile stockpiles, related equipment, and facilities. Iraq's stalling and deception tactics have repeatedly succeeded in turning away UN inspections and frustrating investigations.

President George Bush pledged to support fully the mission of the UN Special Commission, with U.S. military power if required. Consequently, on a number of occasions before his departure from office, Bush had to threaten to use U.S. strike aircraft to compel Iraqi compliance. In September 1991, for example, Bush responded to Iraq's refusal to permit UN helicopters searching for proscribed weapons into Iraqi air space by warning Saddam that U.S. warplanes may be used against Iraq. This threat, which forced Saddam to retreat, was supported by some members of Congress. Senator Robert Dole, who in July spoke out in favor of authorizing the president to use military force to enforce the UN Resolution, said that Bush was making the effort to deliver the message peacefully. "If that doesn't work," he said, "it may be necessary to have the next message delivered by the United States armed forces" [70]. In August 1992, Vice Presidential candidate Albert Gore strongly supported in principle the use of force to compel Iraqi compliance with the UN resolutions [71].

In subsequent months, Iraq continued its practice of "cheat and retreat" and of challenging the right of UN inspectors to operate in the country. On at least four separate occasions Bush approved, but later rejected, military action against Iraq. In January 1993, the United States responded to Iraq's illegal incursions in the southern "no-fly zone" (the movement of surface-to-air missiles into the region) and its refusal to admit UN planes into Iraqi air space by delivering a limited air strike against Iraqi air defenses in southern Iraq. The United States also launched cruise missiles against a nuclear weapons-related facility near Baghdad.

Bush used the air strikes to deliver "a crystal-clear message" to Saddam. Presidential spokesman Marlin Fitzwater underscored for reporters that these kinds of air strikes will not be over "until we get compliance." Senator Dole said that the "surgical strikes" were appropriate to Saddam's violations, and Senator Richard Lugar said that the United States should consider broader bombing operations to topple Saddam. Thus, prior to leaving the presidency, Bush finally set a precedent for the use of air strikes as a tool for controlling Iraqi behavior for as long as the cease-fire agreement remains in effect. This is important given Iraqi refusal to recognize formally UN Resolutions 707 and 715, which provide for long-term monitoring of its weapon systems and facilities. Bush put action behind the words spoken by many within and outside government regarding the value of air strikes for supporting U.S. national security objectives in peacetime [72].

The War in Bosnia. Following the declarations of independence of Slovenia and Croatia in mid-1991, Serbian-dominated Yugoslav forces and Serbian guerrillas began a war to claim territories in those states. In October 1991, the former Yugoslav republic of Bosnia-Hercegovina declared its sovereignty. This move led Serbs in Bosnia and Yugoslavia to refocus their military campaign in early 1992 on "ethnic cleansing" operations, which were aimed at Croats and Slavic Muslims, throughout the state of Bosnia. In coming months, some of the violence also would be directed against UN relief operations. While the United States deplored the Serb aggression, by mid-1992 it had affirmed a decision to stay out of Bosnia.

By late summer of 1992, the tide of public opinion in the United States began to shift. Opinions arose in several quarters that the United States "do something," many suggesting that air strikes should become the tool of U.S. policy in the Balkans. In August, Presidential candidate Bill Clinton said that the United States should go beyond just condemning the practice of ethnic cleansing and should "seek UN Security Council authorization for air strikes against forces attacking the UN relief effort in Bosnia" [73]. During the same month, speculation rose about possible U.S. air strikes against the Serbian military. U.S officials reportedly drew up options that included limited air-based bombing. A senior White House official is quoted as saying that the U.S. would likely attack military targets "to raise the cost [of war to Serbia] rather than putting ground units on the ground willing to fight and take casualties" [74].

In December 1992, while the outgoing Bush Administration reportedly was deadlocked on the issue of using force in Bosnia, President-elect Clinton came out once again in favor of enforcing the UN-imposed "no-fly zone" over Bosnia. He stated that enforcement "can be done from the air without a commitment of ground troops." "Anything we can do to turn up the heat a little there, to try to reduce the carnage, is worth trying." The month before, Representative Frank McClosky of Indiana strongly recommended the use of "selected air strikes" against Serb positions as a signal to Serbia that it cannot take over parts of Bosnia with impunity. McClosky believed that this forceful action would help head off the looming Balkan refugee disaster. At this same time, the Pentagon was busy planning for possible air strikes against Serb targets [75].

Once Bill Clinton assumed office, presidential rhetoric in favor of military action in Bosnia tapered off. The President, however, began a study to consider a wider range of policy options, including the bombing of Serb airfields and artillery positions [76]. While some commentators also continued to urge the use of air strikes to punish the Serbs and assist the victims in that conflict, Clinton's early policy settled on a less interventionist option—air drops of food, medicine, and other supplies to besieged quarters in Bosnia. In April 1993, following a series of Serb military victories and more reports of Serb atrocities against Bosnian Muslims, policy makers again revisited the idea of air strikes by U.S. and other NATO forces against Serb positions in order to bring a halt to Serbian aggression and force Bosnian Serbs to initial the Vance-Owen peace plan [77].

Congressional support for military action in Bosnia mounted despite some fervent opposition from politicians and military leaders [78]. Following an April trip to the Balkans, Senator Joseph Biden recommended U.S. intervention in the war in the form of Western air strikes to eliminate Serb heavy artillery and destroy bridges as well as the deployment of a multinational force to prevent further Serb aggression. Following further stonewalling by Bosnian Serbs, President Clinton again joined the rising chorus for stronger action on the part of the United States and suggested that air raids to enforce a truce was high on his list [79]. Former Secretary of State George Shultz, cognizant of U.S. striking capabilities demonstrated in Desert Storm, also came out strongly in favor of a wide ranging bombing campaign to "go after gun emplacements" and possibly even strike "military targets inside Serbia itself, weapons caches, supply lines, bridges" [80].

In April 1994, U.S. F-16 strike aircraft, under United Nations direction, attacked Serbian artillery that had endangered UN Peacekeeping forces. This action was perceived to have political backing in the United States. Through the end of 1994, NATO air forces sporadically engaged in highly selective, limited air strikes against Bosnian Serb equipment and artillery positions. Fear that these guerrilla forces would target UN forces in retribution prompted the United Kingdom and France to resist U.S. calls to widen the bombing campaign. By December 1994, political momentum had gathered within the NATO countries to pull out UN Peacekeepers from Bosnia, opening the door for stepped-up bombing operations to coerce the Bosnian Serbs to accept a neighboring truncated Muslim State.

Conclusion

Americans have come to see themselves as citizens of an air power nation. Examination of the principal rationale behind the employment of bombing aircraft throughout their short history reveals a remarkable pattern of consistency. Given the geographic situation of the United States, intercontinental bombers, represented in future forces by the B-2, match the strategic needs of the country as does no other weapon system. This class of aircraft makes possible a strategy of air power that Alexander de Seversky held to be "uniquely suited to American genius and capacity."

Since the end of World War II, bombers have been an important element of the U.S. deterrence posture and have been called upon to keep the peace by broadcasting a formidable U.S. capability to project power. Placing bomber forces on alert or moving them to bases near areas in crisis amounts to a display of long-range U.S. forces and signals the willingness and capability of the United States to act decisively abroad. U.S. strike aircraft have been used to great effect with minimum loss of life in several conflicts. They have enabled the United States to use force in cases where the international environment would not otherwise permit action, such as against terrorism.

While the use of aerial bombardment had received support in earlier conflicts, the American people recognized that it had reached unprecedented levels of precision and effectiveness during the 1991 Gulf War against Iraq. The air campaign clearly helped to minimize Allied casualties and the deaths of innocent Iraqis, provided quick and decisive successes, and helped coalition forces weaken Iraq's military capability and begin elimination of Iraq's ability to wage a war using weapons of mass destruction. This left the United States with a new concept of the utility of modern air power as a potential instrument of U.S. foreign policy with unprecedented abilities to wage war, provide a strong deterrent, and protect international peacekeeping and supply operations.

Chapter 3
Defense Planning and the Modern Long-Range Bomber

COLIN S. GRAY AND JOHN J. KOHOUT III

The problem at issue here is the proper role of U.S. long-range bombers in general, and the B-2 in particular, in the distinctly uncertain future that is the new security environment. This chapter explores the degree to which the B-2 and long-range bombardment operations appear to meet the national security needs of the United States [81].

Two routes are taken here to explore and explain the strategic-value of a modern bomber force: (1) with reference to broad principles for the guidance of defense planning in this decade (and beyond); and (2) by means of reconsideration of the bomber force structure for this new, uncertain, era in the light of the "threat" spectrum discussed in chapter 1.

Principles for Successful Defense Planning

It is important to know how the B-2 can contribute to alleviation or resolution of threats in the 1990's. In chapter 1 Figure 1 presented an overall view of "The Structure of the Problem." Here we must focus on the key detail that was purposely omitted from Figure 1: well refined propositions which can serve as principles for the guidance of defense planning. These serve here to test and probe the characteristics of modern U.S. bomber forces. Figure 3 presents a schematic list of these principles.

Figure 3: Military Power in Support of U.S. Foreign Policy
(an expansion upon level 4 in Figure 1)

MILITARY POWER PRINCIPLES FOR GUIDANCE OF DEFENSE PLANNING

1. Capable of winning
2. Sufficient in number
3. Enjoy/merit acceptability at home
4. Diverse
5. Modern
6. Applicable quickly
7. Adaptable to Geography
8. Logistically supportable
9. Able to cope with surprise
10. Focus maximum potential power
11. Able to threaten/protect center of gravity
12. Flexible enough for non-standard missions
13. Earn respect from foes

IMPLICATIONS OF PRINCIPLES FOR FORCE PLANNING

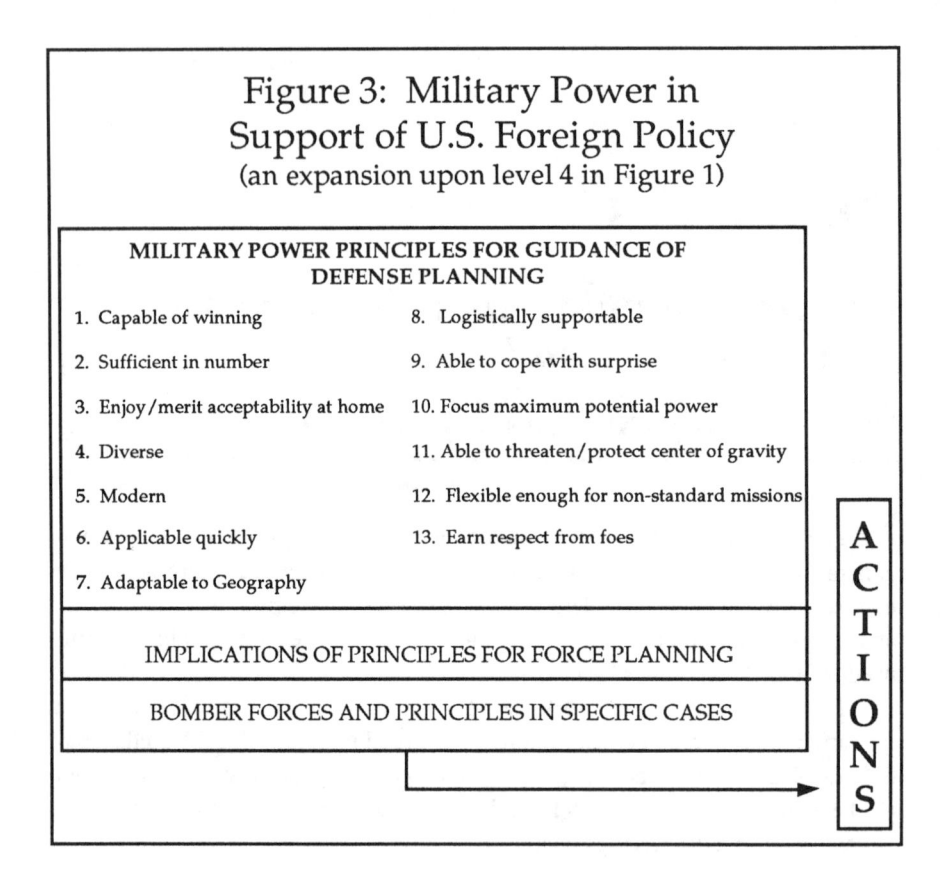

BOMBER FORCES AND PRINCIPLES IN SPECIFIC CASES

ACTIONS

These principles can be questioned at the margin, but that would hold true for any such set of postulated characteristics for armed forces. These principles have been derived to help guide force planning *in toto*, not only bomber forces. This caveat is not a limitation upon the value of the principles, rather it is a strength. A long-standing practical problem for the consideration of bomber forces is that they have been treated as an independent and separate capability. Too often, bombers have been regarded only as nuclear delivery vehicles rather than as an integral component of the forces normally considered for deployment to a theater and designed to function there in conventional roles immediately supportive of other large-scale military operations under the purview of the theater commander. The bomber's reach normally exceeds theater boundaries logical for other forces. No military or political-military capability can fit perfectly with all plausible national needs or strategic requirements at the levels of grand strategy and military strategy. Modern long-range bombers armed with precision weapons, though not a panacea, are a strategic asset of great utility across a wide band of the threat spectrum. What follows are brief general explanations of the ways in which modern long-range attack aircraft reflect, express, or advance the thirteen principles that should guide U.S. defense planning.

U.S. Forces Should Be . . .

1. *Capable of winning* **the wars to which they are committed.** This principle of successful defense planning is the first among equals. It is the ordering principle through which the others obtain their meaning. While military forces or operations may serve in peace and wartime to fulfill other roles, the central military capability of the nation must be shaped in terms of its ability to wage and win wars. As the following principles are considered for the insights each offers in turn, it is helpful to return to this first principle to make sure that the planner does not stray from the central frame of reference to subordinate functions. Defense debates all too easily come to focus on potentially important, but subordinate functions: showing the flag; performing non-traditional peacetime functions; supporting local, domestic economic interests. The modern long-range bomber, as any other element of military power, deserves consideration with this caveat ever in mind.

Modern long-range, land-based bombers are the only U.S. conventionally armed forces that can be employed globally within hours to strike strategic objectives, the destruction of which has the potential to shape the course and outcome of an entire conflict. Without depending on access to overseas basing or preliminary surface operations, long-range bombers can both take offensive action to threaten or penalize an aggressor, or act to spoil or blunt an enemy's offensive operations. As demonstrated in the Gulf War, the technology needed to carry out these roles, long foreseen by air power visionaries, is now clearly in the possession of U.S. aerial forces and is embodied especially in the B-2.

Whatever U.S. forces may be deemed necessary to achieve national objectives in a given conflict, it is the long-range, land-based bomber forces that hold the potential for earliest expression of U.S. intent at a convincing force level. Bombers can serve to delay enemy progress while other U.S. forces are mobilized and can cover U.S. deployments to tactical positions. They can do the same for U.S. allies and coalition partners. They can disrupt the enemy's command and control apparatus, weaken its logistical infrastructure, and engage offensive forces compromising their ability to attain initial objectives. Modern long-range bombers, particularly stealthy platforms, should be able to place at risk those targets deemed by U.S. National Command Authorities and responsible theater commanders to be of the greatest strategic importance. Bombers can do this early, and in a sustained fashion throughout a campaign. The weight of the attack potential of a significant force of modern, long-range bombers, while no substitute for important contributions made by other force elements, has now, more than at any other time in the aviation age, the potential to shape the course and outcome of an entire conflict.

2. Sufficient in number to be employed to decisive military effect. Because of the inherent qualities of modern systems, bombers often can have decisive effect with the fewest weapons and accompanying crew numbers possible among alternative U.S. forces. Because they can operate with decisive effect, and do so with relatively small numbers, there are many cases where political contexts, both domestic and international, find intervention by bomber forces preferable to larger alternatives requiring slow, massive deployments, and putting far more U.S. personnel at risk. Indeed, there are instances wherein modern long-range bombers provide the only practicable option.

As in any military activity, however, numbers remain important for decisive employment. Technology has progressed to the point, though, where the numbers under serious and responsible consideration for bomber forces, shrink to a few hundred rather than the many thousands of World War II, or even the approximately one thousand that bore the brunt of Cold War deterrence in the early 1960's. Several hundred modern long-range bombers embody a great flexibility of strategic contribution to national defense across the widest range of contingencies. Numbers in this range can furnish the mass needed to convert air attack from a form of harassment and disruptive force to a reliable approach to wreaking significant attrition on enemy forces in the field, or upon their assets. Such numbers can turn air attack from a sporadic event into a continuing paralyzing presence. And, such numbers are surely needed for the persistence of effort needed to insure that an enemy cannot attempt to defeat the United States by outlasting it. They can help to bridge the strategic challenge of simultaneous crises in widely separated regions.

It is significant that a force structure of modern, long-range bombers with sufficient numbers to contribute to these military functions is the smallest force structure in terms of weapons, people, and deployed support structure among any similarly capable alternative forms of military presence: land, sea or air. At the same time these numbers hold the potential for reconstituting a nuclear capability for deterrence if that becomes a necessity.

3. Of a kind, scale, and character of behavior such as to merit acceptability at home. Long-range bombardment and the employment of long-range multi-mission, land-based strike aviation has long been a distinctly American approach to the pursuit of victory in armed combat. Long-range, land based bombers have repeatedly shown themselves to be an American weapon of choice. The role of airpower in U.S. military history since the 1930s demonstrates the point, including: the long-range coastal patrol aviation of the mid-thirties through the Combined Bomber Offensive against Nazi Germany; bombardment operations in support of OVERLORD; B-29 offensive against Japan culminating in massive incendiary attacks and the two atomic bombings; strategic and tactical bombing campaigns in Korea; the strategic bombing of Vietnam; the creation of a bomber-heavy Cold War nuclear capability as the core of the deterrence of the Soviet threat; and the delivery of some 29% of all U.S. aerial ordnance dropped on Iraqi targets in the Gulf War [82].

Although not low in initial dollar cost, long-range bombers match the preferences of political leaders, the talents and capacities of U.S. industry, strategic and geographic setting, and have generally served adaptively through operational life times sufficiently long to amortize initial costs comfortably. American society has also tended to value the ability to reach out across the oceans in offensive strikes against aggressors' homelands. American society has seen its bomber force as a uniquely valuable tool in support of American values and interests around the world.

Concerns over collateral damage due to the apparent indiscriminate nature of heavy bomber attacks, long a consideration, should be greatly reduced in the future due to the reduced prospects of nuclear confrontation and the demonstrated precision and discipline of bombing attacks conducted in the Gulf War. Indeed technology demonstrated in Gulf War action should be seen as moving the modern long-range, land-based bomber up from being considered one of the least discriminate military weapons to a position among the more discriminate weapons delivery platforms. That this is beginning to be recognized at policy-making levels can be documented by the interest expressed in various circles about options for U.S. intervention in the Balkans based on airpower. Such options would be frivolous indeed, if they weren't founded on the assumption of impressive accuracy of weapons delivery by bombing aircraft of great range.

4. Suitably *diverse* as to allow for adaptability to unexpected conditions. While the long-range, land-based bomber has the straightforward, simple function of delivering air-to ground munitions at great distances, its basic qualities of range, payload, and operational flexibility have long ensured that bombers can contribute to military campaigns with great diversity. From World War II strategic bombing campaigns in both Europe and the Pacific, bombers switched frequently to tactical support of surface operations.

At the beginning of the Cold War conventional bombers took on nuclear missions; the first dedicated nuclear bombers switched to strategic reconnaissance; high altitude bombers responded to the advent of surface-to-air missiles by penetrating at low altitude and carrying massive electronic warfare suites. As intercontinental range and the need for higher performance came into tension, aerial refueling first became commonplace in the bomber force. With Vietnam the long-range bomber switched back from nuclear to conventional functions against both strategic and tactical targets. And, later in the Gulf War the long-range bomber found its greatest utility in engaging armies in the field while smaller aircraft took on "strategic" targets. During much of the Cold War, the nuclear-armed long-range bombers had collateral missions adjunct to U.S. Navy capabilities in the areas of sea surveillance, mine-laying and anti-surface warfare.

The modern long-range, land-based bomber, particularly the B-2 with its "stealth" characteristics achieves a remarkable potential for adaptability to unexpected conditions. While this is not to deny that there are important tasks that long-range bombers cannot perform well, or at all, progressive adaptation of large airframes to new offensive, defensive and situational awareness technologies has proven to be relatively easy. Advances in "smart" munitions are adding a whole new dimension the roles such aircraft can play. The GPS-Aided Targeting System/GPS-Aided Munition (GATS/GAM) program is one contemporary development. It profits from the inherent capabilities of the B-2 airframe and its advanced computerized avionics to bypass an entire generation of technology to attain low-cost seekerless precision weapons delivery far sooner than it would have otherwise been possible [83]. Such a capability promises accuracy sufficient to enable the B-2 to engage discrete targets with a single weapon, rather than an entire bomb load as was generally the case with bombers in the past.

In defense planning for the future, the modern long-range, land based bomber offers a broad adaptability based on being able to reach any eventual target, with:

- a large quantity of the broadest selection of munitions;
- high confidence of penetrating intense defenses;
- minimal dependence on constrained sets of overseas bases;
- continual availability from the earliest hours of a conflict through to its termination;
- the potential for sequentially changing roles from one category to another as the conflict progresses [84].

Chapter 3   45

5. **Technologically advanced, i.e., *modern*, for effectiveness in action overall.** To the degree that tactical advantage can be obtained through technological progress, such advantage should be factored into force structuring decisions with the greatest care. While some technological advances may generate only transient advantage, others can have enduring influence over decades regardless of enemies' efforts. While it may not become apparent for some time to which category certain technological advances belong, some, like the "stealth" characteristics of the B-2, have such profound impact in terms of fielded capabilities that there is great likelihood of an enduring payoff.

Yet, being advanced or "modern" does not stop at possessing one single technological asset. Far more important in the long run may be a combination of assets in forms such as reliability, so that the new system can remain on the battle line rather than in the repair line; technical adaptability so that the new system can adopt other new technologies that become available during its lifetime, such as new precision munitions; mission adaptability in order to accommodate new battlefield configurations, access or denial of high quality basing, or the need to span great distances. Efficiency in terms of operational overhead such as fuels, maintenance man-hours or ground and air crew numbers may all be crucial parts of the attribute of being "modern" in strategically significant terms.

Seeking advanced capabilities is far removed from actually fielding them. The more restrictive defense budgets become and the more demanding the standard of efficiency, the more modernity needs to be sought in terms of operational systems rather than designs that are only sketches on the "drawing board." The B-2, a modern system that is "flying," has demonstrated the effectiveness of its technology, and is rolling off of a full-scale production line, has enormous reliability advantages over conceptual future alternatives.

6. **Able to be *applied quickly*, when necessary.** Modern long-range, land-based bomber forces are designed, trained, and maintained to be the most responsive element of U.S. military power. They are conceived with direct initial employment to any targets in the world in mind. Initial bomber strikes can reliably attack targets important to the assistance of a threatened ally or forward positioned U.S. forces while deployments of other U.S. force elements are planned and executed. The peacetime posture of long-range bomber aircraft can be advanced to the degree implied by perceptions of increasing tension or U.S. vulnerability in any region.

Recent history provides examples of the range of pre-hostility measures possible to bring bombers to bear as promptly as the situation merits. Abbreviated mission planning in response to the Iraqi invasion of Kuwait had

SAC bombers ready to launch on conventional strikes only a few hours after the invasion began. Years of Cold War nuclear alert saw a significant percentage of these same bombers on runway alert with missions already pre-planned for launch in minutes. During the most stressful of Cold War periods, numbers of these same bombers were kept on "Airborne Alert," maintaining firepower in international airspace, but far closer to target areas, should the attack order be given.

Once hostilities have begun, bombers are amenable to yet other measures to foreshorten the delay before striking time-sensitive targets. Bomber "stream" tactics used in Vietnam and the Gulf War put bombers over targets at frequent intervals. By analogy, AWACS, JSTARS and "Wild Weasel" tactics in the Gulf War demonstrated how, under some conditions, today's modern bombers could be orbited in close proximity to target areas for rapid attack of time sensitive targets when they present themselves. These examples illustrate the degree to which the modern long-range bomber can be applied quickly to gain tactical advantage disproportionate to the weight of weaponry delivered.

7. *Adaptable*, or tailored, *to geography*. Modern long-range, land-based bombers are specifically designed to reflect the strategic geography of the United States. The range and payload capacity of World War II-era conventional bombers reflected the U.S. situation as a continental-sized power with ocean frontiers that had to be crossed in offensive or defensive action. With the true intercontinental bombers of the Cold War period, the B-36s and B-52s, the U.S. bomber force acquired globe-spanning range to match the world-wide span of U.S. interests as a superpower. This class of aircraft is capable of operating over and striking targets on any terrain or at sea. After the last B-52s, and eventually the B-1Bs are retired, the B-2 will be the only remaining strike aircraft in the world that will match the strategic needs of the United States in this way. No alternative system is now on the drawing board or even in conceptual development.

The unique possession of this class of weapon system by the United States often tempts observers to jump to the questionable conclusion that, if other nations do not need intercontinental-range bombing capability, neither does the United States. Recent history is instructive in this regard. The Soviet Union struggled long to maintain a similar fleet of long-range bombers. It was only with the demise of Soviet global imperial ambition, and the dissolution of the Soviet State that they have essentially disbanded their remaining bomber force.

Great Britain furnishes an even more graphic example of the interaction between long-range bomber forces and the span of national influence. In 1982 the British Government determined that, henceforth, Britain would only require military capability in the context of conflict in the European area. The British correspondingly deactivated the aerial refueling systems on their remaining long-range Vulcan bombers and shifted training to short unrefueled missions in support of theater air operations in Europe. Only months later Argentina invaded the Falkland Islands, taking advantage of this unilateral British decision to put aside the only weapon it possessed which could promptly reach the remnants of a once-global empire. Great Britain responded with characteristic determination, but it took months to mobilize and deploy the naval task force needed to retake the Falklands. A part of this mobilization was the reassembly of the refueling systems on a number of Vulcans and the eventual mounting of a few air attacks on Argentina's occupying forces, far too late to serve the strategic purpose that a prompt British response would almost certainly have had [85]. Indeed, the Argentine decision to invade the Falklands had to have reflected, to some degree, the perception that Britain had, by word and deed, renounced its intent to back up residual global interests by the force of arms. If the United States is to avoid any number of similar miscommunications, maintenance of potent modern long-range bomber forces which match in range and combat potential the span and intensity of U.S. interests is warranted.

8. *Logistically supportable* for optimum, or unexpectedly imposed, operations tempo. Because long-range, land-based bombers can be maintained at a high state of readiness at secure U.S. bases and can be launched into initial globe-spanning strike missions without preliminary deployment, initial combat logistical support takes the form of a largely preexisting peacetime logistical train. Bombers can be progressively deployed in the heat of battle to amplify the firepower they can bring to bear and increase sortie frequency to the point that they achieve a measure of mass and surprise unattainable by most other conventional forces. Generally moderately demanding of logistical support in peacetime or for sporadic combat operations, modern long-range, land-based bomber forces significantly increase their demand for logistical support as operations tempo increases.

Tonnage of bombs and volume of fuel tend to drive logistics requirements as increasing tempo adds mass to a bombing campaign. This increase in the support required is in direct proportion to the bomber's efficiency of getting massive tonnages of weapons on target. What is unique about the long-range, land-based bomber in this regard is that it has sufficient range, even operating unrefueled at a high sortie rate, to permit an extremely wide selection of basing options. Bases can be selected for their access to the most efficient surface logistical support system. Inter-theater lift, often highly efficient marine transportation augmented by fuel pipelines, dedicated rail lines and good road nets, can characteristically provide the required logistical support directly to the site of forward-based bomber operations. Most shorter-range or surface deployable force elements more often require significant intra-theater lift to position supplies for distribution to operating forces. The logistical system supporting shorter range or surface forces must extend well into the combat area and accept the level of vulnerability to enemy action to which the supported forces themselves are exposed. This can include challenging underway replenishment for embarked aviation and the restrictions of confined storage volume available on aircraft carriers. In relative terms, the modern long-range, land-based bomber is a logistically responsive approach to establishing whatever operational tempo is chosen by U.S. commanders, or implied by enemy action.

9. **Able to cope with *surprise* and dampen surprise effect.** The great flexibility possible in the employment of long-range, land-based attack aircraft is key to their significance as a U.S. strategic asset. Basing either within the United States or overseas at bases well removed from potential hot-spots insures that the bomber force is as well protected from hostility-starting surprises as military forces can be. Since they do not have to deploy forward, within range of enemy action by shorter-range systems, they and their logistical support structure stay protected throughout the conflict. They are subject to attrition on terms specified by the United States in the form of the choice of patterns of U.S. offensive action.

Modern, high-quality bomber forces are well suited to achieve a rapid response to surprise. Bombers are able to act effectively in a wide range of conflict environments; are capable of acting in imperfectly anticipated situations in response to general orders with additional specific detailed strike orders furnished well after aircraft are launched; and can deliver massive firepower to targets from a relatively small number of platforms. Although bomber forces, along with the remainder of the military establishment, may be caught by surprise, they are well designed to deny an enemy some of the beneficial operational or strategic effect of such tactical surprise as he may achieve. Bomber operations can function to help limit an enemy's gains, slow him down, harass his rear areas and create both fears and the reality of operational overextension on his part. Long-range bombardment activities should be integral to military plans and operations, whether friendly forces are mobilizing and deploying, advancing, withdrawing, or holding.

10. **Adaptable to *focus a maximum potential of military power* on any given conflict.** For the United States of today and the foreseeable future, the long-range bomber is the single conventional weapon system most able to draw together the output of the most productive aspects of

the U.S. industrial base, focus the maximum military potential of the United States, and deliver the resulting destructive power to the enemy. The modern bomber does it in sheer tonnage of explosives, and in terms of accurate application of precise attacks. It produces intense military effect and, even more importantly, focuses that effect sharply on strategically highly significant objectives wherever in the territory of the enemy such attacks are seen as achieving the greatest strategic leverage.

11. Capable of holding at risk the enemy's *center of strategic gravity*, and of protecting our own. This principle highlights the forté of the modern long-range, land-based bomber. With its ability to range the battlefield and the enemy's territory and penetrate any foreseeable defensive array, the modern bomber is often the most suitable U.S. force element for placing the enemy's center of gravity at risk. At the same time bomber forces can react quickly to the need to frustrate enemy efforts to attack important U.S. assets. The bomber's ability to operate from well beyond the threat radius of enemy action also means that bomber bases are not likely to become part of a vulnerable U.S. center of gravity. Bombardment operations with B-2-class aircraft can: threaten the lives or liberty of enemy leaders; place in peril the reputation of an enemy regime by conducting raids that are politically humiliating; challenge the enemy's self-esteem and alter comprehensively his terms of analysis (in favor of pessimism). The Desert Storm combined air campaign demonstrates that the potential of modern bomber forces to threaten the enemy's center of gravity is today far more extensive than even the most visionary of airpower advocates predicted in the past.

12. Sufficiently *flexible* to cope well with the kinds of missions that tend to rank low on service priorities (e.g., low intensity conflict tasks). The challenge here is the ability to ensure that no opponent can challenge the United States in a way that evades the capabilities of U.S. conventional forces and thereby achieves its objectives on the cheap. Terrorism and urban or rural unconventional warfare are broad classes of events that tend to leave conventional armed forces without relevant targets at which to strike, and without attainable military objectives. This area is far from the focus of long-range bomber force design. However, the potential for relatively small forces of bombers to destroy either precisely located finite targets, or area targets within which dispersed enemy assets may be located, exists. Such missions at the low end of the threat spectrum can be executed without deploying U.S. forces into politically tense environments, without significant risk of casualties, and without depending on the cooperation of U.S. allies or coalition partners. Such missions may prove remarkably practical in cases where an aggressor's neighbors find themselves attacked or threatened by proliferating ballistic missile systems or chemical, biological, or even nuclear weapons. In such cases, the deployment of U.S. surface or short-range forces could present politically unacceptable risks, and the establishment of an effective coalition might prove impossible. While such eventualities are most unlikely to constitute a specific rationale for procuring a force of modern long-range bombers, they unquestionably illustrate the range of potential utility that an appropriate modern long-range, land-based bomber force would have.

13. *Worthy of respect* in valuation of would-be foes. Much as U.S. conventional forces collectively embody the attributes of technical competence, large numbers and logistical prowess important to a major, integrated war effort, modern long-range land-based bombers epitomize that American military competence. U.S. ability to strike any enemy target compels a measure of respect from any opponent. The bomber's well advertised deep raiding capability and doctrine can contribute usefully to a potential foe's respect for U.S. power. It is important to note that in some cultures, however, competent local forces may be in surface warfare, modern aerial combat still possesses a mystique that adds to the respect, if not awe, felt for the overall weight of American military power.

The discussion here is intended only to outline the modern long-range, land-based bomber dimension of the military capabilities implied by the thirteen principles for the guidance of defense planning. What stands out from this section of the study is the unique niche that modern bomber forces should fill in the necessary array of U.S. military and political-military capabilities. In some cases, bomber forces may be of little or no identifiable relevance, but the trained and educated habit of consulting these principles of successful defense planning should produce recognition of the broad strategic utility of modern bomber forces.

Long-range Bomber Missions and the Threats of the 1990's

Several streams of argument and evidence must be brought together to review the ways in which U.S. modern long-range, land-based bomber forces could provide strategic utility in the 1990's. The method adopted here is a straightforward examination of bomber missions in the context of the demands and opportunities of threats outlined in chapter 1.

In rough-cut terms there are three broad questions here. First, what security problems will the United States face, or choose to face? Second, what mission and individual tasks will U.S. bomber forces be allowed to attempt? Third, how well will U.S. bomber forces perform?

1. Regional aggression. As the focus and geopolitical scope of conflict narrows from forty years of superpower confrontation, it becomes no less likely that tactically excellent long-range bomber operations will be able to make some critical and identifiable strategic difference to the course of hostilities. In great conflicts, typically both sides are so well endowed with a diversity of assets on a large scale that the outcome can only be secured reliably by an attritional style of warfare. Modern bomber forces make useful contributions to victory in attritional combat, provided they are sufficient in number, whatever substitutions or adjustments the foe can make.

With the Gulf War of 1991, aerial bombardment showed how far it had progressed as a war-winning operational form and how well it suited the United States and its coalition partners as a style of pursuing military goals in regional conflict. Long-range, land-based bombers played recognizably important—if not decisive—roles to facilitate the grand strategy and the military strategy of the war. It is important to note that, if Saddam Hussein had invaded Saudi Arabia immediately after conquering Kuwait, the only conventional forces the United States would have been able to muster immediately in defense of that country would have been long-range bombers. As it was, they added greatly to the air campaign that was the leading edge of the coalition war effort; served to frustrate the Iraqi ground campaign by severely damaging deployed Republican Guard and other field army units; and contributed critically to the impact of psychological warfare against the enemy.

The Gulf War of 1991 was of course unique. The substantial level of long-range, land-based bomber contribution to coalition success in that conflict, however, promises to be far from unique. Long-range bombers cannot themselves wage and win a large-scale regional conflict, but neither are they a merely "nice to have" addition to massive conventional military forces. In regional conflicts modern long-range bombardment air power acts as an important enabler for conventional operational success and as a virtually independent instrument of direct operational, strategic, and political effect. The unique concentration of high quality and capacity air bases in and near the Gulf War theater of action is sometimes overlooked. Future regional conflicts are far more likely to occur where bases are few, far from the action, and logistically isolated (See chapter 4 for details). This promises to place a premium on modern long-range, land-based combat aircraft.

The strategic utility of long-range bomber forces in regional conflict is suggested by historical experience, logic, and common sense. The fact remains that the specific detailed conditions of each conflict, as well as the quality of the bomber forces in question and of the surface and theater air forces that they might assist, always will be critical to the merit of bomber employment. It is necessary to consider both what bomber forces can do well and what specifically needs doing in a particular historical case of conflict. Not only do the bomber forces have to be fit to be employed in the most demanding of military missions, but also political and military leaders both have to know how to use them and need confidence in their prowess. In many instances bomber forces will compete with other kinds of forces to perform tasks that all agree must be performed, while some of the more important stand-alone bombardment operations would "work" strategically more as accelerators of victory (or brakes upon the pace of defeat) than as indispensable keys to victory.

2. Local disorder. Local disorder refers here to war, disturbance or instability within a single country, albeit frequently with one or more of the belligerent parties demanding succession. This category of threat to U.S. interests would exclude the wars in Korea, Vietnam, and the Gulf (1991). By way of contrast the Dominican Republic in 1965, Grenada in 1983, Panama in 1989, and today—potentially the former Yugoslavia, would all count in the column of local disorder. The contemporary Yugoslav-Balkan drama-tragedy is a sad textbook example of local disorder that is teetering on the brink of becoming a truly regional conflict. Indeed, it is only slightly far-fetched to discern in the current Balkan morass the fuel for a general European war. (A familiar pattern of Germans backing Croats and Russians backing Serbs already is apparent, though not yet consummated in a thoroughgoing way).

While not as broadly usable in local conflict as in larger wars, long-range, land-based bombers remain relevant to the "local disorder" category. The frequency of calls for a U.S. role in stopping Balkan violence by the use of air power is evidence that U.S. public opinion and decision-makers are open to the idea of using bombardment air power. The emphasis on long-range of bomber forces comes from the physical setting of the Balkan conflict. Compared to the Gulf War, where Saudi Arabia provided numerous modern and underutilized airfields at a reasonable distance from potential targets, the Balkans find themselves much less well endowed with politically available airfields possessing the surplus capacity and surface logistical potential needed for significant military operations. The pivotal importance of Aviano Air Base as the only full-service NATO Air base near enough to former Yugoslav territory to host combat operations emphasizes this point. Carrier-based operations confront parallel constraints to those they experienced in the Gulf War: vulnerability due to confining waters resulting in excessive distances from targets. If such greater U.S. involvement is decided, it will in all probability include long-range, land-based bomber operations, either actual operations or the political military effect of the possibility of escalation to the level of firepower that such weapons could apply.

Aside from assessments of military performance, the issues with regard to employing bombers here are the structural differences between, say, Vietnam after mid-1965 and Iraq-Kuwait in 1990-91 on the one hand, and Grenada in 1983 and Panama in 1989. Even the Grenadian and Panamanian cases plainly provided conditions where the shock value of aerial bombardment had some utility. In conflicts where U.S. purpose is not recognized as meriting the risk of significant American casualties, aerial bombardment becomes a far more palatable solution than it might normally be seen to be. Still the Gulf War demonstrated the new technical abilities of air power and the capability of shaping and aiming attacks so that they correspond to the conflict and the targets that must be destroyed. Debates over the appropriateness of air attack, particularly if massive or extremely focused by long-range, land-based bombers, will remain extremely contentious. Still in the near-regional conflict in the Gulf in 1991, U.S. political and military leaders were manifestly uncomfortable with the casualty rate inflicted upon enemy soldiers, let alone upon enemy civilians.

On the rare occasions when the United States will be motivated sufficiently to intervene in a local conflict, it is a very safe prediction that intervention, to be viable politically, will need to be swiftly executed and exceedingly discriminating in its application of lethal force. It is important in this regard to realize that bomber operations are likely to be seen as being decisively important to U.S. policy success.

3. **Transnational, non-traditional, "security" threats.** Police and intelligence agencies typically lead in responses to the national security problems that flow from drug-trafficking, other manifestations of organized crime, terrorism (state-sponsored and "private"), and unscrupulous and illegal forms of competitive economic behavior. Nonetheless, when the proper roles of the FBI, CIA, DEA, Treasury and others are duly noted, the fact remains that conventionally constituted or special operations forces are a major, and on occasion an indispensable, resource for policy. In this regard long-range bomber forces probably constitute the extreme-level-of-force limiting case.

The April 1986 raid on Libya is perhaps the clearest example of long-range bombardment in support of a counter-terrorist campaign. While in that case the particular aircraft used were shorter-range aircraft based in Europe or aboard carriers, the success of the operation clearly shows the suitability of modern long-range, land-based air power. Stealthy platforms capable of precision attack of a number of distinct targets at low risk of attrition or loss of American life would certainly have been suitable for the task. The length of the F-111 sorties from England, around Spain to the Libyan target areas was easily long enough to merit use of longer-range assets. Operational security risked compromise by dependence on flight operations in busy European and Mediterranean air space. Effectiveness of the part of the attack performed by carrier aviation was evidently dependent on the fortuitous availability in the Mediterranean of more than the normal single U.S. aircraft carrier.

Had it been necessary to repeat the message to Colonel Qaddafi, the United States would have confronted a very difficult problem. Following the April 15 raid, Colonel Qaddafi redeployed his air defenses into a barrier defense pattern of concentration across Libya's populated Mediterranean frontier. Subsequent attacks would have had to penetrate this reinforced and alerted defensive array. Yet, had B-2-class long-range, stealthy penetrators been available, they could have either penetrated such an array or, even more effectively, flown around it to strike then-unprotected strategic targets far inland.

The point is not to argue that long-range, land-based bombers offer the only answer to terrorism, transnational crime, and economic sanctions-busting (for example). Rather, the point is that modern long-range, land-based bombers have capabilities that other coercive arms of state power might lack. They might only be usable in the few cases where the most extreme pressure for a violent U.S. interjection is merited, but in those cases it is imperative that the United States have the appropriate quality long-range capability needed to do the job.

4. International Emergencies. Modern long-range, bomber forces are least likely assets for responding quickly to emergency calls for help in the face of natural or man-made disasters. However, the complexity of international crisis situations is not to be underestimated, and a rather benign humanitarian operation can turn nasty. The U.S. involvement in Somalia is a case in point. On the surface, there would appear to have been no role for U.S. bombers. Yet, it is clear that the erratic potential for violence that was an ever-present threat to individual soldiers and relief workers could have escalated at any time. That is why the United States took a leadership role in Somalia and why it chose to constitute the U.S. role in famine relief as an armed military intervention. In such a case it is prudent to have overwhelming force available at short notice if a sudden escalation of violence calls for a demonstration of intent and capability. In the Somali case, this force was for a time provided by the off-shore presence of the USS *Kitty Hawk* and its air wing. In the midst of Somali operations, Iraqi contravention of cease fire agreements created another crisis which caused the *Kitty Hawk* to be sent to the Persian Gulf. This left the Somali expedition without its *in extremis* fire power back-up, other than that which could be delivered at intercontinental distances. The equanimity with which the local commander and the press could watch the *Kitty Hawk* sail away from a most unstable situation spoke eloquently about their unspoken confidence in the underlying ability of U.S. long-range airpower to deliver whatever level of firepower might be required half way around the world, and do it in time to cope with any tactical emergency.

Modern Long-Range, Land Based Bombers and National Security Policy

Here we have explained what can be termed the structure of U.S. national security in the 1990's and the apparent fit of modern long-range, land-based bombers such as the B-2 within that structure. The implications of this analysis for policy and strategy and for the value of bomber forces lie in the whole architecture of the argument presented. The strategic value of bomber forces in the new security environment of the 1990's cannot be assessed via an essentially context-free study of the forces themselves. To describe the instrument, in no matter how glowing terms, does not speak to the notion of whether or not the country requires the services of that instrument. Only a comprehensive analysis of all of the major pieces of the (U.S.) national security puzzle can lead to confident understanding of whether, how, where, and when a long-range bomber force structure should "fit."

Chapter 4
Access, Basing, and the Reach of U.S. Combat Power

JOHN J. KOHOUT III

Whatever can be said about the future international security environment and the U.S. role in it, general considerations fail to specify in advance exactly where and why the United States might find it necessary to employ its military forces. The span of U.S. interests is global. Add to "core" U.S. interests those that come with the mantle of responsibility as the sole remaining superpower, and the geographic range of possibilities for U.S. military involvement over the next several decades defies delineation. Recent U.S. military operations in locations as improbable as Haiti, Bosnia, Somalia, Iraq, Panama, Libya, and Grenada illustrate that the prediction of specific threats is neither possible nor necessarily helpful to force structure analysis.

In the course of remarks following his oath of office, then-Secretary of Defense Les Aspin described the security challenge ahead in a way that accepted such geographic uncertainties without resolving them. He alluded to four emerging dangers to our future security. "The first is the new nuclear danger..." stemming from "...a handful of warheads in the hands of terrorists or terrorist states" and "...the second ... from regional conflicts ... potentially threats to the United States' vital interests." Aspin saw the third danger as arising "...from the possibility of a failure of reform, particularly in the former Soviet Union." Finally he described the fourth danger as "...the failure to see our national security interests in a way that includes the economy" [86]. None of these four dangers can be defined by precise geographic location or "sphere of influence". They do suggest that the United States maintain the capability for global action.

It is tempting to see the strategic geography of the United States as a constant in the calculus of U.S. relations with the rest of the world. Over the four decades of Cold War, that was very nearly true. At the beginning of the

58   The B-2 Bomber: Air Power for the 21st Century

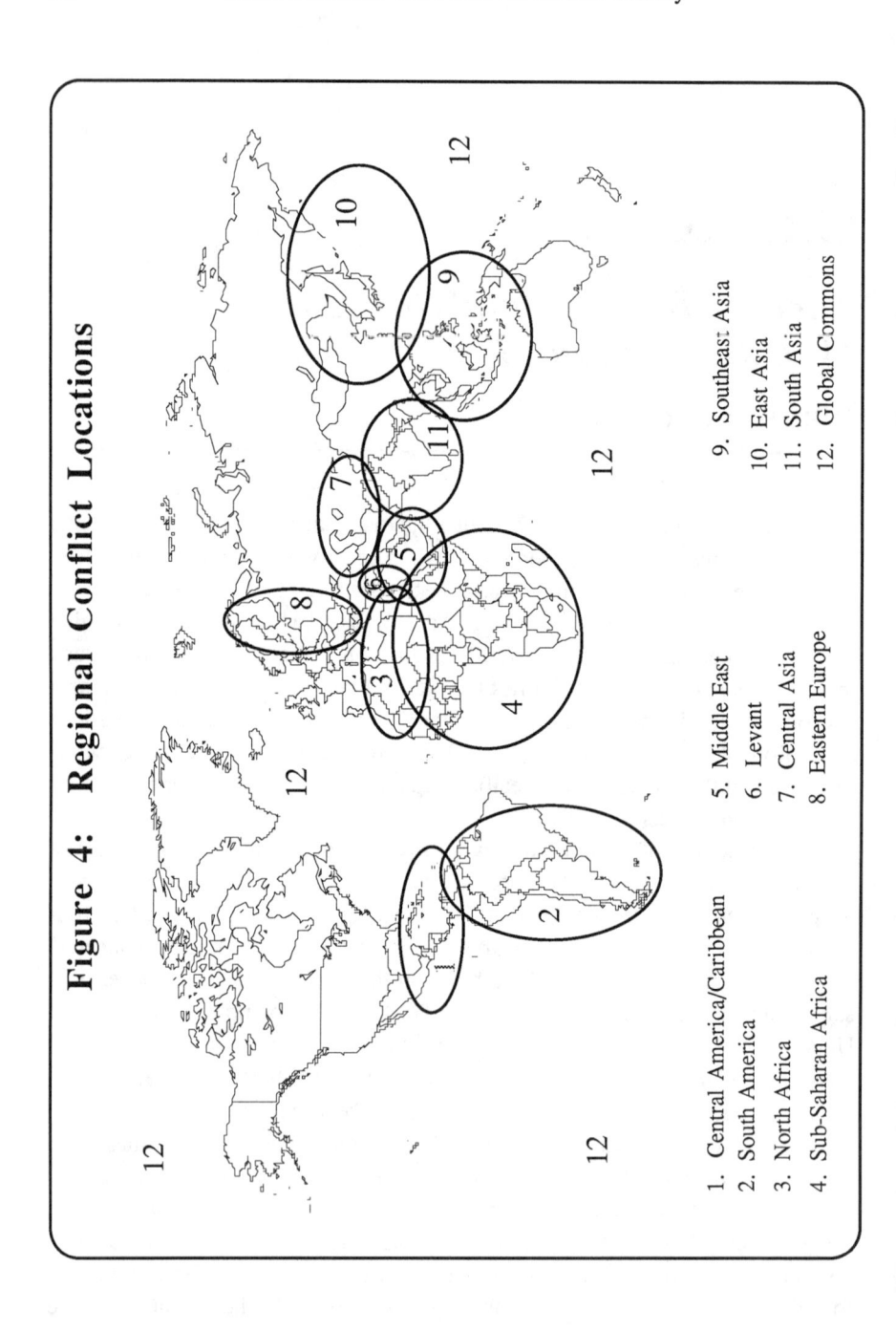

Figure 4: Regional Conflict Locations

1. Central America/Caribbean
2. South America
3. North Africa
4. Sub-Saharan Africa
5. Middle East
6. Levant
7. Central Asia
8. Eastern Europe
9. Southeast Asia
10. East Asia
11. South Asia
12. Global Commons

Cold War a combination of factors gave the United States confident global access. The United States had bases left over from its overseas expansionist period which started with the end of the Spanish-American war (1898) and World War II alliances; it assembled still more bases through the Cold War alliance system. It had overflight access to match. With the Soviet threat gone, the cohesion of that basing and access system has eroded. America's global basing system is a shadow of what it once was. Yet, in a world where regional conflict abounds and opponents can not be predetermined, whatever might be unchanging about the uniqueness of American strategic geography, as an insular continent with global interests, is clearly overbalanced by the need to shape force structure decisions to assure that the United States can meet the geographic challenges of particular regions.

Rather than generalizing about global basing, this analysis proceeds by dividing the world into a number of regions, each of which could at some point in the future host crises of sufficient import to raise the issue of U.S. involvement. This approach generates a series of rather stark caricatures which severally and collectively define the future access and basing challenge for American expeditionary activity. These regional sketches then furnish a frame of geographic reference for evaluating the future strategic utility of U.S. power projection forces in general and modern long-range, land-based bomber forces in particular. Figure 4 presents the range capabilities of U.S. power-projection aircraft as a frame of reference for region-by-region discussion. As the chart shows, long-range bombers have combat radii significantly greater than those of smaller aircraft designed for purely theater operations.

This analysis does not attempt to predict specific conflicts. By dividing the world into twelve regions of likely or possible conflict [87], it seeks to focus thinking about the access and basing situation of various parts of the world with respect to U.S. policy interests. The regions are presented roughly in order of their distance from the continental United States, rather than in order of the importance of current conflicts. Regional perimeters are drawn, less as precise boundaries, than to serve as means of drawing the reader's attention to specific access problems and air base situations.

All regions considered are conceivable focuses of future conflict. Some also involve examples of relatively recent involvement of U.S. combat air power and military actions in thus provide case studies in base access with important lessons for the immediate future. These include the Central America/Caribbean region (Haiti, Grenada and Panama), North Africa (Libya Raid of 1986), the Levant (1973 Arab-Israeli War), the Middle East (Desert Storm), and Southeast Asia (Vietnam conflict). Other regions, where U.S. expeditionary involvement has been limited, absent, or is dated, require one to probe more deeply for applicable insights. These include South America, Africa, South Asia, and East Asia—all of which have various classes of conflict in progress or on the horizon. Two of the regions discussed, Eastern Europe and Central Asia, are significant by virtue of the potential there for conflict following the failure of reforms in states of the former Soviet empire. Finally, the Global Commons category addresses the resources in and strategic value of parts of the earth's surface traditionally outside national territorial limits. The Global Commons is increasingly the locus of international competition as the combination of growing demand and advances in resource exploitation technologies renders them strategically relevant.

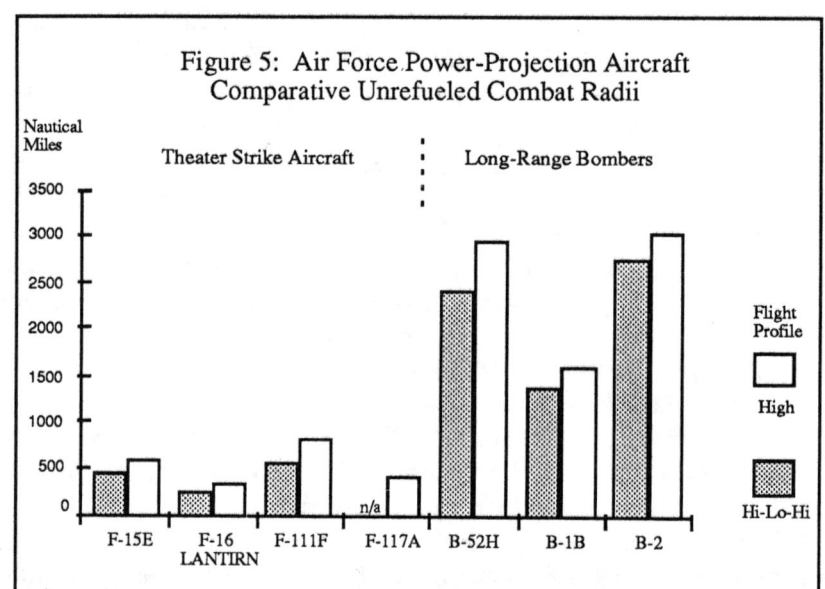

Figure 5: Air Force Power-Projection Aircraft
Comparative Unrefueled Combat Radii

Chart reflects aircraft armed with payloads of 2000-lb bombs. F-16 and F-117, 2 bombs; F-111F, 4; F-15, 5. B-52H and B-2, 16 bombs; B-1B, 24 bombs. Combat radii assume no loitering; hi-lo-hi mission assumes 500 NM low-altitude leg. F-117 does not fly hi-lo-hi profile. F-111F is being retired. Navy aircraft, unlisted in this chart due to concerns for methodological consistency between sources, have combat radii comparable to theater strike aircraft: A-6E, about 584 nautical miles; F/A-18D, about 404 nautical miles.

Sources: U.S. Air Force, Air Combat Command, "Strategic Attack/Interdiction," briefing presented at the Air Combat Requirements Conference hosted by the National Security Industrial Association, November 4–6, 1992 (mimeo, slide 18). Navy aircraft data from DoD, *Conduct of the Persian Gulf War* (Washington: GPO), pp. 661, 707 (data converted from miles into nautical miles).

Observations with respect to each region are then assembled to form a global view of access and basing conditions that the United States is likely to encounter wherever U.S. forces may be required to fight. Implications for the utility of modern long-range, land-based bombers such as the B-2 will then be drawn from these general observations.

Central America/Caribbean

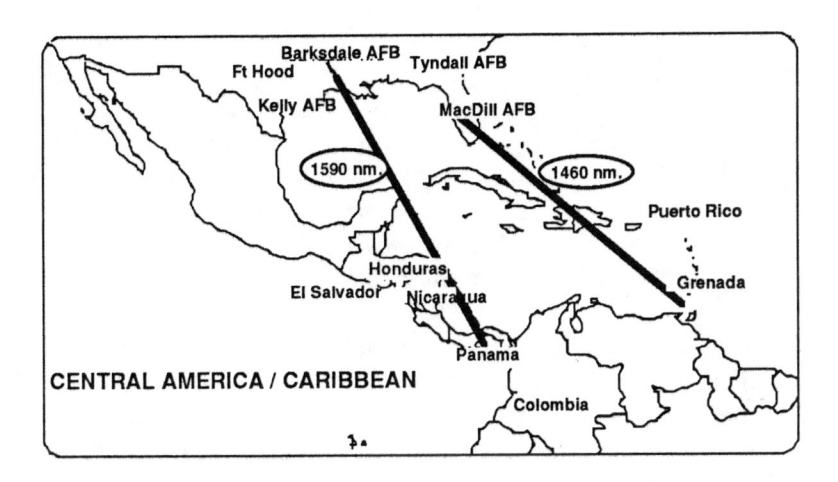

[Map of Central America/Caribbean region showing Ft Hood, Barksdale AFB, Kelly AFB, Tyndall AFB, MacDill AFB, with range arcs of 1590 nm and 1460 nm extending to Honduras, El Salvador, Nicaragua, Panama, Puerto Rico, Grenada, and Colombia]

Proximity to the United States renders the Central America/Caribbean region uniquely important as a potential location for regional conflict, and unusually so in terms of the apparent ease of access that U.S. air forces and surface forces can expect in time of crisis. The United States operates three major military air bases within the Central America/Caribbean region: Howard AFB, Panama; Roosevelt Roads Naval Station, Puerto Rico; and Guantanamo Bay Naval Air Station, a U.S.-controlled enclave in southeastern Cuba. The entire Central America/Caribbean region is within range of long-range aircraft operating from the United States and is the location of frequent U.S. military peacetime flight operations. The Caribbean is an active U.S. Navy training area and, with the exception of central Mexico, all of Central America is within unrefueled range of carrier-based aircraft. Almost all countries in the region have major commercial or joint-use airfields which should be considered capable of hosting some level of U.S. air operations. Military airfields in the region are fewer in number and less capable of hosting the full range of U.S. air combat operations. However, recent U.S. interventions in the Central America/ Caribbean region (October 1983 "Urgent Fury" in Grenada and "Just Cause" in Panama in December 1989) highlight specific impacts of the regional political situation on the U.S. ability to mount military operations.

Triggered in response to a threat to American students on Grenada, "Urgent Fury" included both Marine and Army land forces and special operations units of the Army, Navy, and Air Force. Army forces were airlifted directly from bases in the United States. Their aircraft were either refueled in flight by SAC tankers or staged through Grantley Adams International Airport, Barbados [88]. SAC tankers accomplished 123 air refuelings in direct support of "Urgent Fury" [89]. A contingent of F-15s and AWACS aircraft was positioned at Roosevelt Roads Naval Station Puerto Rico to interdict eventual Cuban efforts to interfere with operations in Grenada [90]. Mediterranean Amphibious Ready Group 1-84, including USS Guam was diverted toward Grenada from a point east of Bermuda [91]. The carrier battle group of the USS Independence also had been diverted from its course toward the Mediterranean [92]. Air operations from the Independence in support of "Urgent Fury" totaled more than 700 sorties [93].

The major political challenge of the Grenada intervention involved turning a U.S. initiative into an international operation, with the United States responding in support of an initiative by the Organization of East Caribbean States (OECS). The six tiny member nations of the OECS, concerned about the chaotic situation prevailing on Grenada after the murder of Prime Minister Maurice Bishop, sought U.S. military help [94]. President Reagan decided to undertake the operation, despite pre-invasion opposition from allies as close as Prime Minister Margaret Thatcher of Britain [95].

Even with this local international endorsement, the popular and political reaction to U.S. military intervention in Grenada was overwhelmingly negative around the world. The enthusiastic approval of most Grenadians for the U.S. action appeared lost on more distant observers [96]. Virtually the only states defending the U.S. action were the tiny Caribbean nations that contributed to the invasion force [97].

The "Just Cause" intervention in Panama involved a surprise night air assault by U.S.-based ground forces joining up with elements of the approximately 13,000 U.S. forces already in Panama to overthrow and seize the Panamanian ruler Colonel Manuel Noriega. Airlift aircraft delivered troops from four major U.S. bases, one of which was 3,500 miles from Panama, directly to their objectives [98]. Military Airlift Command C-130s, C-141s, and C-5s accomplished eighty-four parachute drops and landed the rest of their cargo in Panama. C-130s landed at Howard and refueled before returning to the United States. C-141s and C-5s were refueled in flight by SAC tankers [99]. Air forces involved included Air National Guard A-7 aircraft already on rotational duty in Panama; OA-37s assigned to Howard AFB [100]; AC-130 Gunships, MC-130E Combat Talons, and HC-130 air refueling aircraft operated out of Howard AFB;

and a total deployment of 176 helicopters [101]. The six F-117A aircraft involved [102], of which two bombed the Panamanian Defense Force barracks at Rio Hato [103], operated from Tonopah, Nevada, with air refueling enroute [104]. SAC aerial refueling support for Just Cause involved tanker aircraft flying more than 160 missions and transferring more than 10 million pounds of fuel [105].

International criticism of the U.S. action in Panama, while not quite as one-sided as that over Grenada, was equally vocal. Even Guillermo Endara, U.S.-installed successor to Noriega as President of Panama, denied any role in asking for or authorizing U.S. actions [106]. In the United Nations, of all Latin America and the Caribbean, only the Dominican Republic and El Salvador voted with the United States. Costa Rica, St. Lucia, St. Vincent, and the Grenadines abstained. The rest voted against the United States [107].

Regional Observations: These operations demonstrated that U.S. intervention in Central America and the Caribbean carries strong negative political connotations. These feelings render regional political support almost unobtainable—other than in the face of immediate danger.

- In the post-Cold War world, the absence of an extra-regional threat makes regional acquiescence to basing for U.S. operations even less likely than before.
- Mexico, where drug trafficking, guerrilla activity, economic difficulties, and growing political opposition could give rise to domestic turmoil capable of spilling over the border, is not the least likely location for a conflict that could require U.S. military intervention. Mexico, however, has been among the most vociferous critics of U.S. intervention across the region.
- Even the three long-term U.S. overseas bases in the region, which have a special, near-sovereign status, are politically limited in their utility. The United States would prefer to keep Guantanamo Bay out of the world spotlight. Visible intervention operations from Roosevelt Roads or other locations on Puerto Rico could severely disrupt the political soul-searching that questions the future of Commonwealth status. Howard AFB and other installations in Panama lie at the center of the process of ensuring a stable and democratic Panama when the Canal reverts to Panamanian control on December 31, 1999.
- The nature of the events which trigger U.S. interventions in this region combines with U.S. interest in minimizing negative political

reactions, reducing losses and civilian casualties, and presenting the world with a *fait accompli* to place a premium on the surprise and speed of execution with which such interventions are undertaken.
- These factors combine to cause the United States to perceive great advantage in mounting operations from its sovereign territory (Grenada and Panama) or from naval vessels (Grenada).
- Given the element of chance in the timely availability of appropriate naval units close enough to ensure fast action, long-range air or airlifted operations from the United States itself are likely to remain preferred military options.
- Evidence of the degree to which the United States chooses to rely on long-range air operations from within its own territory in this region is borne out by the quantity of air refueling support employed, even in actions as nearby and as limited as Panama and Grenada.

South America

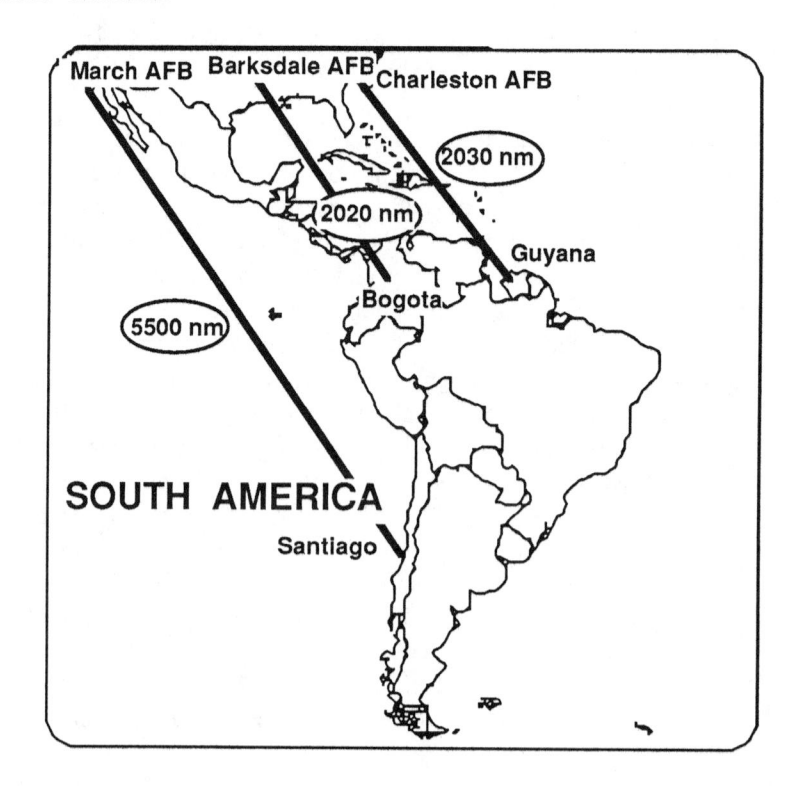

The northernmost tier of countries in South America is about 2,000 nm away from major southern U.S. military air bases. The South American continent itself extends more than 4,100 nm from north to south and 2,800 nm from its western coast near Guyaquil, Ecuador, to Natal, Brazil, in the east. While South America possesses a country-by-country mix of airfields similar to the Central America/Caribbean region, these relatively few facilities are spread over an entire continent. South American countries possess major commercial airports serving capital cities and other major population or economic centers. For the most part, these facilities are in coastal locations. In many cases, they are well integrated into a supporting infrastructure that can provide fuel and other support needed for military air operations. A system of secondary commercial airfields is spread into the interior of most South American countries. These serve a relatively few interior economic or population centers and commonly constitute alternatives to a surface transportation infrastructure.

Purely military airfields in South America, as in the Central American-Caribbean region, are even more widely dispersed and normally have smaller, less capable runways than do the major commercial airports. They also tend to be less well-situated with respect to the surface transportation infrastructure and commercial support. The most capable military airfields appear to be those established as joint-use airfields, locations where military operations can use the fuel and other logistical infrastructure of commercial aviation. While there appear to be sound basing options for small single-base sized deployments, larger ones, seeking to focus massed combat power in a major campaign would be much more difficult.

Military flight operations in the northern two-thirds of South America are generally subject to tropical climatic conditions which, by virtue of heat and humidity, degrade takeoff and landing capabilities of most aircraft to some degree. This degradation is particularly significant in Andean regions, where field elevations are among the highest in the world.

The principal factor affecting the utility of carrier-based aircraft in South America is distance, which constrains timely deployment to the region. Unlike the Caribbean, which hosts U.S. Navy peacetime training operations and is near normal routing to aircraft carrier deployment areas, South America is much less accessible. U.S. carriers are normally far enough away to require significant steaming time before they could confidently be expected to reach station near a trouble spot. Once deployed, carrier-based aircraft would have adequate access to the South American littoral, but their utility diminishes rapidly toward the interior of the continent. While aerial refueling can extend the theoretical range of carrier aircraft indefinitely, operational reality renders combat utility quite low beyond 500 nm from the carrier. Forces that can execute a sustained high-intensity air offensive at shorter ranges can only accomplish a series of raids at longer ranges.

The absence of recent U.S. military involvement in South America reflects in large part the reluctance of the nations in the region to invite U.S. intervention into their affairs. South American governments were unanimous in their condemnation of U.S. interventions in both Grenada and Panama. Washington's characteristic readiness to act to invoke the Monroe Doctrine in order to preclude intervention from powers external to the hemisphere was exemplified by the harsh U.S. reaction to Soviet delivery of weapons and military assistance to the Sandinista regime in Nicaragua and Peru's purchase of Soviet SU-22 fighter bombers. At the height of the Cold War and Cuba's revolutionary activism, U.S. influence was grudgingly accepted within South America. It remains to be seen, however, to what extent any form of U.S. post-Cold War intervention would be supported within the region.

While a major unilateral U.S. military intervention in South America might appear improbable, the United States has forces in the region today. They are involved in the struggle against the illicit drug trade that produces 80 per cent of the cocaine and 90 per cent of the marijuana entering the United States [108]. The magnitude of the drug trade directly threatens the autonomy and democratic character of the affected governments, especially in Colombia, Peru, and Bolivia. As long as the current volume of U.S. drug-dollars continues to flow into the hands of the cartels, none of the affected governments is safe from blackmail or subversion. Viewed against a backdrop of severe domestic economic problems in many of the South American countries, crushing foreign debt, and endemic local violence, the drug trade could lead to domestic crises sufficiently grave to require a call for direct U.S. military assistance. The United States could conceivably see itself bound to intervene militarily on a larger scale if any of its military advisers, security assistance personnel, or drug enforcement agents were killed or taken hostage. There is even a possibility that the United States could find itself confronted by a regime under the complete sway of the drug cartels.

A second category of conflict to be anticipated in South America involves instability linked to severe economic stagnation, and income maldistribution, coupled with the inability of democratically elected political leadership to master these problems. Aggravating this pattern is the frequency with which "strong men" step in and seize control. Although many South American governments moved toward democracy during the 1980's, endemic problems keep the potential for instability and violence high. The ordeal that Chile experienced after the fall of President Salvador Allende's regime in 1973 and the rise of the Junta raises the question of whether the United States might intervene in the case of a similar series of events in another South American country.

A third, less likely, category of possible conflict in South America could involve one country's embarking on a course of aggression against a neighbor—perhaps in order to divert attention from intractable domestic problems. While this has been relatively rare in South American history, it is not unknown. The Argentine invasion of the Falkland Islands in 1982 should be considered to provide a recent example of such an aggression. It also illustrates how precipitously such an event can occur and indicates how geography makes it difficult for an extra-regional power to react effectively.

In order to retake the Falklands, the United Kingdom needed to transit 7,650 nm of open ocean. Ascension Island, the closest U.K. refueling stop, is located 3,470 nm from the Falklands. The United Kingdom's experience in retaking the Falklands is instructive to the United States because U.S. access to the southern extremity of South America, without active support from South American allies, would be little better than that enjoyed by Great Britain.

Future border conflicts between South American nations over such issues as islands in the South Atlantic or fishing rights and access to oil and seabed minerals could easily escalate to the point where they have hemisphere-wide implications. Several South American nations (Brazil, Ecuador, Nicaragua and Peru) insist on 200 nm territorial seas which are contested by the United States as a freedom of navigation issue [109]. A prolonged dispute between Chile and Argentina over three small islands in the Beagle Channel almost provoked full-scale war before being settled peacefully in 1984. An important contributory factor in the conflict was the likelihood that oil deposits lie beneath the islands' territorial waters. The Venezuelan-Colombian dispute in the Gulf of Venezuela and the quarrel between Peru and Ecuador over the disposition of their Amazon River frontier both involved the oil factor. As one press report pointed out, "...the mixture of a disputed boundary with even the slightest trace of oil is highly flammable, so future flare-ups in South America can't be ruled out" [110].

Regional Observations: The United States, if it were to involve itself in any conflict related to such issues, would be faced with very limited basing options. It is almost certain that in such contingencies, the problems associated with deploying any significant U.S. force to the region would raise the issue of seeking alternative approaches or augmentation of small deployments that did not depend on major basing infrastructure.

- Basing for contingency air operations in South America presents significantly greater physical challenges than the Central America/Caribbean region. The South American land mass is vast, and the number of airports adequate for land-based tactical aviation or support of surface operations is relatively small.
- Political limitations on U.S. access to South American basing are probably even more severe than in the Caribbean. The political likelihood of regional basing for U.S. operations in South America is low.
- The demise of Cuba and Nicaragua as externally supported agents of instability makes the likely future political climate even less supportive of U.S. military activity than it has been.
- Even if one South American country under duress seeks U.S. military assistance, its neighbors almost certainly will continue to refuse U.S. access to bases on their territory unless they too feel immediately threatened.
- Aside from the Caribbean coast, much of South America is remote from normal areas of peacetime U.S. naval operations. Considerable preparation and steaming time probably would be necessary before carrier-based air operations could be staged around most of the South American periphery. Much of the interior of the continent is out of reach of carrier-based air operations.
- As in the case of the Caribbean/Central America, these factors probably will cause the United States to perceive a great advantage in conducting operations from U.S. soil.
- All of South America is accessible to U.S. modern long-range, land-based bomber operations with minimal air refueling.

North Africa

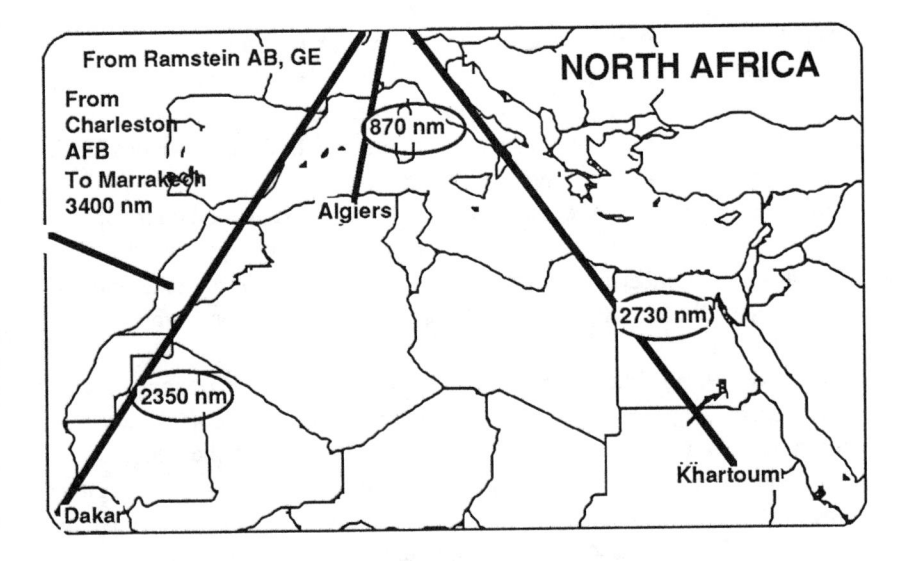

Map of North Africa showing: From Ramstein AB, GE; From Charleston AFB To Marrakech 3400 nm; 870 nm (Algiers); 2730 nm; 2350 nm; Dakar; Khartoum

During World War II the Allies constructed a network of bases and air transit points that stretched across the Sahara through North Africa and to Italy and southern France. Conceptually North Africa served as a long east-west archipelago of strategic bases between the Mediterranean Sea and the "sand sea" of the Sahara. With the advent of the Cold War, this region became an important forward location for basing strategic nuclear bombers that did not possess true intercontinental range. The United States constructed major bases in French Morocco and Libya. Throughout the 1950's B-36 bombers, which could not be refueled in flight, and B-47s, which could be refueled but had shorter inherent range capabilities, were rotated through these bases [111]. These installations later closed under pressure from post-colonial governments. Moreover, as longer-range bombers replaced the B-47s and air refueling capabilities increased, these bases became less acutely important. Most U.S. basing for its forward strategic aerial presence was shifted to the European shore of the Mediterranean.

More recently, the United States and Morocco have maintained defense contacts including an access and transit agreement providing for contingency transit by U.S. armed forces [112] and maintenance of air and naval communication facilities there. Partially in return for these military access privileges, the United States gives Morocco a large economic and security assistance package.

Tunisia is the other Maghrebian country in which the United States retains military access. The two nations have a strategic cooperation agreement. The U.S. Navy makes periodic port visits to the naval bases at Tunis and Bizerte. There are no known agreements for air access, however. Tunisia obtains small amounts of security assistance from the United States.

At the eastern end of the region Egypt has particular strategic importance by virtue of its large population and pivotal location. Egypt too has proved to be a valuable ally in a number of instances—especially as a voice of moderation in the Arab-Israeli dispute. Egypt led the participation of regional states in the Gulf War coalition.

Politically North Africa remains an extremely unstable region. Stable democracies have generally not yet developed in this region. Ostensibly "democratic" governments there may not reflect the will of the people. An enduring source of tension lies in the contests between conservative religious factions and secular leaders. The proximity of this potential for violence to Mediterranean Europe is a source of considerable concern. The proliferation of ballistic missile technology and technologies and materials useful in the production of weapons of mass destruction into this region adds its own note of urgency. While quiescent for the time being, Libya continues to worry its neighbors.

Because North Africa's problems involve bitter domestic contests between secular governments and transnational religious factions, even invited U.S. intervention would risk compromise for lack of reliable access to bases within the region. Libya's manufacture of chemical weapons and Algeria's construction—with Chinese assistance—of a nuclear reactor possibly geared to weapons production typify the proliferation problem. The difficulty of Tunisia's transition from President Bourguiba's one-man rule to a constitutional successor regime, widespread unrest in Algeria, long-term pressure on Hassan II in Morocco, and deep-seated economic and political tensions in Egypt exemplify regional tensions that could ignite major upheavals. The United States has had a usually understated, but occasionally important role in stabilizing such strife.

The U.S. bombing attack against Libya on April 15, 1986, in retaliation for Libyan sponsorship of terrorist activities, is the only recent instance of a major U.S. military intervention in North Africa. The attack also illustrated—and exacerbated—the strains between Washington and the European NATO capitals over the use of bases in Europe for operations against North Africa or other "out-of-area" locations.

The United States used both Air Force and Navy attack aircraft to stage the main attack on Libya. F-111 fighter-bombers based in Britain were refueled in flight over international waters, flying through the Strait of Gibraltar to attack Libyan targets near Tripoli from the sea. A-6 Intruders from aircraft carriers off the Libyan coast hit other targets farther east. Even British bases might have been unavailable had it not been for American support for the British war in the Falklands [113]. The attack, however, reignited controversy in Britain about the desirability of hosting U.S. combat aircraft. The Labor Party made the basing arrangements a major campaign issue in the 1987 general election.

The United States reportedly approached Spain indirectly for permission to use Spanish bases or at least to overfly Spain for the Libyan operation. Prime Minister Felipe Gonzalez after the raid rejected both requests [114]. France and Italy also reportedly refused to grant overflight rights for U.S. bombers enroute from Britain to Libya. The attack raised sensitivities in all the southern European countries about possible U.S. use of bases in their countries for missions targeted against North Africa.

Regional Observations: Even if a country in North Africa felt sufficiently threatened to request U.S. military intervention, its neighbors would probably hesitate to facilitate a U.S. operation unless they too perceived a direct threat.

- Distances both to and within the region are so great, and bases so dispersed as to imply multinational basing for any significant U.S. deployment into the region.
- Unless directly threatened themselves, Washington's NATO allies in southern Europe—Spain, Portugal, France, Italy, Greece, and Turkey—would be unlikely to permit the United States to stage an intervention in North Africa from their soil because of economic ties with North Africa, the risk of political repercussions among their own significant North African populations, and the threat posed by the proliferation of modern weapons in North African states.
- North African countries, for their part, almost certainly would resist U. S. use of bases on their territory for any operations elsewhere in Africa or beyond, except under the most unusual circumstances (As was the case with Desert Shield/Desert Storm).
- The United States cannot rely upon long-term access to military bases and facilities either in the Maghreb or in Egypt. The region is inherently unstable, and local governments would fear the political and cultural impact of a long-term U.S. presence.

- Coastal parts of this region are accessible to U.S. carrier based aircraft normally on-station in the Mediterranean. However, much of the region is beyond the range of carrier-based aircraft. Also, as the Libyans learned from the 1986 raid, a logical counter to U.S. attacks by short-range aircraft (carrier or land-based) is to reorient air defense assets into a coastal barrier defense effective against an attack that can only come from one direction.
- Proliferation of missile technology and NBC warhead capabilities within this area could render difficult the constitution of a coalition of nearby countries to undertake any military action and place at risk U.S. forces deployed into the theater.
- These dimensions of this region place a premium on the availability of long-range combat aircraft that can reach the region from any direction without depending on sovereign U.S. bases or access to the territory of traditional U.S. allies with compatible policies toward North Africa.

Sub-Saharan Africa

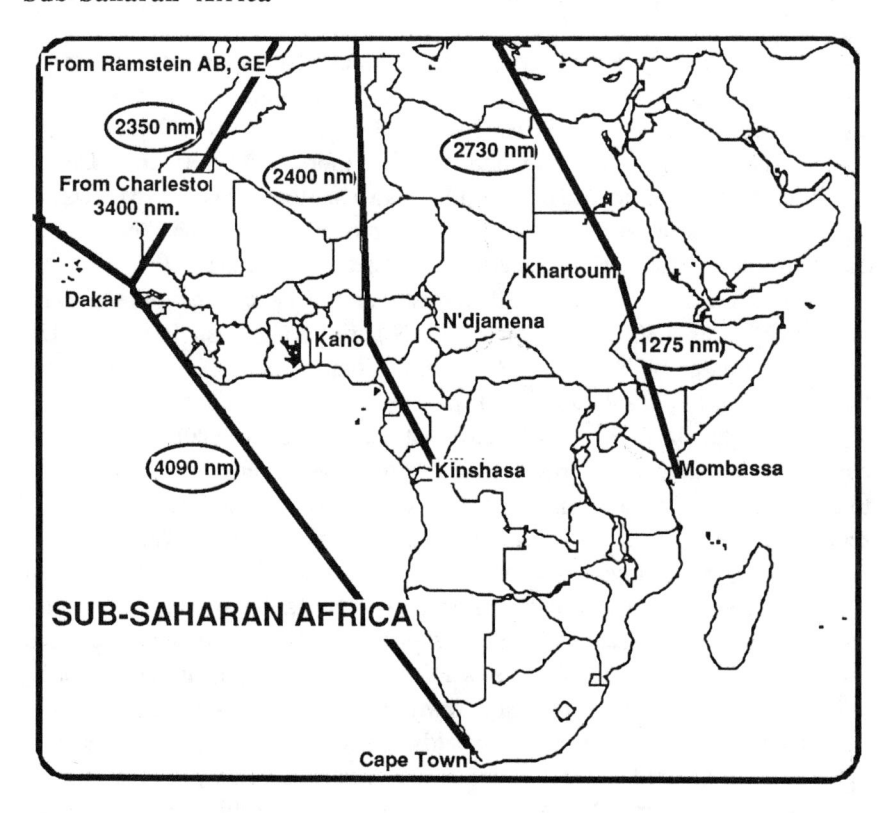

[Map of Sub-Saharan Africa with distance annotations: From Ramstein AB, GE 2350 nm; From Charleston 3400 nm; 2400 nm; 2730 nm; 4090 nm; 1275 nm. Cities labeled: Dakar, Kano, N'djamena, Khartoum, Kinshasa, Mombassa, Cape Town.]

Remote from and lacking important economic ties to the United States, Sub-Saharan Africa nevertheless possesses sufficient political importance for the United States to render this area a focus of basing interest through the foreseeable future. Humanitarian concerns, such as those stimulating U.S. operations in Somalia, and the ethnic ties of important American minorities keep Africa visible in the U.S. foreign affairs process. Reversing South Africa's apartheid policy has been a high U.S. priority for many years. Relaxation of East-West tensions has done relatively little to reduce the frequency and intensity of violence in Sub-Saharan Africa. Post-colonial wars in Africa have demonstrated the particular utility of air power in the African context. Even United Nations actions relating to the recent independence of Namibia involved U.S. military airlift support. United States military air power is often sought in the context of African conflict because the United States, almost alone in the world, has air assets with the range to conduct sustained operations to and within Sub-Saharan Africa.

Great distances characterize potential air combat operations in Africa. Access to Sub-Saharan Africa from the United States is reflected in the 3,400 nm distance between Charleston, SC, and Dakar, Senegal. Even from U.S. bases in Europe, such as Ramstein AB in Germany, it is more than 2,350 nm to Dakar, 2,400 nm to Kano, Nigeria, and 2,730 nm to Khartoum, Sudan. Movement further south is affected by the great dimensions of the continent. Nominally direct air routing from Dakar to the Horn of Africa is more than 4,000 nm. The straight-line distance from the northernmost point of the continent to the Cape of Good Hope is 4,300 nm. From Kano, Nigeria to Kinshasa, Zaire is 1,070 nm; from Khartoum, Sudan to Mogadishu, Somalia is 1,140 nm; and from Dakar to Cape Town is 4,096 nm [115].

Major cities in Africa, particularly national capitals or economic centers, have large commercial airports. Here the term "large" refers almost exclusively to the length and width of runway surfaces. Some relatively large airports are scattered across Africa at even comparatively small cities. Rather simple airstrips are present in variable numbers. Only a few of the larger commercial airports, however, are linked to a surface transportation system sufficiently developed to provide fuel and logistical support beyond that minimally required for scheduled airline service. Even scheduled airlines develop their routes in order to be able to buy fuel at the relatively few terminals which have better access to support, with intervening stops at airfields less likely to have a reliable supply of fuel. The favored terminals tend to be coastal locations, such as Dakar, Senegal, or very rare interior locations, such as Nairobi, Kenya, with an economic and transportation base sufficient to assure reliable resupply.

While there are some military airfields, it is much more common for African air forces, and even for European air forces operating in Africa, to operate from major joint-use airfields. This arrangement facilitates logistical support by allowing the same lines of supply to serve both commercial and military users. Other factors render this solution even more logical. National airlines are often as much government entities as are national air forces. Spare parts for military aircraft usually need to be shipped from European or American manufacturers, and the easiest means of delivery is by commercial air freight. African air forces generally operate at a low tempo that neither conflicts with commercial operations nor merits separate operating facilities. Finally, the precarious nature of many African regimes makes it useful for both national and air force leaderships to keep the major portion of air force assets close to the capital for better control during a coup or other crisis.

Most of coastal Sub-Saharan Africa is remote from normal U.S. Navy peacetime operating areas. Much of Africa is far enough inland to render carrier-based aircraft essentially unusable for sustained combat operations.

Recent European and U.S. Air Force deployments to Africa provide a sketch of some factors that apply to deployment planning. The French Air Force Deployment of "Operation Epervier" to N'Djamena, Chad, in order to protect Chad against air attack from Libya is perhaps the most important example [116]. While the French conducted regular flight operations from N'Djamena, the small number of aircraft and their relatively low fuel consumption kept logistical demands reasonable. "Operation Epervier" was scaled to fit both the threat and the basing support possibilities of Chad.

The only recent U.S. Air Force combat aircraft deployment to this region was the positioning of eight F-15's, two AWACS, and two supporting KC-10 tanker aircraft to Khartoum International Airport, Sudan, to add pressure on Libya to cease offensive operations in Chad and desist from further aggression against its southern neighbors [117]. This deployment too consisted principally of ground alert against Libyan air attacks. It lasted from August 3 to August 23, 1983 [118]. This presence was constrained to very little flying by the limited logistical support that could be obtained in Khartoum.

A general characteristic of the airport system in Africa is that it is much less a supplement to surface transportation, as it tends to be in Europe or the United States, than a substitute for a surface system. This situation has grave implications for the military utility of airfields that would otherwise, by virtue of runway length and location, appear useful to host the deployment of tactical air forces. Even at a low intensity of operations, it has an undeniable impact on the nature of air operations conducted when deployments are undertaken. In order to conduct high-intensity air combat operations, even with relatively small forces, the United States would have to put into place its own massive logistical support system.

These observations are broadly applicable in Sub-Saharan Africa, with the singular exception of South Africa. South Africa has the economic and surface transportation infrastructure needed to turn its numerous modern commercial and military airfields into capable bases from which deployed forces can operate effectively at intense levels of combat activity. During U.S. Air Force support for United Nations peace-keeping operations associated with the independence of Namibia, the realities of African basing geography made it necessary for the United States to obtain some maintenance and logistical support from South Africa.

As limiting as the air base structure in Africa may be, the most serious constraints to reliable basing in Sub-Saharan Africa are political. There is a generalized post-colonial resistance to foreign military presence that even creates problems for successful and invited deployments like that of the French in Chad. Political opposition groups tend to take regimes in power to task for their perceived dependence on foreign assistance [119]. This atmosphere affects dealings with the United States—albeit not as severely as might be the case in Central and South America.

The most important source of basing uncertainty in Sub-Saharan Africa is the frequency and dispersion of openly violent conflict across the continent, coupled with its unpredictability. It is impossible to make arrangements for contingency basing without accepting a large measure of uncertainty over the validity of agreements with a regime menaced by local conflict. Since 1990, as many as fifteen active armed conflicts could be counted on the African continent at one time. These included the reappearance of insurgency in Angola; secessionist wars in Ethiopia; tribal-based violence in Burundi, Rwanda, Liberia, Mali, Mauritania, Senegal, Uganda, and Sudan; civil war in Mozambique with South African involvement; the Polisario war of independence against Morocco in the Western Sahara; guerrilla warfare in Somalia; and war with Libya followed by tribal-based civil war in Chad. This listing does not count violence and human rights problems in Kenya, increasing instability in Cameroon, or the tribal and racial violence in South Africa itself. Fighting that ended recently in Burkina Faso, Nigeria, and Zaire has left embers behind that could flare up again in the near future. Collectively, these hot spots include most of the countries in Sub-Saharan Africa where the United States could expect some sort of air base access if intervention were undertaken.

The United States has been frustrated in preplanning long-term basing in Africa. For example, it has long sought friendly relations with Liberia and contributed to the maintenance of Roberts International Airport as a potential refueling point for access farther south in the continent. Recurring Congressional displeasure with the former Liberian government rendered these efforts difficult, however, and, after the recent overthrow of the Liberian regime the likelihood of reliable access to Roberts Field is even more uncertain. U.S. use of two large former Belgian bases in Zaire—Kamina Base and Kitona Base—was long a subject of mid-level discussions between the two governments. But, there has apparently been no progress in this direction, and none is likely given further disintegration of the Zairean economy and Mobutu's control of his country.

Regional Observations:

- U.S. air power is broadly useful in Africa because of the distances involved and gains further impact by virtue of the basic unfamiliarity of most of the contesting forces with modern aviation technology.
- Much of Africa is beyond the range of carrier-based aircraft.
- Deployment of significant short-range combat air power and its intensive employment is difficult because the African airfield system is sparse for so large a geographic area, and many of the airports that exist are not well served by surface transportation capable of supporting intensive military operations.
- Endemic violence and instability render existing airfields politically unreliable and can place at risk any official American presence, even when U.S. involvement is for humanitarian relief or other peaceful purposes.
- These factors, taken together, argue for the availability of long-range, land-based airpower that can be based selectively either outside the region or at the most secure basing within the region and would be available quickly to counter the fast-breaking escalation of a crisis.

Middle East

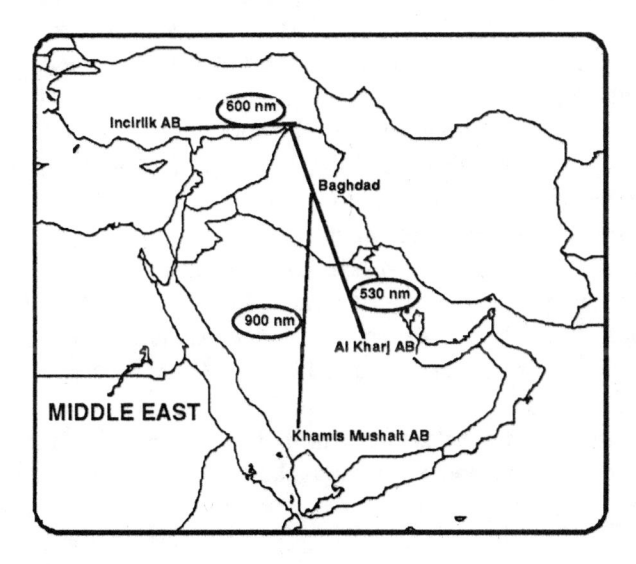

Valuable insights into the basing challenge in the Middle East are to be gained from a thoughtful review of "Desert Storm." This campaign involved U.S. deployment of a large force into existing facilities to fight a well-defined enemy. There was enough time to move forces forward in a planned fashion. Regional allies cooperated, not only by participating in the Coalition, but—more importantly for the purposes of this analysis—by granting the United States access to the most extensive, dense, and modern air base complex in the Third World.

In order to place this case of regional basing in the proper context, this analysis treats as separate regions the "Middle East" of the Gulf War, with its broad coincidence of regional and U.S. objectives, and the separate but overlapping "Levant," which is intended to address the basing situation in the same part of the world, but in a war where U.S. support of Israel puts the United States at odds with its Arab neighbors and, most probably, with European governments. While the precedent of successful coalition warfare holds the promise of a new level of cooperation with states of the Middle East, the intractability of problems permeating Israel's relations with its neighbors renders the pessimistic "Levant" model an unavoidable condition of realistic analysis in the region.

Iraq's occupation of Kuwait on August 2, 1990, required the United States and its Coalition partners to deploy their air forces to bases selected from among more than thirty large modern airfields on the territory of Saudi Arabia and other oil-producing Gulf states. The United States also operated strike aircraft from Incirlik AB, Turkey. The Saudi and Gulf airfields in many cases have longer runways and more modern support facilities than exist in the United States or Europe by virtue of the petrodollars available for their construction.

Even with this extremely favorable basing array, significant numbers of long-range combat aircraft, including many of the 25 SAC B-52s that participated in the war, were based outside of the region at Diego Garcia in the British Indian Ocean Territory; Moron AB in Spain; and Fairford RAF Base in England. Support aircraft operated from Cairo West, Egypt, and still others from European air bases. Six carrier battle groups joined in the air campaign from the Red Sea, the Persian Gulf, and the Indian Ocean [120].

The Desert Storm air campaign provided a unique opportunity to gain quantitative insights into the adequacy of Middle Eastern basing for the conduct of an intense air campaign. Since the highest possible sortie rate was a clear intermediate goal to maximizing destruction of the selected sets of Iraqi targets, strike missions would have been designed to be as efficient as possible. Air refueling adds to the complexity of combat missions; it increases the numbers of aircraft and crews that must be supported in the theater of operations; and it increases the duration of combat missions and the stress on the pilots flying them. With optimum basing, one would expect a surge of refueling during the deployment phase, a minimum of refueling during the employment phase, and then more refueling for redeployment. High levels of refueling support during the employment phase would tend to indicate that basing is more distant from target areas than the combat radius for which the strike aircraft were designed.

The following figures summarize aerial refueling conducted by all Strategic Air Command assets (KC-135s, KC-10s, Active, Guard, and Reserve) in the course of the Gulf War. These figures represent the refueling carried out by the approximately 300 tankers—half of the Strategic Air Command's tanker fleet—that were involved in Gulf War support [121]. Not presented are refuelings accomplished by Navy tanker-modified aircraft (KA-6Ds) or special operations C-130H-to-helicopter transfers.

Table 1: Gulf War Aerial Refueling

	Desert Shield (8/1/90–1/16/91)	Desert Storm (1/16/91–3/5/91)	Desert Victory (3/6/91–4/21/91)
Sorties	17,400+	16,800+	6,500+
Flying Hours	75,000+	66,000+	31,500+
Aerial Refuelings/ Receivers	33,500	51,500+	12,400+
Gallons of Fuel Transferred	70 million	125 million	29 million[122]

There was a massive surge of refueling in the employment phase of the Desert Storm air campaign. In addition to this surge, flight profiles of the attack aircraft were considerably longer than those practiced in peacetime as being typical of combat. For example, the F-117As, which were based at Khamis Mushait AB, refueled both inbound to target and on the return leg. Their missions averaged 5.4 hours in duration. This time compared to an average training sortie length of 1.4 to 1.8 hours at Tonopah, Nevada [123]. F-15E aircraft involved in the Scud-hunting missions averaged missions that lasted from 5.5 to 6 hours. These aircraft received prestrike refuelings; then after searching for Scuds, they retired from the target area to receive a second refueling. Following this refueling they would attack a second set of pre-planned or backup targets. Then they received a third refueling before returning to Al Kharj AB. While it is a tribute to the resilience of crews and aircraft alike that they repeatedly flew such exceptionally long missions successfully, the mission duration certainly had a negative effect on the overall sortie rates attainable in the air campaign. These figures are a significant indicator that even the dense Saudi base array was too distant from targets.

Anecdotal reporting of U.S. Navy carrier-based attack aircraft operations in support of "Desert Storm" indicated heavy reliance on U.S. Air Force tankers for both prestrike and poststrike refuelings. Major General Royal N. Moore, Jr., commander of Marine Air Wing 3 based in Bahrain, was reported to have said that the main limitation to the ability of land-based Marine aviation to keep pressure on the Iraqis around-the-clock was the small number of specialty aircraft available, including, for example, only 19 Marine tankers [124].

The remarkable coincidence of purpose that resulted in successful basing of Coalition air power in Saudi Arabia and other states neighboring Iraq, coupled with the availability of more than thirty modern, major airfields with runways ample for high performance attack aircraft, set the stage for the success of the "Desert Storm" air campaign. It is important, however, to place this success in careful perspective. Basing was still farther from targets than would have been optimum. Hosting so large a foreign military presence was not an easy decision for the regimes of the basing states. For example, at the outset, there was extreme reluctance on the part of the Saudi rulers to accept a foreign presence on their territory. Jordan, normally closer politically to the United States than other states in the region, was a supporter of Saddam Hussein during Desert Storm. Moreover, Israel, by virtue of its status as a pariah to many Arab members of the Coalition, was not only excluded from participation and basing consideration, but became the target of Iraqi efforts to stimulate military involvement in order to break apart the coalition.

Regional Observations:

- The United States demonstrated that it is willing to commit forces in this region by its leadership of DESERT SHIELD/DESERT STORM.

- The physical availability of bases in the Middle East, as defined here, is better than anywhere else in the Third World. They are more numerous, modern and concentrated nearer to potential target areas than elsewhere.
- Yet, the extent of combat-mission air refueling during Desert Storm and exceptionally long combat sorties indicated that even under the favorable conditions prevailing during the Gulf War, regional basing was too dispersed to be optimal for an intensive military campaign.
- Although the circumstances of Desert Storm provided unprecedentedly favorable basing support, the support of regional states was politically qualified and must be considered conditional in future contingencies.
- In spite of the confined seas within which they had to operate, carrier-based aviation was deployed to the region in force, with six carriers on station. The effect of their strikes was heavily dependent on Air Force tanker support and the need to defend the carriers. Tomahawk cruise missiles launched by other ships were effective in precision strikes but contributed only 142 tons of munitions of the 78,581 ton Desert Storm campaign total [125].
- In spite of the large numbers of more modern combat aircraft (over 900 U.S. and 650 from Coalition partners) deployed to the region, up to 75 long-range, land-based B-52's were counted on to deliver over 25,700 tons of bombs in the course of 1,600 sorties [126] from one base in Saudi Arabia, Diego Garcia, Moron AB, Spain; Fairfield AB, U.K.; and Barksdale AFB, Louisiana. These represented over 30% of the total tonnage of bombs delivered during the war.
- The evident utility of long-range, land-based bombers in the Gulf War, combined with that war's evident lesson to future regional aggressors to seek to establish a decisive position at the outset rather than give a coalition time to react, indicates that modern long-range, land-based bombers promise even greater utility in future regional conflicts.
- Shallow, confined waters such as the Persian Gulf and the Red Sea are not well suited for carrier, submarine, or SLCM operations. Potential problems include mines, which damaged the helicopter carrier *Iwo Jima* and the Aegis cruiser *Princeton* during the Gulf War; and vulnerability to nearby ground-launched aircraft and cruise missiles. The vulnerability requires hair-trigger responsiveness on the part of fleet air defense systems, which can result in accidents,

such as the downing of an Iranian civil airliner by the Aegis cruiser *Vincennes* on July 3, 1988. The *Vincennes* had mistaken the airliner for an Iranian F-14.

The Levant

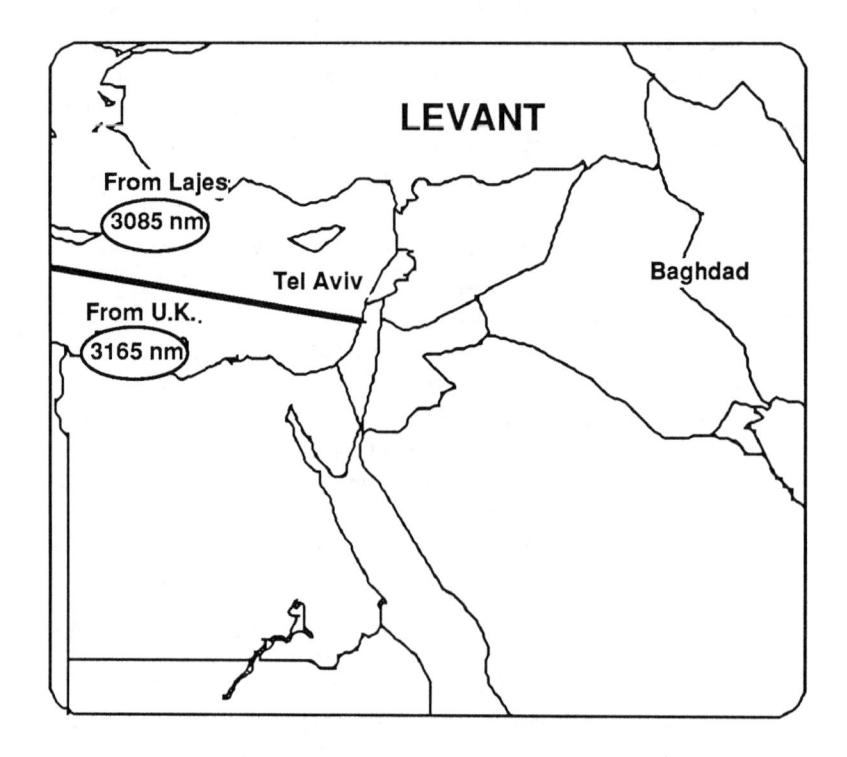

[Map of the Levant region showing Tel Aviv, Baghdad, distances "From Lajes 3085 nm" and "From U.K. 3165 nm"]

Regional Overview: The Levant must be considered separately from the Middle East because of the unique relationship between the United States and Israel. This relationship, in turn, has had a significant impact on U.S. dealings with Israel's Arab neighbors and even strains the ties between the United States and Europe. In the four Arab-Israeli Wars that already have occurred (the War of Israeli Independence in 1948, the British-French-Israeli war over Suez in 1956, the Six-Day War in 1967, and the Yom Kippur War in 1973), except for the Suez conflict, Israel has fought alone against Arab armies vastly superior in numbers. Material assistance from the United States therefore has been essential in turning the tide.

The Israeli-Palestinian agreement of September 13, 1993 may be an historic breakthrough, but its provisions must still be implemented. Future war between these parties remains a possibility. Some of Israel's neighbors continue to perceive the Jewish state with hostility. Syria demands the return of the Golan Heights; and Iraq emerged from Desert Storm with many of its forces intact. While Israel resisted responding to Iraq's Scud missile attacks in order to protect the political cohesion of the U.S.-led coalition against Iraq, the restraint that Israel displayed may be less in evidence in the future.

The United States does not have a single base on Israeli territory. For more than a decade, Washington and Tel Aviv have pondered the implications and utility of establishing U.S. bases on Israeli soil. Such bases could constitute either a complement or an alternative to the unlikely case of securing usable base sites elsewhere in Europe or North Africa for U.S. operations in the eastern Mediterranean. Major drawbacks of U.S. basing in Israel would be the resulting impact on Washington's relations with the Arab countries and the fact that U.S. aircraft would be based so close to the front lines in any future Arab-Israeli War as to be highly vulnerable.

Basing U.S. tactical aircraft on Israeli bases has distinct physical limitations. There are only seven major Israeli bases [127]. While these bases are configured to support U.S.-type fighter attack aircraft, as demonstrated by Israeli operation of these same types, there are already 550 Israeli aircraft distributed among these bases for an average of 75 aircraft per base [128]. Every one of these bases is within 75 km of a potentially hostile border [129]. Three of the bases are even within MLRS-class artillery rocket range of Israel's eastern border [130].

In the past, the United States has relied heavily on European bases to support Israel in wartime. The European NATO countries, however, are not supportive of the level of U.S. assistance extended to Israel and are unwilling to jeopardize their access to Arab oil by pursuing an overtly pro-Israel policy. During the 1973 Yom Kippur War, Portugal was the only NATO ally of the United States that permitted the U.S. to use its bases in support of Israel. Even in this case, the base was not on the Portuguese mainland, but in the Azores.

The extended range of military transport aircraft has greatly facilitated U.S. efforts to airlift military materiel to Israel. In 1973 the United States was able to mount a massive arms airlift to Israel through the sole use of the Lajes Air Base in the Azores, supplemented to some degree by U.S. aircraft carriers in the Mediterranean [131]. In a future Arab-Israeli war, technological advances such as the C-141 aircraft "stretch" program, C-17's, and enhanced refueling capability (such as greater availability of KC-10s) for military transports may enable the

United States to stage a similar airlift from the United States to Tel Aviv without intermediate stops [132]. For the present, however, the United States must continue to rely on at least one forward base, such as Lajes. During the 1973 war, the U.S. Military Airlift Command succeeded in routing 42 flights through Lajes in a 24-hour period [133]. The political sensitivity of this mission in Europe was indicated by the decision by Spain and Morocco to look the other way when the aircraft flew through the Strait of Gibraltar. Ostensibly, they flew down the middle of this waterway in international airspace. Although Morocco later agreed to provide staging access to the United States for contingencies in the Persian Gulf, it emphasized that it would forbid such access on behalf of Israel. Even Britain has drawn the line on the use of its bases for operations in support of Israel. During the 1973 war, Prime Minister Edward Heath claimed to have exercised the "right of veto" when he denied permission for the United States to use British bases in the Mediterranean to resupply the Israeli military forces [134].

Regional Observations:

- The southern European members of NATO remain strongly averse to U.S. use of their bases for non-NATO missions, such as military resupply to Israel. Not only do they continue to disagree with the United States on Arab-Israeli issues, but they want to preserve their relations with the Arab world and to ensure their access to Arab oil.
- Basing significant U.S. tactical air forces within Israel appears to entail too many physical and tactical constraints to be a militarily sound alternative under most circumstances.
- Aircraft carrier operations, while limited by the physical dimensions of the eastern Mediterranean, would be able to bring combat air power to bear in adjacent coastal regions.
- Long-range combat aircraft could operate throughout the region from the United States or from closer extra-regional bases that might become available.

Central Asia

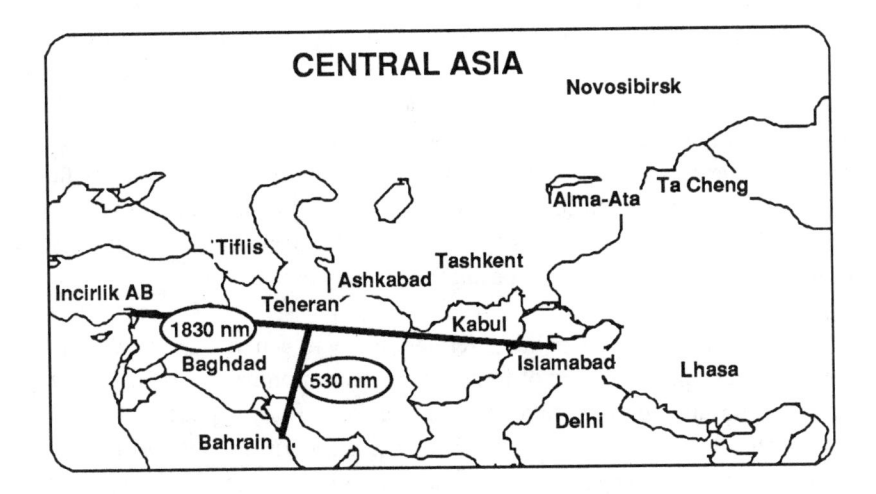

```
                    CENTRAL ASIA
                                    Novosibirsk

                                    Alma-Ata   Ta Cheng
            Tiflis        Tashkent
Incirlik AB        Ashkabad
                Teheran
        1830 nm              Kabul
        Baghdad                Islamabad    Lhasa
                  530 nm
        Bahrain                    Delhi
```

Regional Overview: The former Soviet central Asian republics and their neighbors to the south from the Black Sea to Mongolia present the potential for major instability in the decades to come. Disintegrating Russian control, the demise of the Communist Party, economic stagnation, Muslim fundamentalism, resurgent nationalisms, and other sources of friction could interact in unpredictable fashion to generate violence of a magnitude that exceeds regional importance and impinges directly on both the Middle East and South Asia. The United States is remote from this region. Yet, U.S. dependence on oil from the neighboring Persian Gulf, concern over loss of central Russian control over nuclear weapons deployed in the non-Soviet republics such as Kazakhstan, interest in the spread of democracy, and ties to allies such as Turkey could combine to generate a U.S. need to influence the course of military and political affairs in Central Asia. The reality of this possibility can be discerned from past security ties to not only Turkey, but also to Iran and Pakistan.

The closest U.S. bases to Central Asia are Incirlik AB in central Turkey and the base on Diego Garcia. While there are other Turkish airfields farther east even these are near only the westernmost end of the region. The entire region is out of effective range of carrier-based air operations. Access to the region for U.S. military power has long been an acknowledged problem. Surface forces would be at a particular disadvantage by virtue of isolation from logistical support. Air power is the only conceivable vehicle for extending U.S. military influence into the region. The U.S. factored this problem into its close ties with Pakistan early in the Cold War years, when U-2 reconnaissance flights across the Soviet Union were launched and recovered from significant U.S. air installations in Pakistan. The same issue contributed to the close relationship between the United States and the Shah of Iran. Technical assistance to the Iranian Air Force opened for a few years the possibility of excellent air access to the heart of the region. While air bases close to the borders of the former Soviet Union with the physical characteristics necessary to host major air operations exist in Turkey, Iran and Pakistan, and to some degree in other regional states, it is difficult to foresee significant future U.S. basing of military air power anywhere in the region.

The very nature of the political ferment likely to generate armed conflict in this region renders the basing of foreign air power improbable. Hosting foreign forces would undercut the nationalist credentials of any regime that chose to make such a decision at just the time that those credentials were most important. Even an ally like Turkey, which reasonably could expect to remain outside any open conflict, would see itself as needing to exercise great care in preparing its relations with future neighboring regimes resulting from such a conflict.

As a result of these factors the U.S. Air Force cannot count on bases for the deployment of tactical air power within the region. Even the level of basing cooperation accorded by Turkey in the course of the Gulf War should not be anticipated for future central Asian conflicts. Similarly, basing just outside the region—say in Saudi Arabia, for example—is both too distant to support an intense campaign and politically unlikely for the same reason that prevails with regard to Turkey.

Regional Observation:

- The only form of U.S. military power likely to be effective in this region without a deployment of unprecedented mass, complexity, and vulnerability would be modern long-range, land-based combat aircraft that can operate from U.S. territory or from bases provided by U.S. allies with a common interest in the outcome of Central Asian conflicts.

Eastern Europe

EASTERN EUROPE

Helsinki
St. Petersburg
Riga
Vilnius
Kiev
Belgrade

From Finland and the Kola Peninsula south to the Balkans lies a broad band of former Soviet republics and former Warsaw Treaty Organization countries subject to intense economic and political pressures stemming from the disintegration of Soviet empire. A continuation of the present pattern of ethnic, religious, and politically motivated strife that now affects the Balkans is likely to remain on Europe's door step. The forms by which questions such as the future of the Baltic republics will be resolved are less clear. However the succession to the Soviet empire plays itself out, the United States will play some role in shaping that outcome. The United States will find it useful to at least maintain the capacity to exert some level of military influence across the region. While it is not likely that the United States would actually become involved in military action there, the reality of influence may not be attainable without ensuring that the potential for military involvement is real.

With the exception of the northern and southern extremes of Eastern Europe, the region is beyond the sustained influence of U.S. sea power. U.S. land power similarly would appear to offer only limited utility by virtue of difficult access to a region where large land area traditionally combines with large indigenous armies to minimize the impact of expeditionary forces. Also, the events of the last few years have acted to move any future "threat" and the scene of future conflict 300 nm to 800 nm farther east. Most U.S. combat aircraft were designed to match the set piece concept of a major war across the German plains and do not have the inherent range to operate as efficiently that much farther from existing bases.

Basing for forward-deployed U.S. combat air power capable of influencing Eastern Europe would have to be derived from the basing structure that NATO allies made available to the United States throughout the Cold War. European reluctance to authorize out-of-area use of NATO forces, U.S. reductions in its forward-based forces, political and economic pressure on U.S. basing and freedom to conduct day-to-day training operations in Europe and suggest that the United States will not find itself free to employ those forces it retains in Europe as it might choose. A new trans-Atlantic consensus will have to form before the United States can count on using its forces based in Western Europe for military action in Eastern Europe. The humanitarian air drops to isolated Moslem enclaves in former Yugoslavia, multi-national enforcement of a "no-fly" zone, and ground strikes against Serbian forces threatening UN peacekeepers indicate though that such a consensus is possible, and that the United States sees its long-range aviation as a particularly useful tool in this area. While international consensus over suitable peace-keeping and perhaps even peace-making actions is tentative, future U.S. intervention could be much more assertive.

Regional Observations:

- Whatever basing the United States retains in Europe will be distant from Eastern European areas—300 nm to 800 nm further away than were potential Cold War-era targets.
- Whatever basing for combat aircraft the United States retains in Western Europe will be more subject to European political constraints than in the past.
- Carrier-based aviation has the range to influence only the northern and southern extremities of the region, and that involves carrier operations in particularly confined waters.
- Long-range land-based combat aircraft are likely to remain a weapon of choice for preserving U.S. unilateral military influence across the region.

Southeast Asia

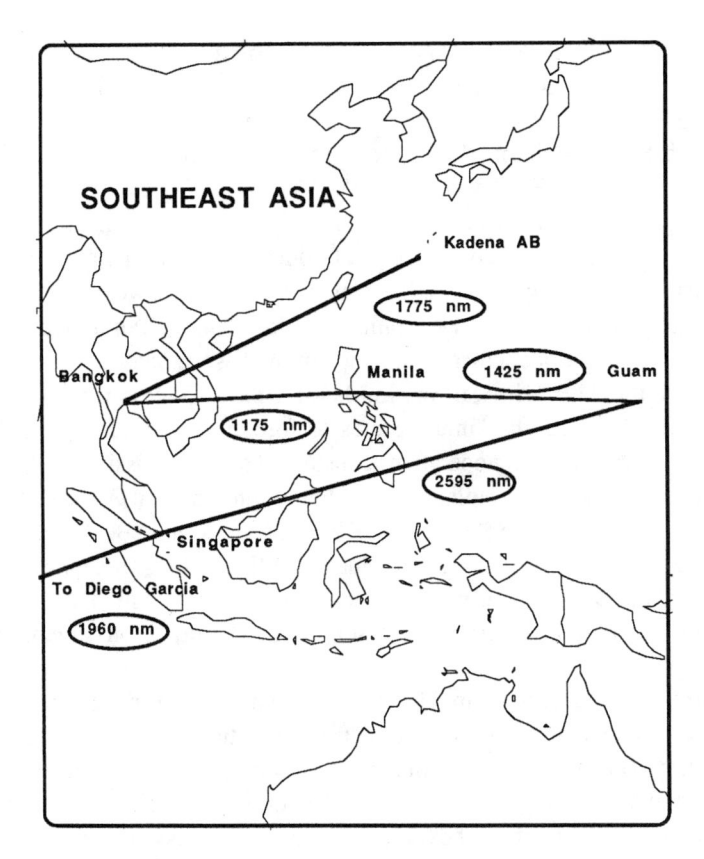

![Map of Southeast Asia showing distances from various locations: Kadena AB 1775 nm, Bangkok, Manila 1425 nm, Guam, 1175 nm, 2595 nm, Singapore, To Diego Garcia 1960 nm]

Southeast Asia is important to the United States for two reasons. First, by virtue of population, resources and productivity, it promises to continue to grow in world importance as the southern anchor of the "Pacific Rim." Second, it provides the locus of a system of bases which enables the United States to extend its strategic reach to and beyond the region to the Asian mainland, South Asia, and the Persian Gulf. Basing considerations in this region benefit from rich lessons learned by the United States through its long, painful involvement in the Vietnam War. Far from the United States, Southeast Asia is made up of insular and peninsular nations separated by great expanses of water. U.S. bases have long formed both the western anchors of the logistical bridge to the United States and the regional hubs necessary in order to further extend U.S. military power. Recent disestablishment of the extensive U.S. basing system across the region cannot fail to influence the implementation of U.S. policy in and beyond the region.

When the United States first deployed large forces to Vietnam, it took advantage of the basing structure built up by the French in Indochina, particularly that which had been developed in post-World War II efforts to reestablish French control. U.S. efforts focused initially on refurbishing and modernizing former French bases [135]. The technological level of the U.S. aircraft used in Vietnam and the intensity of the operations were quickly recognized to require the construction of additional main operating bases and secondary operating facilities [136]. Many additional bases were built outside of Vietnam to support tactical air operations. Udorn, Ubon, Takhli, Korat and U-Tapao in Thailand alone indicate the scope of the base expansion effort required to support the U.S. air war in Southeast Asia. Even these bases were insufficient to enable the United States to forego a massive aerial refueling requirement. Air refueling operations constituted a major mission of Takhli AB, Thailand; U-Tapao AB, Thailand; Don Muang International Airport, Thailand; Clark AB, Republic of the Philippines; Ching Chuan Kang AB, Taiwan; Kadena AB, Okinawa; and Andersen AFB, Guam [137]. It is significant to note that among all these bases, only Kadena and Andersen remain U.S. Air Force operating bases today. Only Andersen AFB, Guam, is on sovereign U.S. territory.

Former base locations in Thailand, Vietnam, and Taiwan are no longer available. Washington has accepted reduced operational freedom in Okinawa in the interest of better relations with Japan. Basing in many other regional states is impractical for a variety of reasons. The only genuine possibility for new access in the region seems to be Singapore; and that access appears to be limited to minimal refueling and "liberty port" rights. Even in "sovereign" Guam local political interests promise increasingly to constrain U.S. military freedom of action. Moreover, Guam is so far from most of the region that its utility for basing combat aircraft is limited to long-range, land-based bombers and their support.

Basing in Southeast Asia is closely linked to both the decolonization process and to post-colonial attitudes on nationhood. In the Okinawan case, it is tied to Japan's progression out of the status of a defeated World War II Axis power. Across the region, it reflects attitudes about appropriate intraregional relations and about the immediacy (or lack thereof) of military threats from both within and without the region. It also relates closely to U.S. relations with Taiwan and China.

To the very end of their service, U.S. bases in the Philippines remained extremely important for regional and extra-regional contingencies. Nationalist pressures, however, had caused the availability of bases in the Philippines to decline steadily. Even as the major remaining base complexes were built up to fulfill their Cold War and Vietnam era functions, the number of bases steadily decreased. U.S. operations conducted from these bases came under ever-closer Filipino scrutiny, with organizational forms imposed to give at least the appearance of turning U.S. bases into joint U.S.-Filipino ones. These trends all converged in the Filipino Senate to trigger the final departure of U.S. forces from the Philippines. Political factors weighed at least as heavily as the volcanic eruptions of Mount Pinatubo in the final lowering of the Stars and Stripes over both Clark Air Base and Subic Bay.

The combination of great distances and strategic significance of Southeast Asia even calls into play the possible need to exploit U. S. military access to Australian bases as an approach to easing the geostrategic bind. The U.S.-Australian defense cooperation relationship is rooted in a bilateral assistance treaty signed in 1951 and the ANZUS Treaty signed the following year. The United States has conducted short-term B-52 training at Australian Air Force bases to include low-level navigation exercises in Australian air space. These activities demonstrated the feasibility of forward operations by long-range bombers from Australian airfields. The U.S. Navy makes port calls at the Australian bases, and the base at Cockburn Sound is a potential U.S. facility that could be expanded to accommodate carriers.

The Vietnamese government has even suggested that the United States might be welcomed back to Cam Ranh Bay—presumably in return for a generous economic assistance package. As far fetched as such a proposal might seem, it represents a valid appreciation by the Vietnamese Government of the strategic value to a United States with global interests of appropriately positioned bases central to this region.

Regional Observations: The great distance between remaining U.S. bases and possible Southeast Asian regional conflict locations reduces the military utility of deployable surface and tactical air power. With extensive aerial refueling support, strikes could be executed, but a sustained, intense air campaign would not be possible.

- Basing access is becoming more limited and more politically constrained.
- While carrier-based aircraft have access to significant parts of the region, the great distances involved in reaching potential trouble

spots render U.S. naval power in the region an asset that will usually require considerably steaming time to deploy, and may be almost as dependent on regional basing as is land-based air power.
- Southeast Asia is generally accessible to long-range air power based either on "sovereign" U.S. Guam or, should political conditions warrant it, outside the region.

East Asia

EAST ASIA

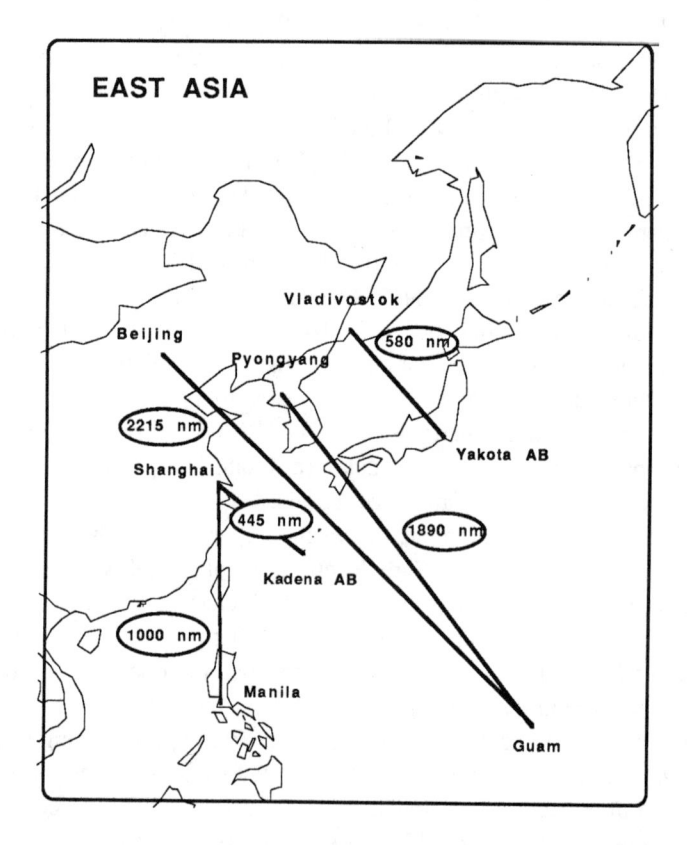

- Vladivostok — 580 nm
- Beijing
- Pyongyang
- 2215 nm
- Shanghai
- Yakota AB
- 445 nm
- 1890 nm
- Kadena AB
- 1000 nm
- Manila
- Guam

Regional Overview: Aside from Europe, the East Asian region contains the largest and most important network of U.S. bases in the world. Most of the basing arrangements stem from the post-World War II period, when the United States presided over the demilitarization of Japan and made arrangements for the protection of U.S. security interests in the East Asia/Pacific region. The North Korean attack on South Korea in 1950 drew the United States into the three-year

Korean War and led to a consolidation of the U.S. basing structure in the Far East inherited from World War II.

East Asia's importance to the United States derives from a recognition of the demographic and economic potential of the region and a need to protect sea lines of communication. These are vital for U.S. trade and freedom of navigation, as well as for the strategic interests of Japan and South Korea, which are among America's staunchest allies. In East Asia, China, Japan, North and South Korea and Russia are in relatively close proximity. A conflict involving one or more of these nations could escalate quickly to involve all four, as well as the United States.

Japan is a world-class economic power with close ties to the United States. China, by virtue of its size, location, huge population, dynamic economy, and powerful military establishment (including its nuclear arsenal), is an important factor in the calculation of U.S. security interests in the region. The situation in Korea remains volatile. The most immediate danger is North Korea's nuclear weapons and missile programs. Although Pyongyang had been a signatory of the Nuclear Non-Proliferation Treaty, it refuses to allow effective international inspection of its nuclear facilities, and it is apparent that North Korea aspires to a nuclear weapons capability. If the North acquires nuclear weapons, it is highly likely that the South will try to follow suit. Even Japan could conceivably get over its nuclear allergy.

The U.S.-Japanese military relationship is based upon the Treaty of Mutual Cooperation and Security, signed in 1960. In addition, the Japan-U.S. Status of Forces Agreement provides land and facilities for U.S. military forces on Japanese soil.

Defense cooperation between the United States and South Korea dates back to a mutual defense assistance agreement signed on 26 January 1950, several months prior to the outbreak of the Korean War. A Mutual Defense Treaty was signed in November 1954. U.S. forces and basing in Korea are currently declining, but remain important to the region. The U.S. presence in South Korea is supported by munitions, ordnance and fuel storage depots and other requirements for combat. The U.S. Navy enjoys access to South Korean port facilities.

The U.S. military presence in Japan and South Korea has been a perennial target of political protest, accompanied by considerable violence. Large-scale rioting in 1980 nearly forced the Japanese government to forego renewal of the U.S.-Japanese mutual security treaty. Japanese radical organizations also have demonstrated repeatedly against visits by U.S. nuclear-capable ships and submarines to Japan's ports. Resentment among Okinawans over the U.S. military presence on their island remains strong.

Political protests against the U.S. military presence in South Korea have erupted on a regular basis. Gestures of U.S. response to Korean sensitivities, however, may be insufficient to prevent further street clashes, particularly since many South Koreans regard the U.S. presence in their country as the chief obstacle to Korean reunification.

An overview of U.S. basing access in East Asia also must mention Taiwan, where the U.S. Navy occasionally uses the Kaohsiung and Keelung naval bases. Although the U.S. military presence there is designed to be infrequent and as inconspicuous as possible to avoid offending the People's Republic of China, it presumably could increase in size and tempo if a crisis erupted between China and Taiwan [138]. Although relations between the "two Chinas" currently seem to be relaxed, a future confrontation in the Taiwan Straits certainly cannot be ruled out and would impinge directly on U.S. security interests in the region.

Regional Observations:

- East Asia will remain of paramount importance to the United States because of military and trade relationships with Japan, the proximity of Russian military power, the pivotal geostrategic position of China, and the uncertain future of the volatile Korean Peninsula.
- The acquisition of ballistic missile technology by Japan and Korea and of a possible nuclear weapons capability by North Korea are driving the growth of military power within the region.
- The political instability of both China and Russia and the possibility of closer military cooperation between the two will bear close watching by the United States.
- The distance between the United States and East Asia mandates either continued U.S. forward deployment in the area, with the concomitant need for basing access which is under increasing pressure, or the fielding of forces with range sufficient to exert military power from outside the region. Long-range, land-based air power ranks high in this category. To the extent forward-deployed forces in East Asia are reduced further, the adverse diplomatic consequences of such reductions will be lessened by the manifest ability of long-range bombers to reach that region quickly and with substantial firepower.

South Asia

SOUTH ASIA

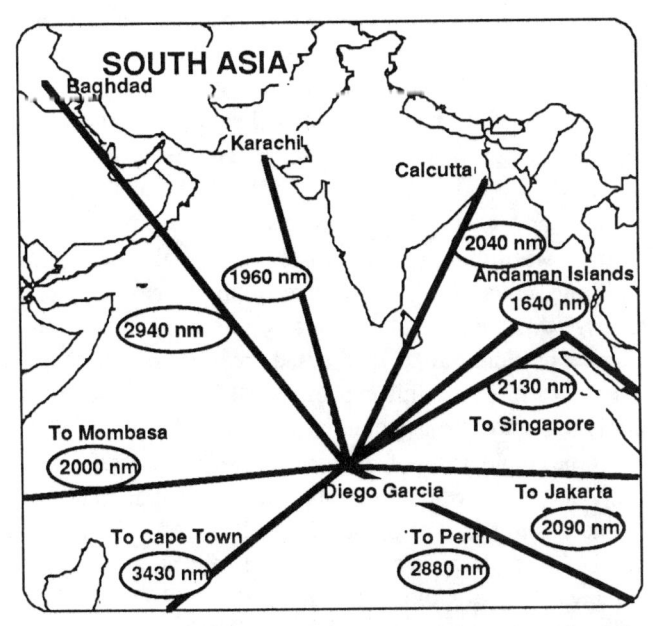

Baghdad — 2940 nm
Karachi — 1960 nm
Calcutta — 2040 nm
Andaman Islands — 1640 nm
2130 nm
To Mombasa — 2000 nm
To Singapore
Diego Garcia
To Jakarta — 2090 nm
To Cape Town — 3430 nm
To Perth — 2880 nm

The strategic importance of South Asia has been recognized for centuries. India was the crown jewel in the British Empire. More recently, U.S. concern about Soviet designs on Afghanistan reflected Washington's desire to maintain the neutrality of that country, which traditionally was the gateway to South Asia. These concerns operate against the background of a post-colonial history of bitter and sometimes violent conflict between India and Pakistan, and between India and China. These conflicts are chronic potential ignition systems for war in South Asia.

The stability of South Asia also is put at risk by India's aspirations for hegemony in the region. For example, India sent some 50,000 troops to Sri Lanka to help the government quell an uprising by the Tamil minority. Indian troops also were dispatched to the Maldive Islands during civil strife there. The Indians already have interfered massively in the internal affairs of the small Himalayan nations of Nepal, Sikkim, and Bhutan; the latter two have become virtual Indian protectorates. India's naval expansion and ambitions in the Indian Ocean are an even more immediate cause for U.S. concern. An Indian naval buildup in the vicinity of the straits leading from the Indian to the Pacific oceans could jeopardize unfettered maritime access through these strategic choke points.

Military operations in South Asia are difficult for the United States. The entire region is as geographically remote as any where the United States may be required to act. Its access depends on access to chains of intervening bases through either Europe, North Africa and the Middle East or the Pacific, East Asia, and Southeast Asia. Basing in this expansive region is severely restricted by both the availability of adequate air bases and political realities.

By far the most significant U.S. base access in the region is at Diego Garcia, part of the British Indian Ocean Territory. The base offers fuel, water and munitions storage and hosts the "Near-Term Prepositioning Force," which consists of large Maritime Prepositioning Ships with equipment to outfit Marine amphibious units [139]. Extensive improvements to the facilities at Diego Garcia give this base the ability to host relatively intense operations by significant numbers of long-range, land-based combat aircraft. B-52 operations against Iraq serve to illustrate this capability. It is important to consider that Diego Garcia is so remote from potential targets in the region that it is not a feasible base for the employment of shorter-range tactical aircraft.

The U.S. presence elsewhere in South Asia is minimal. The United States no longer has access to bases or prepositioned supplies in Pakistan [140]. In Sri Lanka, the U.S. Navy makes occasional port calls at the Trincomalee naval base, and the naval base at Colombo is available for R & R for U.S. military personnel. There are no prearranged air access privileges for U.S. combat aircraft in any of the South Asian countries. Even the refueling of Military Airlift Command aircraft passing through India generated a political crisis during the Desert Shield build-up. The Congress Party leadership threatened the incumbent Socialist regime over the refueling of U.S. C-130s and other transports at Bombay, Madras, and Agra. Critics saw the refueling of U.S. Air Force aircraft as alternatively an effort to draw U.S. support away from Pakistan, and as subservience to the United States and support of the war against Iraq [141].

Large relatively capable airfields do exist in India and Pakistan. The better tend to be commercial fields, but military airfields are up to standards sufficient for the significant force structures of the Indian and Pakistani air forces. However, the scope of potential conflict in South Asia reflects the size and population of the principal antagonists, and they are so large that the potential regional basing structure is minute in comparison, and far too dispersed for more than an isolated air campaign if the United States relies on deployed fighter-attack type air forces.

While aircraft carriers are usable in the region, they too are at the end of a long, tenuous supply line. Carrier-based aircraft also have access only to coastal regions of sub-continent-sized countries. Their utility would be at its maximum in terms of frustrating Indian attempts to extend regional hegemony across the Indian Ocean. They would have far less potential in affecting the outcome of major regional land campaigns.

South Asia is beset by severe instabilities. Secessionist movements are strong in India. The most serious involves Kashmir, the object of past wars between India and Pakistan and the site of recent clashes. Kashmir is a legacy of the upheavals that accompanied Pakistan's creation as a separate nation in 1947 and the massive population transfers between Hindus and Muslims. The bitter feelings engendered by Pakistan's separation from India at that time and by the Indian-assisted secession of East Pakistan (now Bangladesh) in 1972 remain. Adding to the tensions are efforts by both India and Pakistan to develop a nuclear weapons capability—public disavowals notwithstanding [142].

The future of U.S. access to Diego Garcia too is affected by the politics of the region and must be considered far from certain over the long term. India has conducted vigorous public diplomacy campaigns to eliminate the U.S. presence on the island. The Indians strive to restrict the U.S. naval presence in "their" ocean. Already India is capable of exercising sea denial in the northern part of the Indian Ocean in close proximity to the Indian subcontinent; in the future, its capabilities will extend further. U.S. presence and operations anywhere in South Asia draws critical Indian attention and comment. Even the U.S. cyclone relief operations in Bangladesh drew considerable Indian press comment attributing to "official sources" consternation over the "arrival of thousands of American troops in South Asia" [143].

Pakistan, a former member of the Southeast Asia Treaty Organization (SEATO) and the now-defunct Central Treaty Organization (CENTO), was a major U.S. ally for many years and most recently served as the principal conduit for the delivery of U.S. weapons and equipment to the anti-Soviet insurgents in Afghanistan. Nevertheless, since the murder of Pakistani president Gen. Zia ul-Haq, in 1988, relations between Islamabad and Washington have slid downhill. A major bone of contention is the U.S. insistence on linking military assistance to Pakistan to assurances that the country is not moving to acquire nuclear weapons. The future of U.S. defense cooperation with Pakistan will have a major bearing on any attempt by Washington to intervene militarily in the South Asian region.

Regional Observations:

- South Asia will remain important to the United States because India is one of the most populous countries in the world and is the largest democracy.

- Instability in South Asia and various ongoing conflicts might at any time ignite larger (even nuclear) wars that could have a negative impact on U.S. security interests. Many of the problems in South Asia predate the Cold War, and most are likely to persist into the "new" era.
- The ability of the United States to intervene in South Asia is hampered by distance and limited access to bases in the region.
- The base at Diego Garcia is the most important U.S. staging area for South Asian intervention, but political agitation by India could impede its usefulness in the future. India's expanding naval and air power also could complicate efforts to supply the base and stage operations from it.
- The United States would have to rely heavily upon long-range aircraft for projection of power into South Asia, whether such operations are based inside or outside of the region.

Global Commons

GLOBAL COMMONS

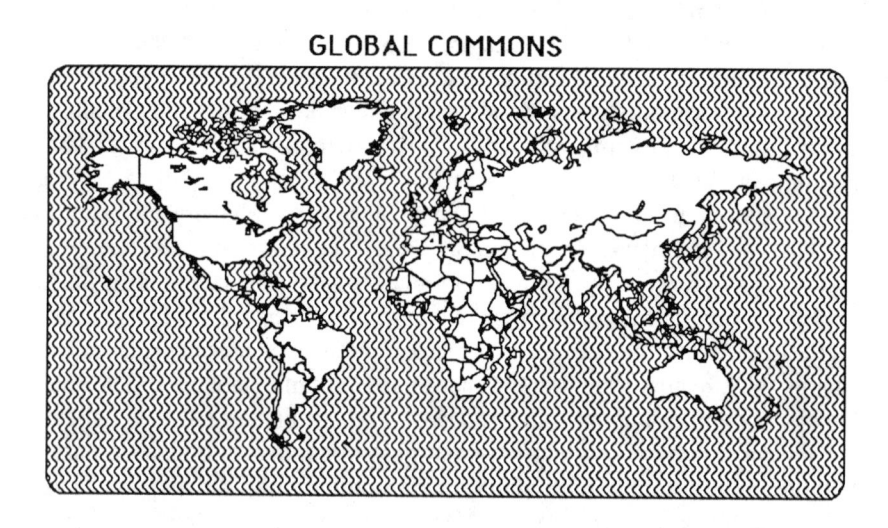

Possible future conflict may transcend regional categories. One must also consider potential conflict focused on resources or strategic advantage beyond the bounds of national territory in a broad expanse that can be labeled the "global commons." This area includes the high seas, seabeds, Arctic and Antarctic regions, and international waterways. Such conflict is increasingly likely in the future as important resources become more scarce, as Third World nations gain the capability to reach out beyond their own borders in search of coveted resources, and as technology permits exploitation of resources only recently considered to be beyond the reach of profitable exploitation.

This trend was recognized over a decade ago as a pattern of conflicts over such regions became discernible.[144]. Oil exploration, for example, is pushing out into ever deeper waters, farther from shore, and farther into the Arctic. Undersea oil exploration has spread wells across the North Sea, far out into the Gulf of Mexico, and across the Persian Gulf, and even generated conflict between China, Vietnam, and the Philippines over the Parcel and the Spratly Islands in the South China Sea. Engineering work is underway to transform shallow reefs into real islands. Traditional territorial claims are aggravated by efforts to extend territorial waters and exclusive economic zones around these islands.

Other resources also are subject to such Global Commons disputes: pelagic fishing, sea bed mining for various metals, and perhaps in the not too distant future, pressure for mining of a variety of minerals in Antarctica. All of these could generate international conflicts. Passage through international straits, the regulation of exclusive economic zones, and a variety of other freedom of navigation issues also are increasingly contested.

By virtue of geographic remoteness, where these Global Commons problems tend toward violence, basing access presents a problem. The Global Commons tend to be far from major air bases. Much of the military activity associated with Global Commons issues tends to involve a "quick grab" tactic intended to present more distant competitors with a *fait accompli*. The potential distribution and remoteness of such conflict locations is illustrated by the number of countries in the world (95) which have exclusive economic zone or maritime claims or notification regimes that are excessive or inconsistent with the UN Law of the Sea Treaty and with U.S. views of the law of the sea [145].

While much of the Global Commons is traditionally perceived as a marine environment where ships and carrier-borne aircraft are the primary military actors, the scenes of much of this competition takes place far from normal peacetime operating areas. Since coastal states are likely to be at odds with maritime nations such as the United States, land-basing for deployable U.S. tactical aviation probably will be unavailable.

Regional Observation:

- Since land basing for deployable tactical power is unlikely to be available, and since carrier-based aircraft involve relatively slow transit times, long-range, land-based combat aircraft probably will be particularly useful in this context.

Conclusions

This analysis by region implies a number of specific observations regarding the availability of basing and the significance of this availability in terms of the various approaches to power projection, including the conventional attack utility of modern long-range, land-based bombers such as the B-2. These observations are summarized in Table 2.

1. The distance from the United States of all of these regions save the first implies a lengthy deployment process and major logistical support burden if expeditionary forces are to be fielded as the major U.S. force involvement. As successful as such deployments may be under favorable conditions, such as those in DESERT SHIELD/DESERT STORM, the build-up of deployed power is slow and initial elements can be quite vulnerable.

2. The number of available air bases with facilities and surface transportation infrastructure capable of supporting an intense tactical fighter/short-range attack air campaign and the proximity of such bases to potential combat locations is probably inadequate in all regions save one—the Persian Gulf—where such conflict is likely. Even the Gulf War, fought under the best Third World basing conditions, saw remote basing of some combat aircraft, long sortie durations, and massive employment phase aerial refueling which indicated how tenuous basing actually was.

3. While adequate basing for a single base-sized presence such as the U.S. Air Force presence in Khartoum and French air defense presence in Chad is more generally available, these are severely constrained in combat effectiveness by the widespread absence of logistical support.

4. Political factors reduce the likelihood that U.S. air forces will obtain relevant basing rights, and even where basing is accorded, employment options may be restricted. These take the form of strong feelings against U.S. intervention such as in Latin America, frequent unpredictable violence such as in Sub-Saharan Africa, concern over cultural impact of a Western presence, or opposition to U.S. policy, such as is the case with U.S. support for Israel.

5. Aircraft carrier basing varies greatly in its potential utility. In regions where the terrain is insular or coastal and the carriers can be supported nearby, it has good potential. Reach inland is poor. Initial response time varies greatly as a function of steaming time from peacetime carrier locations. The vulnerability of carrier forces in confined waters is also a factor in determining the part of the carrier task force's efforts that must be reserved for self defense.

6. Modern long-range, land-based bomber utility is good in any of these regional settings. B-2 class bombers can range all of the regions from the United States with nominal refueling (none in the case of Central America). This yields excellent initial combat effectiveness within hours. For sustained operations in the more distant cases, the less demanding runway requirements and greater range of the B-2 class bombers (3,000 nm combat radius unrefueled and 6,000 nm combat radius with one refueling) open up a far broader selection of bases than for any other combat aircraft. This eases both the logistical support and political availability criteria and increases tactical flexibility. The B-2 adds two main categories of operational advantage over earlier long-range heavy bombers (B-52 class) in regional conflict: B-2s can operate from essentially any major airfield within or outside the region in question without concern for load bearing capacity or logistical support beyond that common to commercial air carrier or indigenous military operations; and, beside nominal refueling for more distant targets, B-2s, by virtue of their stealth technology, require no protective support package of fighters and ECM aircraft, all of relatively short range that itself would depend upon forward bases.

While not presuming to suggest that the B-2 can do other than its bombardment mission, this regional survey indicates that the B-2 can indeed range across the world from bases where the United States has sovereign control or is accorded near-sovereign rights by traditional allies with a great coincidence of policy interests. It can operate with particular efficiency without a complex fleet of support aircraft and can bring its firepower to bear throughout a conflict, from its first hours to conflict termination. These factors give the B-2 the unique status of being the only current or planned U.S. combat aircraft with the ability to exercise full conventional combat potential across each of the twelve regions that together constitute the world regional conflict arena.

Table 2: Regional Basing Summary

	Distance from U.S. (Atlantic Ocean Equivalents)	Adequate Basing for Intense Campaign (Gulf War standard)	Adequate Basing for Single-Base Campaign (with Logistical Support)	Political Reliability	Aircraft Carrier Utility	Long-range Bomber Utility
1. Central America	<1	No	Yes	Poor	Good	Excellent
2. South America	1	No	Probable	Poor	Fair	Good
3. North Africa	>1	No	Probable	Fair	Fair	Good
4. Sub-Saharan Africa	2	No	Improbable	Poor	Poor	Good
5. Middle East	2	Yes	Yes	Fair	Fair	Good
6. Levant	2	No	Improbable	Poor	Fair	Good
7. Central Asia	2	No	Improbable	Poor	None	Good
8. Eastern Europe	>1	No	Probable	Fair	Poor	Good
9. Southeast Asia	>3	No	Probable	Fair	Fair	Good
10. East Asia	3	No	Probable	Good	Good	Good
11. South Asia	4	No	Improbable	Poor	Poor	Good
12. Global Commons	1-4	No	Unknown	Unknown	Fair	Good/ Excellent

Chapter 5
The B-2 and U.S. Domestic Politics
BERNARD C. VICTORY

The President and the Secretary of Defense lead the government in making and implementing defense policy, but Congressional authority, stemming from Congress' control of the public purse, is at its height and can be dominant when the issue at stake is a large acquisition program, such as the B-2, requiring sustained funding. Party politics and the views of congressional leaders influence the direction of these major programs. The change in party control and leadership of Congress resulting from the 1994 elections could lead to a decision to proceed with the B-2 program beyond the force of 20 bombers approved in 1992.

The B-2 in the Executive Branch

The President and Vice President are the only officials elected by the United States as a whole, and are charged with preserving national security. The Department of Defense, whose Secretary is appointed by and responsible to the President, is the principal executive-branch agency charged with carrying out this task. The Air Force, under the Department of Defense, has a mission to "defend the United States through the control and exploitation of air and space" [146]. Accordingly, the Air Force directs programs, including the development and deployment of weapons, enabling it to carry out its official mission. The B-2 bomber is one such system. The B-2 program was initiated in 1978 in response to perceptions of need for a class of nuclear-armed weapon systems to guarantee future deterrence of the Soviet Union in a Cold War. The existence of the stealth bomber program was announced in 1980 and the program was supported in turn by Democratic President Jimmy Carter, and Republican Presidents Ronald Reagan and George Bush. Due to the incorporation of revolutionary materials and design technologies in the B-2, development and testing of the aircraft was conducted out of public view until 1989. Up to that point, the B-2 program had been shaped mostly by the Air Force. This would change when the program became public.

The B-2 in the Congress

The roots of congressional power are local rather than national. Congressmen and women generally are not held accountable for formulating national strategy. Rather, their job is to represent their local constituency on the entire spectrum of public affairs issues. The power to encourage orderly and nationally-oriented decisionmaking in Congress rests largely with its committees and the committee chairmen. The chairmen and members of the House and Senate Armed Services committees particularly have power over the annual defense funding requests. They tend to shape debate and form the cadre around which floor opposition and support coalesce. Committee proceedings, hearings, and reports provide much of the congressional "big picture" and the "long view" about national issues. The committees are also the chief, if not the only, recipients of classified information from the executive branch in their areas of specialization.

While the B-2 remained a classified program, the Air Force's budgetary requests for the B-2 were consistently approved, after secret review, by elements of the House and Senate Armed Services and Appropriations Committees. There was no public committee or floor action on the B-2 program; the funds were approved on the House and Senate floors along with the entire defense authorization and appropriation bills.

By the time the B-2 program came out of the "black world" in 1989, and debate moved into the public and politicized fora of normal congressional action, it faced an unexpected revolution in the international security environment. The B-2 program has since then largely been shaped by Congress. The Air Force, in initial public hearings, touted B-2's conventional capabilities, but justified the aircraft primarily in traditional terms of superpower deterrence—as a penetrator of Soviet air defenses, and deliverer of nuclear weapons [147]. The B-2 program's force of 132 aircraft were justified as being the number necessary to cover the Soviet target set in a nuclear conflict [148]. Another pro-B-2 argument that tended to portray the aircraft as almost exclusively a Cold War nuclear deterrent invoked a counting rule in the U.S.-Soviet negotiations toward a Strategic Arms Reduction Treaty (START). Each bomber, though carrying up to 16 warheads, was counted as only one warhead under START limits, allowing the United States to maintain a strong deterrent against the Soviet Union, despite the START treaty reductions [149].

In 1989, however, the Soviet empire was crumbling; after two more years of political upheaval the Soviet state itself disintegrated. While these events did not point to a future without danger, they were devastating to the nuclear rationale for the B-2 program. In the Congress, consistency in voting records is a quality most members try to maintain. The shift from a rationale emphasizing the B-2's nuclear capability to one highlighting its conventional potential, however valid, did not restore much of the support lost by the withering of the nuclear requirement. Few congressmen who rejected B-2 as the Soviet threat receded found it easy to consider supporting the program to counter regional, conventional threats. The Department of Defense, in response to budgetary pressures and the declining threat, reduced in April 1990 the planned B-2 buy from 132 to 75 aircraft [150], and at the end of 1991, decided to limit the B-2 program to 20 operational bombers [151]. General John Michael Loh, USAF, Commander, Air Combat Command, makes clear that budgetary pressure was the primary driver in the decision to reduce the B-2 buy:

> I think it fair to say [sic], having been a part of these councils over the last few years, that the Air Force has always sought more than 20 B-2s, and the decision to go to 20 B-2s was made because of budgetary considerations, far more than operational considerations [152].

Congressional debate on the B-2 program was subordinated to a pervasive sense that, with the collapse of the Soviet Union, the defense drawdown will be a fact of future political life. The drawdown is understood to include: declines in manpower [153]; base closures, particularly overseas [154]; reduction in force structure [155]; and reductions in the number of new types of weapons systems being produced [156]. Many in Congress are seizing the post-Cold War opportunity to press for significantly increased spending on domestic programs and trying even harder to reduce the federal budget deficit. Congressional appreciation of the continued utility of major defense programs, such as the B-2, remains, and may have increased as a result of the 1994 elections. In the 1990-1994 period, this sentiment, however, was weaker than the post-Cold War determination to shift resources away from defense.

Past congressional resistance to funding a full force of B-2s was manifested by efforts to find technical fault with the basic design, execution of the construction of the aircraft and its subsystems, overall program cost control, and real and imputed changes in its primary mission. Specific narrow accusations of one or another failing served as stalking horses for opponents unwilling to base criticism of the program on larger issues of strategy, policy, or national need for the capability such a system provides [157]. In 1992, even when the House

Armed Services Committee agreed to the Bush Administration's request to fund four more B-2s and close out the program at 20 aircraft [158], funding was made contingent on reports of a satisfactory solution of low-observability questions and Northrop's ability to hold constant complete program costs of the B-2 force in the face of required modifications and drastic reductions in funded production [159]. Both concerns now appear well on their way to solution. The replanning of B-2 production undertaken in March 1992 to accommodate the reductions in aircraft numbers actually authorized is promised to hold total costs level at $44.4 billion while accommodating the technical adjustments required [160]. Adjustments to low observables characteristics are the subject of continuing scrutiny under a series of congressionally mandated System Maturity Matrix Milestones [161].

In all, 58 technical performance requirements set by Congress had to be met before some B-2 funds could be released by DoD to the contractor. In October 1993, then-Secretary of Defense Aspin certified that the B-2 had met all those requirements, and the money was made available [162].

Party Positions on B-2

The B-2 debate has had some partisan aspect, but support for and opposition to B-2 procurement have existed on both sides of the aisle. In 1980, a stealthy bomber was championed by the Democrats as an alternative to resurrection of the B-1 program, which had been terminated by then-President Carter in 1977 [163]. Resurrection of the B-1 program was a 1980 Republican campaign promise [164], and in 1981, President Reagan made development of both the B-2 and B-1B bombers a part of his strategic force modernization plan [165]. The B-2, being blessed by both the Democrats and Ronald Reagan, received bipartisan approval throughout the 1980s [166].

In 1990, Democratic support for the B-2 program in the House of Representatives began to waver. The House Armed Services Committee (HASC), led by then-Chairman Les Aspin, Democrat of Wisconsin, voted to terminate the B-2 program at 15 aircraft; this decision, made over the votes of most Republicans on the committee, was approved in the Defense Authorization bill by the full House. In the Senate, support for the B-2 remained bipartisan, and the program was funded in a compromise reached in the House-Senate authorization conference. This pattern essentially repeated itself in 1991 and in 1992, although in 1992 Aspin and the House supported funding for four more B-2s with the understanding that the program would terminate at 20 operational aircraft. Democrats in the Senate, led by Senators Sam Nunn of Georgia and

Daniel Inouye of Hawaii, then-Chairmen of the Armed Services and Defense Appropriations, both have favored continued production of the B-2.

The Republicans have generally been consistent supporters of B-2 requests in both the House and the Senate. John Warner of Virginia, who served as ranking minority Member on the Senate Armed Services Committee (SASC) from 1987-1992, is a backer of the B-2. Other supportive Armed Services Republicans include Senators Trent Lott of Mississippi, Dirk Kempthorne of Idaho, and Kay Bailey Hutchison of Texas [167]. Exceptions to the strong Republican support for the B-2 are Senators William Cohen of Maine, who has attacked the B-2 largely for its acquisition costs [168], and John McCain of Arizona, a former naval aviator and member of the Projection Forces and Regional Defense Subcommittee of the SASC, who has championed naval power-projection capabilities [169].

In the House, B-2 supporters include Bob Stump of Arizona, Duncan Hunter and Robert Dornan of California, Herbert Bateman of Virginia, and Jim Hansen of Utah, among senior members of the National Security Committee (formerly the Armed Services Committee). These members were among 133 House Republicans—three quarters of the Republican delegation—who in 1994 supported funding for studies of the bomber force and for maintaining the capability to produce the B-2 through fiscal 1995 [170]. Rep. John Kasich of Ohio has been the most vocal critic of the B-2 among Republicans. Kasich has used a wide range of arguments. Initially, he argued that its nuclear mission was fulfilled by other systems such as cruise missiles, and that the plane cost too much [171]. Kasich later opposed the B-2 on grounds that the program had "the greatest concurrency we have ever seen," and that it would be unable to fulfill what Kasich saw as its primary mission, finding mobile targets. Kasich opposed the B-2 as a conventional platform because he was "deeply concerned about spending $800 million to a billion [sic] dollars for an aircraft that is going to be used primarily as a carpet bomber." Air Force Secretary Donald Rice countered most of Kasich's assertions, citing the elimination of most concurrency, the record of deemphasis of the mobile target mission, and the B-2's projected use as a deliverer of precision-guided conventional weapons. Kasich has nevertheless remained opposed to the B-2 program [172].

Over the last 25 years or so, the Democratic Party has developed a reputation for spending less money on defense than Republicans and favoring fewer major weapons systems, but this perception is at best only partially correct. There are many Democrats who support a strong U.S. defense posture. In the Senate, James Exon of Nebraska is ranking minority member of the Strategic Forces and Nuclear Deterrence Subcommittee of the SASC. As subcommittee chairman from 1987-1994, Exon was consistently supportive of long-range air power and the B-2 bomber [173]. The ranking minority member and former chairman of the Defense Subcommittee of the Senate Appropriations Committee, Daniel Inouye, followed then-Chairman of the Armed Services Committee Sam Nunn's lead by supporting the B-2 and other initiatives to maintain and develop land-based air power. In a letter to then-Secretary of Defense Les Aspin, Inouye in 1993 called for continued B-2 production, declaring that "there is a ground swell of support for the B-2 program in the Senate as more and more members become more and more informed on the important role it will play in U.S. force projection in the contemporary global security environment" [174].

In the House, Democratic Congressman Ike Skelton of Missouri is widely respected as a serious student of defense policy. Skelton has long been a proponent of strategic offensive forces in general and of bombers in particular. His support for the B-2 also has benefited his constituents—Whiteman Air Base, the operational location of the B-2s, is in his district. The ranking minority of the Defense Subcommittee of the House Appropriations Committee, John P. Murtha of Pennsylvania, is quietly supportive of strong defense spending and long-range bombers [175]. In contrast to Murtha's low-key approach, Norman Dicks of Washington State has been extremely active in drumming up support for the program, at one point in 1994 obtaining signatures of 211 House members on a letter sent to then-chairman of the HASC Ron Dellums supporting the Senate's plan to devote $150 million to maintaining the industrial capacity to produce B-2s.

Nevertheless, many Democrats in both houses have consistently opposed what they see as excessive defense spending. Often they have focused on high-profile weapons systems such as the B-2 and B-1 in their efforts to cut the defense budget in favor of spending on domestic programs. Ronald Dellums of California, ranking minority member on the House National Security Committee, is clearly in this group. Since his election to the House in 1970, he has generally criticized U.S. military involvement and use of force abroad [176], and has expressed opposition to both strategic defensive [177] and offensive weapons. His opposition to the B-2 bomber first challenged the aircraft's rationale as a nuclear delivery system. Dellums then dismissed assertions that the B-2 would be useful as a conventional weapon as "folly," asking (during Desert Shield) why the nation's other advanced long-range bomber, the B-1B, was not being sent to operate in the Persian Gulf area [178]. Dellums in 1989 allied B-2 opponents in the Democratic Party with a number of anti-B-2 Republicans led by John Kasich in a move to terminate the program;

Dellums was successful in 1990 when he was joined in his effort by Les Aspin [179]. In the Senate, Carl Levin of Michigan is among Democrats who have sponsored amendments to cut or eliminate B-2 funding; the most recent of these failed, 55-45 [180]. The turnover of the House and Senate to the Republicans should mean reduced influence for members with views akin to Dellums and Levin and an increased congressional willingness to consider funding weapons programs such as the B-2, for which a compelling military justification can be made.

Congressional Leadership and the B-2

Party positions on the B-2 and opinions of rank-and-file members are greatly influenced by the stances taken by the chairmen of the House and Senate Armed Services committees, as well as by the party congressional leadership. Most recently, the committee chairmen have often exerted their influence within their committees and on the floor of the Congress to shape the contents and direct the policy orientation of the annual defense authorization bills [181]. For example, in 1989, Les Aspin, Democrat from Wisconsin, then-chairman of the House Armed Services Committee, supported continued production of the B-2, over the objections of many Democrats led by Ronald Dellums and some Republicans led by Kasich. But in July 1990, Aspin moved to terminate the B-2 citing high cost, uncertain technical capability, and a capability that was neither unique nor necessary [182]. Many House Democrats followed Aspin's lead and terminated the B-2 (the program was maintained by a compromise with the Senate in conference). Aspects of those Congressional leaders' understanding of national security issues, and particularly how the modern long-range, land-based bomber fits into future U.S. force structure accordingly bear close examination.

Floyd Spence of South Carolina became chairman of the House National Security Committee (formerly the Armed Services Committee), in January 1995. Spence, first elected in 1970, has a low-key approach. Although he has made few public statements regarding the B-2, Spence has consistently supported the program. Spence's general comments on force modernization provisions in the FY 1995 Authorization Act indicate the likelihood of his continued support for the B-2 program:

> In essence the administration's long-range modernization strategy is to do little more than delay important and costly decisions until such time that a future administration will be confronted with the need to breathe new life into the remnants of our defense industrial base in order to modernize the military services. The administration's "not on my

watch" approach to investing in modernization is cause for great concern, and this bill's modest enhancements represent at least a small step in the right direction [183].

Senate Armed Services Committee Chairman Strom Thurmond of South Carolina is one of the longest-lived figures in American politics. Born in 1902, he is the "Dean" of the Senate, having served there since 1954. Thurmond is one of the Senate's most staunch proponents of defense. He has always supported the B-2, most recently opposing an amendment to the FY 1995 Authorization bill that would have eliminated the funding to maintain the B-2 suppliers' network, in order "to preserve capacity and reduce the cost of future acquisitions if we find them necessary during next year's hearings on bomber requirements" [184].

Although he is no longer chairman of the Senate Armed Services Committee, Senator Sam Nunn's views are widely respected throughout the Senate and beyond. Nunn often has supported defense policies and weapon systems, such as the B-2 bomber, in the face of opposition from many in his own Democratic Party. On the other hand, he has successfully parried defense initiatives of Republican presidents a number of times. For example, one need only recall his successful battle with the Reagan Administration to retain the "narrow" over the "broad" interpretation of the ABM Treaty. Nevertheless, Nunn often worked closely with the Republicans the last time that party held a Senate majority (1981-1987); moreover, Nunn is probably Congress' most articulate and effective proponent of the B-2. Accordingly, his statements will be reviewed here in some detail.

Recognizing the continuing trend of declining resources available to the Pentagon, Senator Nunn in 1992 called for a review and overhaul of the services' roles and missions. Nunn sees considerable wasteful overlap among the services, costing billions of dollars yearly [185]. According to Nunn, the change in the size, location, and urgency of the threat, combined with the ongoing federal budgetary crisis, makes reorganization necessary if the United States is to get the most military efficiency out of its remaining forces.

Senator Nunn speaks of ten areas where he sees duplication in service roles and missions. Projection of air power is first on the list [186]. Specifically, he sees sea-based and land-based capabilities as duplicative:

What is the most cost-effective way to provide air interdiction in the future—with long-range bombers from the United States or with large numbers of aircraft carriers with medium-range bombers on their decks?

Chapter 5   111

... Could Navy aircraft carriers utilize shorter-range bombers—like F-18s—and let the Air Force provide the long-range bombing capability [187]?

Nunn asks that the capabilities and costs of these projected force elements be examined to determine the tradeoffs. Nunn maintains that he is not advocating an either/or proposition; he sees both capabilities as necessary and is thinking of changes at the margins. It nevertheless may be inferred that Senator Nunn may be prepared to support augmenting land-based, long-range air power over procuring new naval strike platforms. He noted that the projected development and procurement cost of the AX bomber (since cancelled) was $60 to $80 billion, while upgrading the B-1B force will cost $5 billion [188].

Senator Nunn has continually gone to great lengths on Capitol Hill to maintain the B-2 program. In 1990, when the House agreed to terminate B-2 production [189], the Senate, led by Nunn, voted to maintain production [190], and the program survived in the House-Senate conference. Similarly in 1991, the House refused to fund production of any more B-2 bombers; this would have terminated the B-2 program at 15 aircraft. But the Senate, led by Nunn, approved the Administration request to continue the B-2 program with four additional aircraft, and suggested building the entire fleet of 75 B-2s at efficient, high-production rates, calling the B-2 "a necessary and affordable capability" [191].

The SASC described in some detail the basis for the committee's decision to fund the B-2 program in fiscal 1992. Nunn's Committee saw merit in using the B-2's combination of stealth, long range, and large payload for conventional conflicts, citing the Gulf War as a case in point. The committee agreed with the Air Force's assessment that the plane was able to accomplish the mission of a much larger and more expensive assembly of non-stealthy aircraft; that in doing so, B-2 clearly put fewer personnel at risk from enemy fire than the non-stealthy armada; and that B-2 operations required no expensive and vulnerable bases nearby and could be conducted in a more timely manner. Figure 6, which the SASC reproduced in its FY 1992-93 Authorization Act Report, vividly illustrates the operational advantages and efficiencies the B-2 has over alternative systems [192].

The 1991 SASC decision led to another House-Senate conference compromise which kept the B-2 alive by approving the 16th aircraft plus long-lead funding for the next four [193]. When in 1992 the administration decided to terminate the B-2 program at 20 the required funds were approved in part because

112   The B-2 Bomber: Air Power for the 21st Century

The Value of Stealth

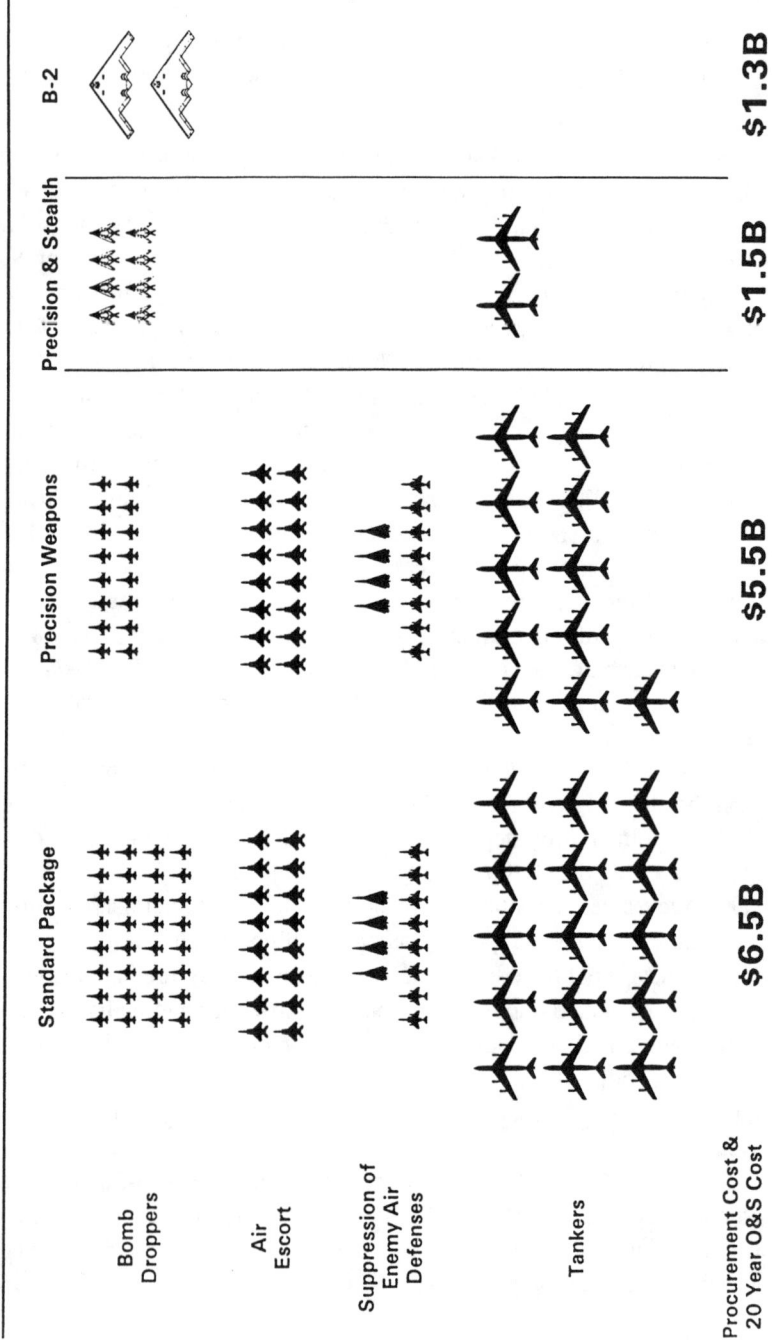

	Standard Package	Precision Weapons	Precision & Stealth	B-2
Bomb Droppers				
Air Escort				
Suppression of Enemy Air Defenses				
Tankers				
Procurement Cost & 20 Year O&S Cost	$6.5B	$5.5B	$1.5B	$1.3B

the long-lead funding for the last four aircraft had already been authorized and appropriated the previous year. And it appears that Senator Nunn had hoped to continue building B-2 bombers; the SASC report for the FY1993 authorization act expresses "disappointment" that the administration capped B-2 purchases at 20 aircraft [194].

The year 1993 saw almost no debate on the size of the B-2 force [195]. Nevertheless, the SASC FY 1994 Authorization Report, reflecting Nunn's views, criticized the Air Force Bomber Roadmap for not considering the numbers-stressing bomber requirements of stopping an armored invasion. The report also expressed concern with the projected capabilities under "demanding scenarios" of the non-stealthy bomber force, particularly the B-1B. Concern was noted with regard to the reliability of the B-1B force as well as the tactical effectiveness of the aircraft in making use of projected precision-guided weapons capabilities [196]. The final FY 1994 Authorization Act required a study and report, based on an actual exercise evaluating the operational readiness of the B-1B fleet [197].

In 1994, Senator Nunn led a congressional initiative to develop a coherent policy regarding the future bomber force. There were two major aspects to this effort. The first was the addition of $150 million to the defense authorization bill, to fund a study of future U.S. bomber requirements, and to maintain the supplier network for B-2 components, enabling the manufacturing base to survive, keeping the option open to produce more B-2s [198]. Second, Nunn's measure rejected the administration's programmed reduction in the B-1 and B-52 bomber forces, and prevented retirement of any of the bomber force through fiscal year 1995. The House agreed in the inclusion of this measure (at $125 million in funding) in the Authorization and Appropriations Acts [199].

Clinton Administration Perspectives

Les Aspin served as Secretary of Defense for the first year of the Clinton Administration (January 1993 to January 1994). During this time he undertook a reexamination of U.S. military forces. This DoD effort, called the Bottom-Up Review (BUR), sought to determine the size and composition of U.S. armed forces for the coming post-Cold War years. Much of the work behind the Bottom-Up Review was undertaken in 1992 by Mr. Aspin while he was Chairman of the House Armed Services Committee.

Aspin decided that U.S. military forces could be smaller than the Bush Administration's "Base Force," which, though formally announced in January 1992, was developed while the Soviet Union was still intact and constituted a potential regional threat of considerable concern [200]. Aspin believed that the dissolution of the Soviet Union had obviated any serious conventional threat from that quarter for the near term. He considered potential U.S. involvement in Major Regional Conflicts (MRCs) as by far the most stressing of future requirements for U.S. military forces. Assessing such contingencies would accordingly be most important in determining appropriate forces to meet them.

Aspin posited that potential regional aggressors, such as North Korea or a revitalized Iraq, may field as many as 2,000 to 4,000 tanks, 3,000 to 5,000 armored fighting vehicles, 2,000 to 3,000 artillery pieces, and 500 to 1,000 combat aircraft [201]. He chose hypothetical scenarios of a North Korean attack on South Korea, and an Iraqi attack on Kuwait and Saudi Arabia, to determine the level of forces required to defeat regional aggressors. Aspin created a yardstick, the "MRC Building Block," as a measure of U.S. military strength required to meet *one* major regional conflict [202]. The MRC Building Block includes, among other forces, 100 Air Force heavy bombers [203].

Aspin and his DoD analysts decided that the United States must field two MRC Building Blocks—forces sufficient to fight and win two nearly simultaneous major regional conflicts. Aspin determined that forces capable of fighting two such wars simultaneously are necessary due to the following factors. First, the United States, while engaged in a major regional conflict, needs forces to deter aggressors who might otherwise take advantage of U.S. preoccupation by attacking neighbors. Second, having forces sufficient to defeat two "Iraqs" or "North Koreas" provides capabilities to deal with a greater-than-expected threat, should one emerge [204]. Aspin's plan also included additional forces for nuclear deterrence, overseas presence, and force training and maintenance.

Aspin expressed considerable respect for air power in the Bottom-Up Review, and in earlier statements. Just before the Gulf War, he said: "Advocates of air power will likely get a full opportunity to see if air power alone can win the war" [205]. And the subsequent HASC report on the lessons of the Gulf War recognized that air power had been the most significant factor in winning the war [206]. In the Bottom-Up Review, Aspin repeatedly acknowledges the value of the heavy bomber force in major regional conflicts. A major regional conflict was assessed to have four phases. The first would involve initial defense of friendly territory from invasion. Bombers are understood to be important in this capacity, in that they can reach the battlefield directly from the United States, and can "delay, disrupt, and destroy enemy ground forces." Moreover, bombers are capable of destroying "enemy high-value targets, such as weapons of mass destruction" [207]. The bomber force also would have high utility for accomplishing objectives of phase two, including "grinding down the enemy's military potential while additional U.S. and other coalition combat power is brought into the region" [208]. Bombers could also support phase three, the decisive counteroffensive, and would help provide for postwar stability, in phase four [209]. This analysis would seem to imply a bomber force in excess of 200, since 100 bombers are deemed to be necessary to handle a single Major Regional Conflict. But the Bottom-Up Review calls for "up to 184 bombers," and declares that "certain advanced aircraft, such as B-2s ... that we have purchased in limited numbers because of their expense would probably be dual-tasked." The BUR also declared that, in addition to being available for conventional conflicts, the B-2 and B-52H fleets must be tasked to constitute a significant portion of our remaining nuclear deterrent forces [210].

The Bottom-Up Review also tried to consider the maintenance of the nation's defense industrial base in the modernization of U.S. forces. Since U.S. submarine forces, for example, will be declining from 87 in 1994 to about 45 to 55 in 1999, no new submarines will be needed for some years. Submarine construction, however, was funded in order to preserve the industrial infrastructure to construct submarines against the day in the future when new submarines are needed [211]. The Bottom-Up Review also aimed at preserving the industrial base for aircraft carriers [212]. In addition, programs were funded that would preserve the nation's capacity to build tanks and armored fighting vehicles [213].

In what can only be characterized as a striking disconnect, the Bottom-Up-Review failed to address the future of the strategic bomber force in its section on modernization. Although ostensibly concerned with operational need, new technologies, the changing nuclear threat, and the defense industrial base, the Bottom-Up-Review looked at almost every key defense acquisition issue, except maintaining a force of long-range bombers that is adequate to implementing the strategy just described [214].

Bomber Issues in 1994-1995

Controversy has continued over the size and composition of the current and future U.S. bomber force. The Clinton Administration's FY 1995 budget request envisioned just 107 active bombers, including 7 B-2s, 40 B-52Hs, and 60 B-1Bs. This force is considerably smaller than even the lean bomber force of 184 aircraft envisioned in the Bottom-Up Review. The current Secretary of the Air Force, Sheila Widnall, claimed that this force is sufficient to fight two wars, but General Loh of Air Combat Command expressed doubts about a two-war capability given its small size [215]. Then-Chief of Staff of the Air Force General Merrill McPeak acknowledged that there is a bomber shortfall, and claims it is due to near-term cost-cutting measures. By this he implied an understanding that the bomber force must expand in the future [216]. Bomber force levels since 1946, including The Administration's programmed levels to 1999, are graphically illustrated in Figure 7.

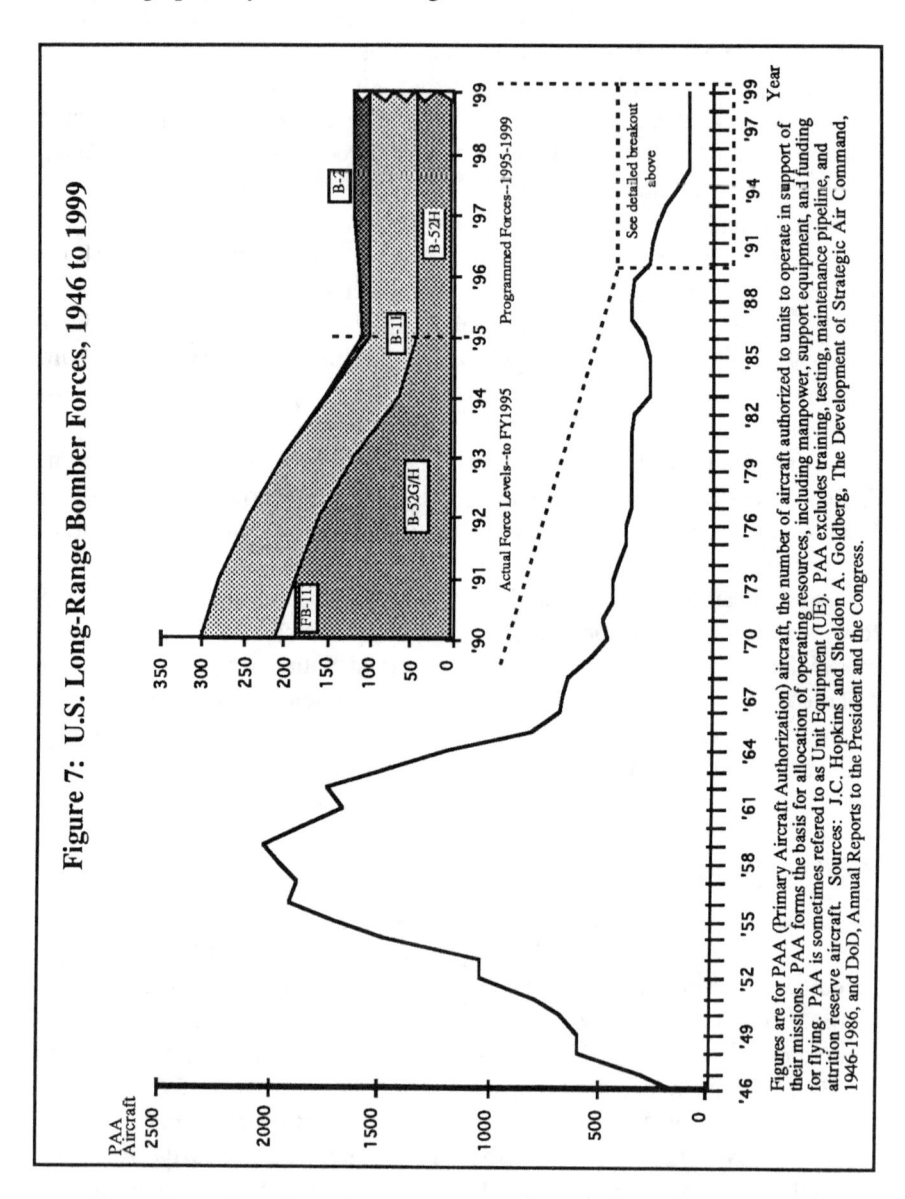

Figure 7: U.S. Long-Range Bomber Forces, 1946 to 1999

Figures are for PAA (Primary Aircraft Authorization) aircraft, the number of aircraft authorized to units to operate in support of their missions. PAA forms the basis for allocation of operating resources, including manpower, support equipment, and funding for flying. PAA is sometimes referred to as Unit Equipment (UE). PAA excludes training, testing, maintenance pipeline, and attrition reserve aircraft. Sources: J.C. Hopkins and Sheldon A. Goldberg, The Development of Strategic Air Command, 1946-1986, and DoD, Annual Reports to the President and the Congress.

In 1994, a number of senators and congressmen expressed concern over current plans for the bomber force, leading to the actions described earlier: Funding to maintain the B-2 supplier base, to maintain the entire existing force of B-1B and B-52H bombers, and funding to study future bomber requirements. Some tensions have arisen between supporters of the various components of the bomber force--based on the belief that the three bombers are in competition for funds. Congressman Norman Dicks, Democrat from Washington State, strongly supports additional production of the B-2 bomber, even if funds have to be raised by retiring B-1B bombers [217], although he would prefer not to retire that aircraft. He termed the 107-bomber force called for by the Air Force as "pathetic" [218]. Senator Kent Conrad, Democrat from North Dakota, also criticized the bomber shortfall, but instead called for retaining B-52s to remedy the problem[219]. Despite incoming Senate Majority Leader Bob Dole's statement that "we need all three bombers" [220], it is unclear whether these legislators will be able to unite behind a long-term modernization program that includes new production of the B-2. A group led by Senator John Glenn, Democrat from Ohio, supports continued spending on improvements to the B-1B Force [221]. Representative Dellums staunchly opposed additional B-2s [222]. However, the B-2 appears to have the support of the new Republican Chairmen of the Defense Subcommittees of the Senate and House Appropriations Committees, Senators Ted Stevens of Alaska and Representative C.W. "Bill" Young of Florida, as well as Senators Inouye and Nunn, and Representative Murtha [223].

William Perry, Aspin's successor as Secretary of Defense, was an early proponent of stealth technologies. In his confirmation hearing, however, he indicated that purchasing more B-2s "does not appear to be appropriate" unless there are "dramatic changes in world events" [224]. Subsequent statements, while maintaining Perry's official opposition to more B-2s [225], have sometimes been ambivalent. For example, in March 1994 before the SASC, Perry said: "We don't have anything in our program to sustain a bomber industrial base. This is a weakness of this program that we are presenting to you." And, "The most logical way of maintaining a bomber industrial base was to continue to build more B-2s. That's not only because that is the best, most effective bomber we can describe to you right now, but because we could make very good use of the extra B-2s if we had them" [226].

Two major studies of the U.S. bomber force were completed in 1994. One is a RAND effort that considered how the bomber force would be able to meet the requirement of stopping enemy attacks in major regional contingencies. The report stressed the importance of modifying the bomber force to use precision weapons. It also determined that the administration's programmed bomber force of about 60 B-1s, 40 B-52s, and 20 B-1s, if properly modified would be able to handle a stressing major regional conflict, but would have very little margin for attrition, no extra firepower to compensate for unexpected situations, or to withhold for nuclear deterrence, and only a limited capability to support a second major regional conflict. On the other hand, the report determined that a properly modified force of 60 B-2s and 40 B-52s would have "considerably more capability to support a stressing major conflict as well as a moderately demanding, near-simultaneous second major conflict" [227].

The second major analysis was undertaken by Major General Jasper Welch, USAF (retired), at the request of Senator Nunn. Welch concludes that a bomber force headed by 30-50 B-2 bombers would actually fulfill U.S. requirements to operate in two major regional contingencies *at much lower cost* than a force of 40-80 B-52s and 40-80 B-1s, augmented by only 20 B-2s. The B-2 force costs less because it does not require the very expensive standoff munitions that the B-52 and B-1 bombers must use, due to their vulnerability to air defenses. Instead, the virtually invulnerable B-2 can drop precision glide bombs that are much less expensive. Over two major regional contingencies, the large quantity of standoff munitions that must be launched by the B-52s and B-1s, and the required modifications to the aircraft, eclipse the costs of more B-2s and their cheaper munitions by $17 to $41 billion, depending on the size of the bomber force envisioned. Welch calls for a force of 30 to 50 B-2 bombers [228]. DoD continues to study the bomber issue, as directed by Congress in the FY 1995 Defense Authorization and Appropriation Acts [229]. These studies will be completed in early to mid-1995 and will be important in influencing congressional opinion on the B-2 program.

The cost of additional B-2s is beginning to take shape. The initial outlays required for the decision to produce more B-2s present its most difficult political obstacle. The Congressional Budget Office estimates that 20 additional B-2s will cost 26 billion FY 1995 dollars [230]. DoD indicated the cost of full funding for 20 additional B-2s will be about $20 billion [231]. The prime contractor, Northrop Grumman, has offered to produce 20 additional B-2s at a firm-fixed-price flyaway cost of 570 million FY 1995 dollars each, ($11.4 billion)—with total program costs estimated at $13.529 billion. This would provide 20 additional fully-equipped aircraft configured to match the most mature aircraft ("block 30" avionics) in the original B-2 buy.

Besides the analyses of the costs and capabilities of the B-2, at least three issues may bear on a 1995 decision to reopen B-2 production. They include: the future of a number of other defense acquisition programs; the fate of "non-traditional" programs being funded by the Defense budget; and the decision by President Clinton to add $25 billion to the defense budget over the next six years.

Other defense acquisition programs impact on B-2 procurement in two ways: operational and budgetary. Systems seen as having capabilities or missions similar to B-2 are regarded by some as substitutes. One of these is the Tri-service Standoff Attack Missile, (TSSAM), a stealthy cruise missile which initially was to be launched by nonstealthy aircraft The TSSAM was cancelled in December 1994. Previously, then-Undersecretary of Defense for Acquisition John Deutch had agreed that, should the TSSAM run into difficulty, additional stealthy B-2s might be needed [232]. Regarding budgetary competition, cancelling the TSSAM may save up to $13.3 billion; this could free up funding for the B-2.

The Republicans, now the congressional majority party, have been critical of defense expenditures on "nontraditional" programs being funded in the defense budget. These programs, ranging from environmental activities, to peacekeeping, to defense conversion, are consuming over $11 billion of the FY 1995 defense budget; this figure is up from about $3.5 billion in FY 1990 [233]. Republicans, including incoming National Security Committee Chairman Floyd Spence, charge that these programs, whatever their merit, do nothing to contribute to the capability to defend the United States, and should either be cut back, or shifted to other agencies' budgets [234]. In either case, Republicans argue, DoD monies saved should be used to fund traditional readiness, operations, and procurement accounts in the defense budget. If some DoD monies are saved this way, it will be that much easier to fund continued production of the B-2.

President Clinton, recognizing a shortfall in planned defense budgets over the next six years, declared in December 1994 that he will add $25 billion to defense over that period. These funds are expected to include provision for 1% annual real growth to modernization [235]. This move will ease pressure on procurement accounts and could facilitate a decision to renew production of the B-2. It is even possible that President Clinton in 1995 could request more B-2s as part of a policy aimed at responding to the apparent public perception that his administration had moved away from mainstream opinion on a wide range of issues.

The Republican victory in the House elections is widely perceived to have been the result of the House Republicans' support of a number of national policies contained in Newt Gingrich's *Contract with America*. The *Contract* author Gingrich and the Republican leadership accordingly are expected to play a very powerful role--more powerful than that played by their Democratic predecessors--in many policy areas, including national security.

The *Contract's* section on defense does not address specific weapons programs (aside from missile defense), but does say that the Clinton Administration's Bottom-Up Review has been criticized for (among other things) envisioning too few "long range attack aircraft" [236]. In response to the Bottom-Up Review, the *Contract*'s proposed National Security Restoration Act aims to establish "a blue-ribbon panel to conduct an accurate and comprehensive review of the U.S.'s national security needs, force readiness and modernization plans" [237]. The author of the *Contract*, Newt Gingrich, has not been at the forefront of the B-2 debate, but has supported the B-2, most recently signing the letter to Representative Dellums supporting the $150 million to maintain B-2 production capability. Representative Richard Armey of Texas is the new Majority Leader, replacing Democrat Richard Gephardt of Missouri. Armey supports the B-2, citing its versatility and long-term future utility [238]. Majority Whip Tom DeLay, also of Texas, replaces David Bonior, Democrat of Michigan. DeLay is similarly on record as being in favor of the B-2, citing the stealthy aircraft's potential to minimize casualties on both sides in a conflict [239]. In the Senate, incoming Majority Whip Trent Lott favors the B-2, as does Majority Leader Dole and Texas Senator Phil Gramm.

Conclusions

The Defense Department has attempted to procure a force of B-2 bombers that will make a long-term contribution to U.S. national security. The consensus in the Democratic-majority Congress from 1990 to 1994 was that the threat is declining and defense spending should and will decline with it. Competing claims on scarce resources have been seen as representing more immediate needs. The current B-2 bomber program, however brilliantly it has passed technical challenges, has suffered setbacks due to this thinking [240].

Yet, the Congress and its new leadership are sensitive to the international security environment and willing to respond to its implications for U.S. policy and requisite supporting military capabilities. The Congress is well aware of the degree to which air power demonstrated its effectiveness in the Gulf War, and that new regional flare-ups—such as in North Korea—are a real possibility. This awareness supports the place of modern long-range, land-based bomber forces as an important part of American air power. Since the B-2 represents the future of long-range, land-based U.S. power projection capability, it should be at the center of congressional thinking about U.S. defense needs for a dynamic international security environment.

Chapter 5

The weakness of the current debate is epitomized by the Bottom-Up Review which recognizes the strategic value of the B-2, but stops short of the obvious point that funding of additional B-2 production is required. Political will is the key to reinitiating production. Eventually international events will demand that the United States be ready to take effective action against new dangers. At that point, the American people will not fail to recognize the value of a robust bomber force. Today's challenge is to make those decisions necessary for the nation to be prepared for that moment.

Chapter 6

The B-2 and the U.S. Defense-Industrial Base

BERNARD C. VICTORY AND JOHN J. KOHOUT III

In adapting its military establishment to the security demands and economic constraints of the post-Cold War world, the United States should exploit those elements of military and industrial strength that give it a long-term comparative advantage over potential adversaries. Air power and its supporting industries are among those comparative strengths. No nation can match the combination of technological advancement, force size, multimission capability, operational experience, technical proficiency, and tactical skill possessed by U.S. air forces. In the last half century, the air arm has played an indispensable role in all major conflicts fought by U.S. forces, including a global war (World War II) and three large-scale regional wars (in Korea, Vietnam, and the Persian Gulf). Modern air power is well-suited to both the geostrategic position of the United States (interests and allies overseas, hostile powers nearer to possible theaters of war, fewer and fewer forces deployed abroad) and its preferred style of war (pursuit of quick victory, low tolerance for casualties and collateral damage, direct attack of the enemy's centers of gravity, reliance on firepower rather than manpower, use of high-technology weapons) [241]. If they are maintained, the impressive capabilities demonstrated by U.S. air power in the Gulf War—precise and lethal attack, stealthy flight, suppression of enemy air defenses, routine aerial refueling, comprehensive surveillance and reconnaissance, high sortie rates, round-the-clock bombing, carefully orchestrated operations—will help prevent not only regional aggression, but the emergence of "peer competitors" (e.g., a resurgent Russia) bent on challenging the United States [242].

The U.S. aircraft industry likewise offers a competitive edge. The United States is preeminent in the development of aircraft and associated technologies. According to one assessment of the international standing of the United States in a variety of critical technologies, U.S. industry is "strong" (the highest rating) in the military aerospace applications of air-breathing propulsion, composites, high-performance computing and networking, sensors and signal processing, and systems engineering, and "competitive" (the rating below "strong") in avionics [243]. All parts of the U.S. defense industry are suffering as defense budgets decline, because civil aircraft production is so competitive. This is true even though U.S. procurement of combat aircraft is dropping sharply. For example, no production of USAF combat aircraft was requested or authorized in FY 1995![244]. Plans for substantial cutbacks in naval construction mean significant shipbuilding capacity will be difficult to maintain, given that this sector is sustained by Navy contracts rather than commercial orders. The small number of firms involved in building combat vehicles have limited opportunities for generating commercial business, and with the end of the Abrams tank and the Bradley fighting vehicle procurement programs, their future will depend on foreign sales, Abrams and Bradley upgrades, production of repair parts, and research and development (R&D) work.

The important defense advantages growing out of U.S. industrial strengths can be reaped only if those specific capabilities required to focus generalized U.S. industrial capacity on the timely production of specific weapons systems are protected. Major defense cutbacks in response to the end of the U.S.-Soviet rivalry, tighten fiscal constraints, and the higher priority assigned to domestic needs are seriously weakening important parts of the defense-industrial base as weapons programs are reduced or cancelled. Without careful planning, the current shrinking of the military could diminish the high-tech edge that enables smaller U.S. forces to both compete with those of other first-rank powers and win regional conflicts; limit the ability of the industrial base to mobilize expeditiously and turn out sufficient arms to deter a new challenger or fight a large-scale war; and make it difficult for industry to build advanced weapon systems at affordable prices. The protection of selected major weapons programs must constitute the central axis of policy efforts to protect the U.S. defense-industrial base.

Under current plans, defense budgets in the late 1990s will be more than 40 percent less than what they were in the mid-1980s, during the peak of the last arms buildup. In 1999, given current projections, only 2.8% of the gross domestic product will be devoted to defense [245]; this will represent the lowest level of U.S. effort on defense since 1940 [246]. Funds available for force modernization are expected to decline by more than 50 percent, greatly reducing the market for the defense-industrial base [247]. With large cuts in acquisition expenditures, key weapon programs are canceled or scaled back. The defense industry is left with overcapacity. Many defense contractors have insufficient orders to operate efficiently and profitably. As a result, they downsize, join with other contractors, diversify into civilian work, divest their defense operations, or shut down. Without continuing orders, subcontractors, suppliers and vendors that manufacture the components for larger systems may leave the defense business altogether, making rapid military reconstitution problematic. Some even predict the number of military aircraft manufacturers could drop from a half dozen today to as few as three in the future [248]. Once lost, the plant, equipment, teams, and skills essential to producing certain weapon systems may be neither easy nor cheap to rebuild.

Preserving the vital elements of the defense-industrial base as R&D and procurement budgets decline will require concerted efforts by both industry and the government. Besides restructuring measures, defense companies will need to take steps to increase their productivity. While the government can help protect the base in a number of ways (e.g., by reforming the procurement system, by fully funding future weapon prototypes), one of the most valuable would be to promote a more stable planning environment, thereby facilitating industry adjustments to the changing defense market. As one prominent aerospace executive has argued, a strategy for maintaining the defense-industrial base should, among other things,

> [p]lace the utmost emphasis on reducing turbulence in the acquisition process, ending the seemingly interminable starting, stopping and stretching of virtually every project. This is where the true inefficiencies and large losses of money are to be found. Asking Department of Defense and industry executives to operate their enterprises effectively in such an environment is tantamount to asking them to manage an earthquake [249].

Eliminating abrupt and frequent changes in program buys, schedules, and funding through an acquisition approach like low-rate procurement (discussed below) would increase industry incentives to adopt production methods like lean manufacturing (also discussed below) aimed at improving efficiency and reducing costs. At the same time, greater stability in weapons acquisition would make future force modernization more predictable and aid long-term military planning.

The government furthermore may want to ensure the continued development of critical defense technologies and the maintenance of production capacity for pivotal weapon systems that will not be supported adequately by capabilities found in commercial industry. Technologies incorporated in precision-guided munitions and night-vision equipment, for example, have few, if any, commercial applications. While components of various weapon systems may be dual-use items manufactured by the commercial sector, the systems themselves lack commercial counterparts. To retain the ability to build major weapon systems, including the requisite "intellectual capital," then Deputy Secretary of Defense William Perry has argued for protecting a "small but modern production base for those systems which are defense unique," such as submarines, fighters, air-to-air missiles, tanks, and anti-tank missiles. This would include keeping open a minimum of one production line for each type of the major weapon systems. Lines would be sustained through limited production runs and work to refit and upgrade existing aircraft, combat vehicles, warships, and missiles [250]. This thinking was reflected in the decision by the Clinton Administration to procure a third Seawolf attack submarine, despite planned reductions in the size of the attack submarine force, in order to maintain a shipyard (and the associated "intellectual capital") capable of building nuclear submarines [251].

Production capabilities for heavy bombers are also elements of the defense-industrial base that seem worthy of preservation. Given enduring U.S. interests, the nature of international politics, the characteristics of long-range air power, and the limitations of other types of military forces, there will be a need for heavy bombers for decades to come. Bombers have demonstrated value for a wide range of contingencies, from shows of force to general war, from independent air campaigns to combined-arms operations. The attributes of heavy bombers fit the military requirements of the emerging security environment. A future reconstitution effort to counter a new global threat to U.S. interests almost certainly would benefit from a bomber buildup.

Retaining bomber production capabilities would be an important part of a strategy for ensuring the survival of a sizable and effective bomber force over the long run. The current force of B-52 and B-1B bombers, while potent, is aging, faces increasingly lethal air defense systems among possible enemies (due, in part, to the proliferation of Soviet/Russian equipment), and will confront retirement in the first part of the next century. (By 2000, the average age of the B-52H aircraft will be approaching 40 years. The average age for the B-1Bs will exceed 23 years in 2010.) [252] New heavy bombers to augment or replace these aircraft are being built by a single production line, the B-2 final assembly facility at Palmdale, California. Although this line originally was intended to turn out well over 100 aircraft, present plans call for the production of just 20 operational aircraft. The B-2, an advanced warplane optimized for long-range, stealthy strike missions, has no commercial equivalent. With the shutdown of the B-2 line, the ability to produce heavy bombers quickly will atrophy. Already many suppliers have completed their work for the B-2 program and at least one major subcontractor soon will lose its capacity to manufacture critical subassemblies for the aircraft [253]. The United States may give up a defense-industrial capability it has found wise to maintain for more than a half century, a capability unmatched by any other country, except the former Soviet Union.

Once the physical, organizational, and intellectual assets needed to design, develop, and produce heavy bombers disappear, they may require considerable, and perhaps unacceptable, time and expense to regain. Since no follow-on to the B-2 is in prospect, and the B-52Hs and B-1Bs that now make up the force eventually will be scrapped, a decision to end B-2 production also signals the gradual demise of the U.S. bomber fleet. Closing the B-2 line will have significant, long-term, and possibly irreversible consequences. The United States will be foreclosing valuable force structure options (i.e., the potential to improve or increase its capabilities for rapid nonnuclear or nuclear global power projection) in an uncertain and dangerous era in which there are distinct advantages to keeping options open.

In addition, the B-2 program is at the core of the key military edge the United States holds in low-observable technologies. The many operational and tactical benefits afforded by stealth are outlined in the next two chapters. These benefits, evident in the performance of F-117As in the Gulf War, are sufficiently great that the Vice Commander of Air Combat Command (ACC), Lt Gen Stephen Croker, flatly predicts the United States "will never pursue combat aircraft development again without stealth" [254]. The United States leads the world in stealth technologies, primarily because of defense-related investments. According to a Defense Department report on critical technologies, "Signature control [including signature reduction from stealth technologies] is primarily a military need, and the industrial base will be largely dependent on government funding. Few significant commercial applications exist" [255]. Keeping the R&D, engineering, testing, and production facilities for the B-2 in operation would support not only the future effectiveness of the U.S. heavy bomber force, but also the U.S. strong suit in the military applications of stealth.

Continued production of the B-2 beyond the 20 aircraft now programmed would be consistent with the "resource strategy" then-Secretary of Defense Les Aspin has proposed to protect key elements of the defense-industrial base. He outlined this strategy in February 1992, during his tenure as Chairman of the House Armed Services Committee [256]. In a speech and related report, Aspin argued that the defense-industrial base must be able to "deliver goods currently on contract," "maintain/upgrade existing equipment," "produce next generation systems—with high quality and at affordable rates," "develop new technology at home," and "provide a basis for reconstitution of a more robust industrial capacity." To achieve these objectives, he advocated an acquisition approach involving "selective upgrading," "low-rate procurements," "rollover-plus," and "silver bullet procurements." This same strategy has been endorsed by then-Deputy Secretary of Defense Perry who succeeded Les Aspin, as Secretary of Defense on January 20, 1994 [257]. In addition, its merits for the acquisition of aircraft have been highlighted by ACC, the command that operates and maintains heavy bombers, including the B-2 [258]. The ways in which the different parts of Aspin's resource strategy apply to a continuing B-2 program are discussed below [259].

In pointing to the need for the defense-industrial base to "deliver goods currently on contract," then-Secretary Aspin recognized that procurement cutbacks create overcapacity, eliminate vendors, increase overhead, and drive up unit costs. As a consequence, the government may find it necessary to spend more to complete certain contracts. In the case of the B-2, reductions in the planned buy, funding restrictions, schedule changes, and program delays have increased costs. When the B-2 force was cut by nearly 75 percent (from 75 to 20 aircraft) in January 1992, total program cost dropped by only 25 percent, from $62 billion to $47 billion (in constant 1992 dollars) [260]. The B-2 production line, originally designed to build 36 aircraft per year, has been scaled back to support the reduced, 20-aircraft buy. As noted, the number of suppliers and subcontractors supporting the B-2 program already has begun to shrink. Unit flyaway cost increased by almost 80 percent, from $422 million to $750 million (1992 dollars) as the program buy decreased from 75 to 20 aircraft [261]. An increase in the production run, along with the stability of low-rate procurement and the use of lean manufacturing techniques should yield more aircraft with lower unit costs.

With tighter defense budgets, smaller numbers of new weapon systems will be procured, making it important, in Aspin's words, to "maintain/upgrade existing systems" in order to extend service lives and counter changing threats. Heavy bombers are among the longest-lived and most adaptable of major weapon systems. Through improvements in avionics, engines, airframe, and munitions, they can accommodate changes in technology, threats, and missions. The venerable B-52 is testament to the longevity and adaptability of heavy bombers. Appropriate maintenance and modifications have kept the B-52 bomber an effective part of the U.S. arsenal for almost 40 years, a period four times longer than originally anticipated [262]. The B-1B likewise incorporates various improvements over the B-1A design. There are, however, limits to how much older bombers can be upgraded. They can never, for example, gain the stealthiness inherent in the B-2. And though their life spans are impressive, they become more difficult and expensive to maintain with age. With a projected service life of at least 30 years, the B-2 is the bomber the United States will rely on for decades into the next century. As with the B-52, refits and retrofits should assure the B-2 a long and useful career.

According to Aspin, continuing production of some weapon systems may be required to ensure the future availability of capabilities to "produce next generation systems—with high quality and at affordable rates." If production ends, those capabilities may evaporate, especially in "certain sectors that have no commercial analog." The long-range air power offered by heavy bombers has been and will remain an essential component of military strategies for defending U.S. interests. The B-2 is the sole heavy bomber in production. No follow-on is in development. Bombers and stealth technologies have no "commercial analogs." Without the B-2 line in operation, the capacity to produce heavy bombers may be lost. It may be possible to resurrect this capability and build bombers again, but not necessarily at "affordable rates." (Indeed, in 1992, then-Secretary of the Air Force Donald Rice voiced his concern that "the B-2 is the last bomber that we will ever build in this country given the way things are going.") [263] Keeping the B-2 line open would prevent the emergence of a "production gap" (Aspin's term) as the Defense Department and the Congress map out the long-term future of the bomber force. Moreover, low-rate procurement of B-2s over an extended period promises an affordable way of adding high-quality aircraft to the bomber inventory.

A defense-industrial base that enables the United States to "develop new high technology at home" gives U.S. forces qualitative advantages that offset the military power of numerically superior foes and minimize U.S. casualties. Aspin argues this edge must be preserved without undue reliance on foreign technology and suppliers. Heavy bombers, their critical subsystems, and low-observable technologies are indigenous defense products. Stealth is among the highest and most militarily significant technologies. The United States has invested more than any other country in developing low-observable technologies and surpassed all other countries in fielding systems that are highly stealthy—an estimated $65 billion between 1975 and 2000 [264]. With the B-2, the United States is acquiring a low-observable combat aircraft with the long range and large payload that will convert this technological edge into a significant and lasting military advantage. To gain the maximum return on this substantial investment, B-2s must be procured in numbers sufficient for the aircraft to play major roles in a wide range of contingencies (e.g., a large-scale strategic air campaign requiring thousands of strike sorties). Capping the B-2 force at 20 operational aircraft limits the utility of this advanced weapon system. Increasing the size of the force would allow the full potential of the stealthy bomber to be realized.

Aspin says that as the last of its five basic functions, the post-Cold War defense-industrial base should "provide a basis for reconstitution of a more robust industrial capability." Reconstitution would involve an expansion of defense production and an increase in military forces to meet a new global threat to U.S. security from a belligerent Russia rebuilding its armed might or another nascent superpower pursuing aggressive aims. A threat of this magnitude would take years to emerge, during which time reconstitution would be under way. Yet reconstitution would be successful only if the necessary design capabilities, manufacturing processes, production facilities, and labor skills had been kept up. Since all probable global rivals are located at intercontinental distances from the United States, and long-range nonnuclear—or nuclear—bombardment forces for attacking enemy military strength and war-making potential will be valuable in deterring or defeating such adversaries, reconstitution very likely will encompass an increase in the size and effectiveness of the heavy bomber force. Extended, low-rate production of the B-2 would preserve the capacity to build heavy bombers, allow a buildup of the bomber force against a future superpower threat, and, at the same time, magnify the contribution of the B-2 fleet to more frequent efforts aimed at preventing or winning regional conflicts.

Each part of the Aspin/Perry acquisition approach to bolster the defense-industrial base also is applicable to the B-2 program. Consider "selective upgrading." Aspin contends that for some types of major weapons, upgrading systems or their subsystems will be sufficient to permit force modernization without the acquisition of new systems, sustain capacity to "surge" (rather than reconstitute) production in response to lesser emergencies, and safeguard a base for the development and production of future systems. As indicated above, heavy bombers like the B-2 are major weapon systems highly amenable to assorted and repeated upgrades to enhance their performance, striking power, and efficiency. During the last 35 years, numerous upgrades of B-52s—e.g., new engines, structural modifications, improved bombing and navigation systems, advanced electronic countermeasures equipment, better power subsystems, different weapons—have been an important factor in both modernizing the bomber force and supporting its production base. Over a decade ago, the original configuration of the B-1 was upgraded with new offensive and defensive avionics systems and "stealth" modifications to yield the B-1B, a bomber intended to bear chief responsibility for penetrating Soviet air defenses pending the deployment of the B-2. Previous upgrading of the bomber force has bought the time and saved the resources needed to develop low-observable technologies and design the B-2.

Producing a larger number of B-2s would fully capitalize on past efforts and result in a force of advanced bombers well-suited to future upgrades to prolong service life and ensure combat effectiveness.

In some cases, as then-Secretary Aspin acknowledges, selective upgrading alone will not stop portions of the production base from contracting to the point where defense preparedness is endangered. Low-rate procurement then might be indicated to keep critical suppliers in business. Since the last of more than 740 B-52s rolled off the assembly line over 30 years ago, bomber production in the United States in fact has been a matter of sporadic low-rate procurements: 76 FB-111As in the late 1960s and 100 B-1Bs in the mid-1980s [265]. These limited runs nourished the production base, but did not replace the aging B-52 force. Low-number procurement of the B-2 beyond the 20 operational aircraft now planned would sustain suppliers and subcontractors supporting the program and provide a way to maintain the size of the bomber force as superannuated B-52s finally are retired. Such an approach to future B-2 production would be consistent with views expressed by the leadership of Air Combat Command. General John Loh, the ACC Commander, believes "[i]ndustrial base considerations should be almost equally as important, perhaps even more important, as operational need," and sees low-rate production as a means of balancing the two [266]. His deputy, Lieutenant General Croker, has suggested low-rate procurement of "an airplane like the B-2" as a "replacement-based strategy" that would forestall force deficiencies related to future B-52 and B-1B retirements and "eliminate the peak or valley acquisition cycle we have had in the past" [267]. In addition, low-rate procurement of B-2s to some extent would hedge against technical obstacles, delays, stretch-outs, and cancellations in current programs for modernizing Air Force and Navy inventories of shorter-range strike aircraft.

To help assure the affordability of low-rate procurement within constrained defense budgets, "lean manufacturing" techniques could be adopted in the production of the B-2. "Lean manufacturing" is a rubric for concepts, principles, and methods the Air Force and private industry are examining to decrease costs (overhead, unit, operation and support), increase production efficiency, and improve quality [268]. They include modifications of production processes to decrease waste, time, and costs, as well as various measures to enhance the quality of finished items. A number of lean-manufacturing ideas already have been implemented in the production of some aircraft (e.g., the F-15E), and many undoubtedly could be applied to reduce B-2 costs as well [269].

For the "rollover-plus" element of the Aspin/Perry "resource strategy," prototypes of new systems and components would be under continuous development, but a prototype would not be put into full-scale production unless three criteria were met: 1) the technology "worked"; 2) changes in the threat environment required procurement of the system or component; and 3) the prototype represented a military breakthrough. If the prototype fell short of these standards, its technology and the knowledge gained in the course of its development would be "rolled over" into a follow-on program. If the prototype met the mark, it also would need to be readily producible and suitable for rigorous operational testing, and not merely an experimental model. (Hence, "rollover-*plus*.") Such an approach, Aspin asserted, will allow the United States to continue to field highly advanced weapon systems in the absence of the modernization imperative of the U.S.-Soviet arms competition and the larger defense budgets of the past [270]. It also

> preserves design and engineering expertise and continuity; ...advances production technologies and processes, thereby lowering production problems and therefore the ultimate cost of a system; ...keeps us at the forefront of technology developments; and does each of the above without the current attendant costs of a full-up production program [271].

The B-2 is entirely compatible with the "rollover-plus" concept. In line with the first of the three deployment criteria, the B-2 technology works. Its design brings together: (1) the span-loading aerostructure prototyped decades ago in the Northrop XB-35 and YB-49 flying wings; (2) low-observable techniques more advanced than those used in building the SR-71, B-1B and F-117A; (3) the operations value of stealth shown by the F-117A force in the Desert Storm air campaign; (4) the large-payload nonnuclear bombing capability combat-tested by B-52s in the Vietnam and Persian Gulf conflicts; and (5) the precision weapon delivery demonstrated in the Gulf War. Moreover, results of the B-2 flight-test program confirm the airworthiness, low observability, subsystem performance, and reliability and maintainability of the aircraft [272]. In the future, given the inherent adaptability of heavy bombers, new components, subsystems, and weapons can be "rolled into" the B-2 to increase its effectiveness and service life.

With regard to the second deployment criterion, the B-2, though a product of the Cold War, clearly will be valuable in countering the new military threats confronting the United States. U.S. military operations in future nonnuclear regional conflicts may benefit from the employment of even more heavy bombers than were required by recent plans for strategic nuclear attacks against the Soviet Union. Progressive improvements in the air defense systems available to hostile powers in the developing world underscore the need for

Chapter 6   133

stealthy bombers. And increasing elite and public sensitivity to U.S. combat casualties—reinforced by the remarkably low losses suffered in Desert Storm—also point to the political as well as military value of bombers able to evade enemy air defenses.

Few dispute that the B-2 is a military breakthrough—the third condition for prototype deployment—that can change the terms of aerial warfare. Stealth shifts the advantage to the offense, undercuts all radar-based defenses, reduces combat attrition, diminishes or eliminates the need for defense suppression, leverages non-stealthy aircraft, provides greater freedom of action, increases effective range or payload, and promotes tactical surprise. Yet unless more than 20 aircraft are deployed, the impact of the B-2 on the course and outcome of military operations will be limited. The B-2 force will be restricted to serving as what Richard Cheney, predecessor to Les Aspin as Secretary of Defense, called a "special-mission squadron" [273].

It should be noted that the 20 operational aircraft do permit the "rollover-plus" field testing to determine the B-2's "operational contributions and requirements," including its "potential contribution to tactics and doctrine" and "battlefield maintenance requirements." Rigorous operational testing in fact is well under way. The aircraft already built under the current program also prove the "producibility" specified by "rollover-plus." And, consistent with the need to "advance production technologies and processes," the production of the B-2 has involved pioneering work on hundreds of new processes, including computer-aided design and computer-aided manufacturing.

"Silver bullet procurements" are the fourth and final part of the Aspin/Perry acquisition approach. "Silver bullets" are highly capable weapon systems that even in limited numbers give U.S. forces a large military advantage. F-117As have been described as the "silver bullets" of the initial phase of the Desert Storm air offensive. F-117As were only a small fraction of the combat aircraft participating in the operations against Iraq, yet they played a key role in quickly taking down enemy air defenses, thus increasing the survivability of non-stealthy strike aircraft. Along with the F-117A, Aspin has labeled the B-2 a "silver bullet," saying that it could be used early in a conflict to conduct "leading edge" strikes against opposing air defenses and attack critical targets that were too well defended or too far away to be hit by other aircraft [274]. It might be argued, however, that F-117As in the early days of the Gulf War were less "silver bullets" than the tip of a very large "silver bullet" made up of over a thousand sophisticated fighters, fighter-bombers, heavy bombers, and attack aircraft. With U.S. force structure declining, the "silver bullet" role will become considerably more demanding. Even a B-2 force several times larger than the one now programmed might not be excessive for the "silver bullet" role in future wars.

Continued, low-rate production of the B-2, then, would met the objectives and follow the acquisition approaches of Department of Defense "resource strategy." The procurement of more low-observable heavy bombers not only would serve various military requirements discussed elsewhere in this report, but would help sustain the vital aircraft sector of the defense-industrial base. Air power and the aircraft industry are long-standing U.S. strengths. A sizable bomber force will be valuable in defending U.S. interests in a wide range of future political-military contexts. Ill-conceived or poorly executed cutbacks could undermine the ability of the United States to maintain its presently planned bomber force, augment that force in a reconstitution effort, and preserve the technological and industrial base for acquiring next-generation systems. Keeping the B-2 production line open would help avoid these dangers. A production line turning out aircraft at a low rate over an extended period would offer industry a measure of stability that would aid it in adjusting to significantly smaller defense budgets. Lean manufacturing techniques could be used to limit or lower the costs of low-rate production. At the same time, low-rate production would support a "replacement strategy" that would facilitate orderly retirement of older bombers while maintaining the overall size and long-term effectiveness of the bomber force.

Chapter 7
Stealth in Context
JOHN J. KOHOUT III

The low-observable or "stealth" design of the B-2 is popularly seen as the defining characteristic of the modern long-range, land-based bomber. But, "stealth" does not exist in isolation. It interacts with other technical characteristics to yield an overall system capability. The standard against which such systems are measured is the effective and efficient application of firepower. The National Aeronautic Association, which is oriented toward aeronautical technology, recognized this in its selection of the B-2 for the 1991 Collier Trophy:

> The Air Force/Industry B-2 Team addressed and mastered the infusion of revolutionary low observable characteristics with a highly aerodynamically efficient airframe incorporating unique raw materials. The resulting aircraft possesses unequaled competitive advantage, and will furnish the Air Force with the capability to support national objectives in peacetime or in time of crisis anywhere on the globe well into the 21st century. The B-2 will provide the centerpiece of a security strategy based upon the employment of air power anytime, anywhere, without the constraints of foreign bases [275].

The B-2, as any other attack aircraft, contributes to operational success in accomplishing its missions primarily in terms of four traits: the firepower it delivers, the range over which it delivers that firepower, the speed with which it can reach designated targets, and its ability to penetrate enemy defenses. Each of these characteristics contributes directly to the strategic utility of the weapon system. Range determines whether or not the bomber can reach strategically significant targets, firepower whether or not the target can be destroyed once reached, speed whether or not the destruction is timely enough to achieve the required tactical or strategic effect, and ability to penetrate enemy defenses whether or not the enemy's efforts to frustrate an attack can be overcome. At the same time, each of these characteristics interacts with the others, either to support or to compromise their effect. If the weight-carrying ability allocated to firepower versus fuel is increased and range drops off; add more fuel and weapons delivered are reduced; increase speed and more fuel is required cutting into both range and firepower. Improve the ability to penetrate defenses, and both effective range and firepower are increased.

The ability to penetrate enemy defenses is particularly important to such tradeoffs. A technical advance that significantly enhances the ability of a combat aircraft to defeat enemy defenses influences the other traits of the long-range bomber and the sum total of its effectiveness. Low-observable technology or "stealth" represents an enormous advance in the ability of aircraft and other vehicles to penetrate defenses. Placing "stealth" in context, however, requires both that the nature of stealth's inherent contribution be understood in terms of the full range of traits of the long-range, land-based bomber.

The Nature of "Stealth"

The *International Military and Defense Encyclopedia* gets right to the heart of "stealth."

> Stealth is a weapon system characteristic involving a variety of techniques to reduce detectability... Weapon systems cannot be made totally undetectable: the idea is to reduce the range and probability of detection so as to gain the critical advantage of time [276].

Stealth reduces detectability by minimizing the observable characteristics of a vehicle. This means that an observer cannot detect the "stealthy" vehicle until it is much closer than an "unstealthy" vehicle would be at detection. If a limited number of observers is distributed across a wide area, increasing the stealth of a vehicle increases the probability that the vehicle can pass through that area without ever being detected. If the vehicle does come close enough to the observer to be detected, it will remain under observation for a shorter period. This greatly complicates tactical response to the stealth vehicle. Initial detection is rendered less likely and probably delayed if it does occur. Tracking is rendered more difficult because there are fewer data points and they are less precise.

"Stealth" has a cascading effect in terms of the applicability of low-observable technologies across the range of ways vehicles can be detected. "Stealth" has come to be popularly associated with its effect on the utility of radar. While this is one particularly important focus of low-observable technology, it is not the only one. Others include infra-red detection, visual detection, the detection of electromagnetic signatures transmitted by systems on board the vehicle, acoustic detection of noise generated by the vehicle, the detection by various means of other physical disturbances generated by the vehicle within its operating medium, and even, for some stealthy vehicles, the detection of magnetic disturbances. These latter examples show that contemporary stealth aircraft and missile systems have a century-old ancestor in the form of the submarine—a vehicle that operates in a different medium, but which has the same ability to profit from reduced detectability.

The Submarine Precedent

On the surface, a submarine can be detected by the same means as any other ship. Its only real advantage is its relatively small size above the waterline for radar or visual detection and identification [277]. As it submerges, however, the submarine is cloaked from visual and radar detection. While it cannot stay submerged indefinitely, a well-trained crew can use the submarine's stealth to approach within lethal range of potential targets or evade enemy threats with a significant advantage over any surface weapon system. While submerged, however, the submarine is neither invulnerable nor invisible. Its operation creates sounds that can be detected and localized. A destroyer's active SONAR systems can bounce sound pulses off the submerged submarine and, subject to the characteristics of the submarine environment, obtain relatively precise location information. The same technology is resident in sonabouys dropped by patrol aircraft. The distortion of the earth's magnetic field by the large iron mass of the submarine provides anti-submarine aircraft with yet another means of locating submerged submarines. Such detection methods however require extremely sensitive instrumentation and require the marshaling of considerable resources over time to reliably cope with submarines' stealth-induced uncertainty of location.

Modern high technology approaches may hold out the promise of finding submarines in large expanses of ocean. The detection of minor water temperature variations due to the submarine's thermal energy emissions, radar evaluation of surface disturbances, and the passage of certain wave lengths of energy through the water to obtain essentially a radar image of a submarine all have been the subject of experimentation. These three approaches can even involve space-based sensors. A great effort has been sustained in the area of harnessing high-capacity data processing techniques to correlate bits and pieces of sensor data within a computer model of the anti-submarine situation of entire ocean basins. All these techniques have demonstrated some potential.

Yet, the submarine remains a deadly weapon system by virtue of its stealth. Modern submarines hold the potential for combat utility far into the future, and no foreseeable breakthrough threatens that utility in the near or even mid-term. The submarine illustrates how a century-old vehicle that has evolved only slowly from the World War I U-boat to the Cold War SSBN can still get value out of stealth technology to stay one step ahead of enemy countermeasures.

The submarine teaches important lessons about stealth, lessons that are important for understanding the potential and utility of stealthy airplanes. The stealth of the submarine was never perfect. Submarines were detected and sunk during World War I, during World War II, and throughout the Cold War. Yet, submarines remain potent. The contribution of stealth to this fact is highlighted by the observation that submarine speeds increased only very slowly through the century; submarines can dive only hundreds of feet deeper than they could at the beginning of the century; and they carry anti-ship weapons that have ranges not that much more capable than the torpedoes of earlier years. It is the low observable characteristics of the submarine that have kept the modern submarine as viable today as it was in the past. There is no way to predict precisely how long this will be the case. But, what one can say is that the utility of the submarine is linked to its stealth, and as long as the submarine retains a stealth advantage over competing systems, it will likely retain a utility advantage as well. The technologies of stealth in the air differ from those that produce stealth in the sea. But these differences are insignificant in the conceptual sense. The submarine illustrates the past and present military utility of stealth, while the B-2 and other stealthy air vehicles embody the potential for stealth's future utility.

Options for Reducing Detectability

Approaches to reducing the detectability of air, and eventually space, vehicles must address the full range of phenomena that can signal a vehicle's presence and location. Since radar is the primary technology for locating aircraft, it has become a central focus of the development of stealth technology. Primitive anti-radar countermeasures were sought earlier in the history of military aviation. Radar depends on bouncing a focused beam of high frequency electromagnetic radiation off a target and using the azimuth and time delay of the reflected pulse to determine the vehicle's location. The intensity of the reflected energy, Doppler changes in its frequency, the vertical component of the vector of the returning energy, and even differences between reflective energy at different wavelengths and polarization add information about a potential target. What is important to realize is that only a minute portion of the energy transmitted from the radar installation is returned to it to convey information about a target vehicle.

In early approaches to defeating radar, false targets were created in order to confuse radar operators. This was accomplished by releasing small pieces of metallic foil into an aircraft's slipstream. These created relatively persistent radar returns as strong as those produced by the target aircraft. Dropping of this "Chaff" or "Window" was widely used in Europe during World War II. The tactic has evolved considerably and is still a part of today's anti-radar tool kit.

As the Strategic Air Command built the early Cold War nuclear deterrent force to confront a massive Soviet defensive array, emphasis shifted toward active electronic means for clouding enemy radars. This electronic "jamming" of radars proceeds from the observation that since only a small percentage of transmitted energy is reflected to the receiver to convey information about the target, the introduction of other transmissions on the same frequencies can confuse radar images. If small radar transmitters are carried on the bomber aircraft, or another aircraft in the vicinity, they can transmit energy on the same wavelength as the air defense radar to either mask the bomber's return or be tailored to generate specific false information. These electronic countermeasures techniques and sets of equipment have become exceptionally capable and quite complex. Some require dedicated operators and others push back the bounds of complex automatic function.

Two basic technical limitations bound the effectiveness of active countermeasures tactics. The first is the fact that any transmission of electromagnetic energy from a bomber, even a well designed pattern of pulses specifically tailored to defeat a perceived threat, is vulnerable to interception by passive receiver stations and can provide exactly the location information that countermeasures are intended to conceal. The second is the fact that the closer a target vehicle comes to a radar site, the greater the energy required to conceal the bomber's location. For a large bomber such as a B-52, which reflects a large amount of incident radar energy, large amounts of jamming power are required in order to delay "burn through" until the bomber gets closer to the radar site. Since more electrical power is available to the ground station than is available to the defensive systems of even a large aircraft, the ground station will eventually locate the approaching aircraft, assuming other tactics are not introduced.

Early recognition of aircraft vulnerability to increasingly capable defenses resulted in the first major stand-off munitions programs such as the AGM-28 Hound Dog cruise missile (IOC 1961), followed by the Short-Range Attack Missile or SRAM (IOC 1972). Unarmed decoys such as the ADM-20 Quail also entered service in the early 1960's.

Starting in the early to mid 1960's SAC's bombers began serious planning for other defense penetration measures. Jet bombers designed for high altitude flight began to train and plan for flight at low altitudes, below the optimum range of air defense radars where the radar "horizon" was foreshortened. As terrain avoidance tactics and equipment were perfected, penetration altitudes were further decreased to permit employment of terrain features to mask the penetrating bombers from transmitted radar energy. These approaches to compensating for the high inherent visibility of large intercontinental range bombers to radar oriented defenses placed increasing operational constraints on the bomber force. More payload was dedicated to defense penetration versus firepower on target, more fuel was used to circumnavigate defensive concentrations or to fly at inefficient low altitudes to penetrate below radar coverage, and low altitude speeds were increased requiring even greater fuel consumption and shortening range available to reach deep targets. High aerostructural stresses generated by low altitude, high speed flight weakened aircraft structures, added weight to new aircraft designs, and reduced the service life to be expected of the bomber fleet.

This panoply of measures intended to maintain the ability of non-stealth attack aircraft to reach defended targets is effective, but enormously expensive. In theater conflicts it has become necessary to mount truly massive operations to cover the attack of a relatively few bomb-laden aircraft. The bombers are informed by electronic and radar-equipped sensor platforms, covered from interceptors by fighter escorts, shielded from radars by dedicated jamming aircraft, protected by disabling attacks on defensive radars by "Wild Weasel" anti-radar aircraft. The entire armada required refueling by a fleet of aerial tankers. Magnificent tactical expertise and coordination make such force packages marvels of effective execution, but the resource costs and number of crews and aircraft at risk is high. Logistical burdens grow to unprecedented levels. Once-potent force elements such as the carrier air wing are gradually marginalized because the numbers of aircraft required for such tactics, when coupled with those required to protect the carrier, exceed the ship's capacity. This then is the offensive air combat trend that resulted largely from the challenge of defeating increasingly lethal, radar-based defenses with non-stealthy attack aircraft. (See "value of stealth" diagram, in Chapter 4.)

The introduction of low-observable or stealth technology to the penetration of radar-based defenses equation completely upsets the terms of the offense-versus-defense struggle. By significantly reducing the radar energy that is reflected by a penetrating vehicle back to the threat radar, the effective range of that radar is significantly reduced. An array of defensive radars that created bands, or large areas of continuous radar coverage against non-stealthy threats, now provides only isolated residual points of radar coverage threatening to stealth systems. The radii of these points are so small that the stealthy attacker can either fly around them undetected or, if need be, pass through them at jet aircraft speed providing a period of detectability so short that minimal tracking data can be obtained and likelihood of successful interception low. Because a stealthy attack is conducted largely outside of effective radar range, supporting attack aircraft packages are not necessary, and active radar jamming, though a possible adjunct to stealth, a far less normal penetration tactic. The only support required for stealthy attack operations would normally be any aerial refueling necessary to get the attack aircraft to the target and back. Considerable operational experience has now been accumulated by stealthy aircraft precursors to the B-2. Patterns of SR-71 operations where stealth design refinements combined with exceptional speed and altitude capability document this understanding of stealth aircraft employment. The same is true for the F-117A's employment against targets in Iraq. Both of these aircraft demonstrated how stealthy penetration enables a modern combat aircraft to defeat defenses autonomously while placing sensors where needed or delivering modern precision munitions to heavily defended targets. The validity of SR-71 and F-117A experience as an indicator of future B-2 effectiveness is high. Moreover, the B-2 design is significantly stealthier than its predecessors. It has the range, payload and inherent flexibility to employ its stealth advantages to full effect.

It is important, in the context of stealth versus radar, to address the operational resilience of low-observable technology as an approach to overcoming defensive initiatives aimed at overcoming stealth's effects. Because stealth takes radar defenses "head-on" by reducing the reflected radar energy, thereby reducing the effective range of a given radar installation, it implies that to be effective against stealth, any defensive system requires a massive proliferation of radar installations to reestablish radar barriers or area coverage that exists for non-stealthy aircraft. Certain technological approaches may have an effect on the margin, but they do not replace large, potentially unaffordable numbers of separate radar sites. Some of these approaches to countering stealth include so-called bi-static radars with transmitter and receiver(s) separated by some distance. The idea here is to receive and analyze energy reflected or absorbed by the stealthy vehicle but not returned toward the transmitter. Another approach is the use of long-wave radar such as that used by over-the-horizon radars. These would be of a wavelength chosen to see the entire stealth aircraft as a reflecting dipole, yielding some return regardless of low-observable treatments or vehicle configuration. These techniques add enormous complexity to the detection system, but appear to return at best imprecise location information that contributes little to effecting an intercept. Stealth attacks the cost-effectiveness of a radar-based air defense system at its core. It takes away the most effective technology for finding airplanes and obliges the defender to look to other technologies that are fundamentally less helpful in air defense.

Among the other ways an aircraft can be detected are: infra-red imagery, either from engine heat or the aircraft's surfaces; visual detection by ground observers or fighter interceptors; electromagnetic transmissions from the vehicle's radios, radars, or other equipment; acoustic detection of noise generated by the aircraft; or physical disturbances to the atmosphere created by the aircraft's passage, particularly those rendered visible by smoke, temperature differential, or contrail formation. Any of these, as well as radar, could be enhanced to a degree by the selection of optimum sensor platforms, including space-based systems. While some of these observable characteristics have high utility for specific phases of an intercept, none are as broadly useful or as independent of the influences of the particular operating environment or aircrew tactics as radar. A few examples might be useful.

Infra-red sensors have particular utility at short range. But, infra-red radiation attenuates in the atmosphere, particularly through the effects of suspended moisture. The ability of an infra-red sensor to discriminate between a valid target and a background also giving off infra-red radiation is problematic. Under many conditions a sensor would have the greatest difficulty in identifying a target vehicle at low altitude against terrain background. If the target vehicle's crew suspects attack by infra-red guided missiles, they can deploy flares likely to defeat the attacking missile. Stealth design characteristics of the F-117A and B-2 include a configuration intended to minimize infra-red signature. Engines are buried in the body of the aircraft, and hot exhaust streams spread and mix with cool air to reduce temperature extremes.

Visual detection is rendered difficult by the stealth vehicle's small size, low profile, and dark matte surface treatment. Both the B-2 and F-117A have a configuration that would make it difficult to judge distance and heading in the quick glance a searching fighter pilot might have. Operations in clouds would greatly restrict visual detection. As demonstrated in the Gulf War, limiting stealth attacks to hours of darkness is entirely feasible and greatly reduces defense effectiveness. The extent to which this is true was demonstrated not only by the success of the F-117A, but also by the AC-130 which operated for prolonged periods at night in close proximity to troops in the field. The one AC-130 lost in the Gulf War stretched its visual stealth too far in the interest of the troops it was supporting by lingering in the target area until the first light of dawn made it vulnerable.

Electromagnetic emissions, intentional or unintentional, from the target aircraft itself can be an important source of location information to the enemy. Any electromagnetic signal that is transmitted by the aircraft can be received and analyzed by enemy stations as well as by the intended recipient. Those very few transmissions that might be deemed acceptable can be rendered difficult to detect by a variety of techniques such as burst transmissions, frequency-hopping, or aimed laser communications, but the basic rule is radio silence. Radars for bombing and navigation of stealth aircraft such as the B-2 use a variety of techniques to minimize transmissions, disguise them, and make them hard to exploit for position location.

Detection of attacking aircraft by virtue of sound is possible but subject to atmospheric irregularities to an even greater degree than submarine sonar used against submarines is subject to thermal layering in the water. In World War II slow aircraft at low to middle altitudes could be detected by sound sensors. With greater speed and extremes of altitude, either very high or very low, sound becomes less useful. Wind, ambient noise, atmospheric layering, and rather rapid dissipation in the atmosphere all combine to make sound a rather unreliable and indeed expensive approach to detecting an attacking force. Stealth aircraft such as the B-2 are designed to be relatively quiet to further reduce the utility of this approach to localization.

Physical disturbances to the atmosphere are a significant challenge for stealth engineering. Any aircraft produces vortices as a by-product of the lift it generates in flight. While it is theoretically possible to detect the energy contained in these vortices, it is much more important that these vortices not become visible by virtue of contrails or smoke from the aircraft's engines. Contrails are minimized primarily by tactics selected to avoid altitudes of predicted contrail formation. There may also be supporting technologies aimed at reducing the contribution engine exhaust may make to contrail persistence. Smoke is a serious consideration in stealth, or indeed non-stealthy, combatant aircraft. Smoke can lead an enemy straight to a penetrating bomber otherwise totally invisible to the enemy interceptor pilot. Even under conditions where atmospheric or lighting conditions do not produce the contrast needed to make smoke trails visible, their shadows can be equally revealing. Some otherwise superior combat aircraft were infamous because they smoked enough to compromise their effectiveness; the Vietnam era F-4 Phantom was first among these.

The most fundamental truth about defense penetration through the application of stealth is that no vehicle is 100% invisible. The object of stealth is to reduce observables to the point that each part of the air defense problem is rendered more difficult. Air defense has several functional components. First, intruder aircraft must be detected to activate the entire defensive systems. Second, the incoming aircraft must be tracked with enough accuracy to determine location, direction, and speed. This tracking eventually has to be consistent enough to allow vectoring of interception close enough to identify the intruder aircraft and, eventually, to engage them or trigger the commitment of surface-to-air missiles. Next, the engaging aircraft in missiles must be able to hone in on the intruder. Finally, the warhead fuzes and intercept missiles must actually detonate close enough to destroy the intruder.

Stealth effects "cascade" across the various components of solutions to the air defense problem to render successful engagement of a penetrating vehicle improbable. Stealth needs to be good enough to reduce the likelihood that the attacking vehicle is detected and recognized as a threat in time to alert defenses and focus their attention. Stealth needs to prevent controllers from establishing a track sufficiently precise to permit interceptors to be vectored or missiles to be programmed. Stealth should then reduce the likelihood that an interceptor or missile will successfully acquire and home on the vehicle. Finally, stealth even reduces the likelihood that a weapon's warhead will fuse within range of the target.

Because the probability of successful interception is the product of the likelihood of achieving each of these sequential functions, measurable reductions in the enemy's ability to perform all of these functions massively reduces his likelihood of achieving a successful intercept. Similarly, nearly complete success in frustrating any one of these actions can reduce the likelihood of successful intercept to near zero. While in any given situation there remains uncertainty about the degree of success that a stealth vehicle has in avoiding detection by a particular sensor element of the defensive array, effective emphasis on low-observable technologies across the full range of possible sensor wavelengths generates an extremely high confidence of successful penetration. The overall effect is cumulative in its disruption of defensive effectiveness.

The Operational Potential of Stealth

The real military product of stealth is not perfection in penetrating defenses. It is the creation of military options that, successfully pursued, are capable of achieving strategic objectives with a resource constrained force structure. Stealth technology combines with the basic characteristics of the long-range, land-based bomber to significantly expand upon the utility that can be expected from traditional non-stealthy systems. The following ten capabilities demonstrate some of the breakthroughs in utility that are to be anticipated from fielding a rational number of B-2-class stealth bombers, and how stealth contributes to each.

1. Early effectiveness against defenses. The lethality of current and anticipated air defense systems has created the necessity to engage enemy defenses before beginning an offensive air campaign focused on tactical or strategic target systems of broader significance to larger campaign objectives. In the Vietnam War and Libya Raid, this translated into the assembly of massive mutual support packages within which the bombers constituted a rather small fraction of the airframes committed. The Gulf War saw for the first time the employment of stealthy F-117As and cruise missiles that penetrated directly to strategically significant targets in the first moments of the war and proceeded to unravel key elements of the enemy's command and control and air defense systems. The unchallenged success of F-117As against Iraqi targets and the strategic impact these missions documented the contemporary utility of stealth but only suggested a much greater future utility. They only suggested future utility because the F-117As were subject to a lengthy deployment process before they could see their first combat employment. Fortunately Saddam Hussein accorded the Coalition sufficient time to get the fully deployed attack aviation force into its forward wartime basing. Future aggressors should be expected to have learned from the Iraqi's fate and spare no efforts to interrupt U.S. deployments or present the United States with a *fait accompli*.

Full utility of stealthy attack is, however, realizable by modern long-range, land-based aircraft. B-2-class aircraft can execute initial attacks on world-wide targets from peacetime locations in the United States. This means that stealth allows a sufficient B-2 force, launched in response to an aggressor's surprise attack, to attain the quality of early strategic impact that the F-117As had as lead elements of a carefully planned campaign prepared over many months. The F-117As served magnificently in the opening minutes of a campaign requiring months to prepare. In Gulf War terms this means that, given the political will, a force of stealthy B-2s could have participated in the initial defense of Kuwait, rather than waiting and preparing for months before mounting the massive DESERT STORM to dislodge entrenched Iraqi occupation forces from the pillaged victim state. U.S. ability to conduct such early bomber attacks against an undegraded modern defensive array would certainly weigh heavily in the mind of a potential attacker. It would complicate his attack planning, compromise his ability to execute whatever plan he sought to implement, and might convince him to reconsider precipitate action and stand deterred.

To the United States confronting an act of aggression, the B-2 presents the military potential to execute a response while the initial attack is in progress, to shape a military response of the same violent nature as the attack in progress, and to have some military effect in preventing the enemy from achieving his initial objectives. To a decided and resolute national leadership, this capability offers the possibility of amplifying the effect of U.S. purpose by accelerating a response in timing, rather than by multiplying the mass of force structure invested and placed at risk or the volume of firepower directed at the enemy.

2. Wide range of attack axes and tactics. The range, payload, and effectiveness of offensive weapon systems of all types are highly sensitive to their routing to the combat zone and tactics that are applied to penetrate defenses and place weapons on target once within it. Non-stealthy combat aircraft characteristically have had to accept circuitous rather than direct routing and other than aerodynamically optimum flight paths in order to counter enemy defenses. B-17 missions to Germany in the course of the Combined Bomber Offensive were carefully structured to avoid enroute defensive concentrations and commit to the real target only late in the mission. Similarly, successive B-52 missions against the Hanoi/Haiphong area during LINEBACKER II were studiously conceived to approach on different routes and axes. To produce the highest likelihood of reaching the target, the planning of SIOP bomber missions long involved routing that variously avoided defensive concentrations or sought to overwhelm them. Low-altitude penetration tactics adopted by B-52s and the combination of low altitude and high penetration speed available to SAC's FB-111s and B-1s accepted considerable degradation of fuel efficiency in return for higher likelihood of penetrating defenses. All of these tactics reduced the reach that bombers could exercise with respect to their targets, the payload they could deliver to those targets, and the frequency with which the bombers could revisit the target system.

It is also significant that, even beyond the threat of enemy anti-air defenses, combat aircraft mission planning has often been subjected to political constraints that severely compromised operational efficiency. The April 15, 1986 raid on Libya provides a graphic example. Normally cooperative European allies found it politically unacceptable to associate themselves with the raid. Since agreeing to all-too-visible overflight of their territory by strike aircraft would have provided evidence of willing participation, the United States was reluctant to press for, and the allies involved unwilling to grant, overflight. The raid had to be carried out by carrier-borne aircraft and F-111s that had to fly a long endurance routing from England, around Spain, back across the Mediterranean to Libya, and then retrace their routing after the attack was complete. In both directions the F-111 force threaded its way through the Straits of Gibraltar, maintaining the transparent but effective fiction that it was proceeding down the center of the waterway without penetrating either Spanish or Moroccan sovereignties.

Stealth technology unquestionably offers the potential for reducing this mission-planning effect of enemy defenses. Sensors cover less area against stealthy targets, so bombers can follow more direct routing and still stay beyond range of radars and defensive systems. The bombers can also remain at optimum altitudes and speed longer so that more weapons can be delivered to more distant targets.

It is also possible, in the new security environment, that effectively stealthy attack aircraft can open up entirely new options for routing and target selection. Consider for a moment the challenge of planning a follow-on military alternative against Libya should it again take the lead in supporting international terrorism. The April 1986 raid against Libya in response to its terrorists actions struck coastal targets of considerable military value. Following the raid, Colonel Qaddafi took action to redeploy his air defense assets from a relatively even area—defense posture to a coastal-barrier defense. It was apparent from the first raid that any future attack would have to cross the Mediterranean coast. The United States could not expect acknowledged overflight approval from Libya's neighbors and carrier-borne aircraft did not have the range to fly around this region. By assembling a barrier defense Qaddafi increased the likelihood that any future raid would produce greater losses than the first. At the same time though, some of the barrier defenses had come from inland locations including the system of Libyan strategic bases reaching south toward Niger, Chad, and Sudan, a system that provided the armature for Libyan military influence over much of its African neighbors. Absent a force of modern long-range, land-based bombers such as the B-2, U.S. military planning options for a second raid might be limited to a reprise of the first raid, albeit of a grander scale or more dependent on expensive precision munitions, including small-payload cruise missiles. With a B-2 force it would have been entirely conceivable to rely on stealth to devise a second strike planned around the Sahara, the great sand sea separating North Africa from the distant south. A raid could overfly the Sahara from west to east, destroy Libya's strategic base network and depart back to the West encountering neither defenses nor notice. Unacknowledged diplomatic acquiescence to an overflight that would never be detected from the ground would be far more likely than approval for visible overflight. Stealth technology coupled with the long-range bomber thus holds the potential for widely expanding the range of strategic utility of U.S. forces normally constrained to a much more confining concept of operations. The payoff is in terms of greater strategic impact for less force applied.

3. Reliable destruction of difficult targets. The combination of stealth and the basic range, payload, and flexibility of the long-range, land-based bomber yields a high-confidence ability to destroy the broadest range of defended and technically difficult targets. F-117A employment in the Gulf War bore witness to the ability of stealthy aircraft to penetrate even intense modern defenses and to attack finite targets with unprecedented precision. However, this initial employment of stealth was limited in terms of radius of action, albeit with aerial refueling, from deployed operating locations. It was also limited in terms of the small number of weapons deliverable with each sortie (2) and the small force size. While the weapon most commonly used, the laser-guided 2,000 lb. bomb, had impressive destructive effect, the number available required targeting against precisely known targets of crucial value to the progressive accomplishment of the total air campaign. While targets vulnerable to F-117A attack had enormous value in terms of the success of DESERT STORM, particularly its air campaign, F-117As contributed much less to the destruction of important classes of targets which were either imprecisely located, well concealed, or spread out across multiple installations and considerable area. Such target systems implied the need for high-payload bomber aircraft.

Proliferation of ballistic missile technology to Iraq and Iraq's ability to produce weapons of mass destruction in the future remain a serious concern on the part of Iraq's neighbors, the United States and other Coalition members. That this concern survives the Gulf War has serious implications for the future. A number of Third World states possess ballistic missile technologies. Many are developing weapons of mass destruction. Among these are states which show evidence of coveting regional influence to a degree that they can be expected to threaten their neighbors or reach for regional hegemony. The military potential of these states reposes on weapons development installations which resemble all too closely the Iraqi installations that the United States and its Coalition partners were unable to effectively negate during the Gulf War. Press attention to underground CW facilities in Libya, expanding military capabilities in Iran, reported recent confrontation between India and Pakistan, and North Korea's renunciation of the Non-Proliferation Treaty and its apparent debut as a nuclear power highlight the strategic significance of the ability to attack the difficult targets at the core of ballistic missile, nuclear, chemical, and biological technologies quickly and massively should the occasion demand.

Chapter 7

In each of the cited cases, as well as the many others that exist or can be foreseen, the B-2 long-range, land-based bomber provides a military capability well endowed with the characteristics most likely to produce successful destruction of such target systems, before the weapons they produce can be employed against neighbors, allies of the United States, or U.S. forces in the field. Wherever such facilities are located, however they are defended, whatever hardening or concealment is employed, and however many aim points such targets may represent, the B-2 is likely be considered a weapon of choice against them.

4. Contributing to effectiveness of non-stealthy air forces. In the present climate of defense retrenchment, it is unrealistic to expect that sufficient resources will be made available to effect a sweeping conversion of entire air forces to stealthy systems. Stealth aircraft will, for the foreseeable future, provide the cutting edge, the "door-openers" for the larger non-stealthy force. Stealth today is the primary technology around which future "high-low mix" force structures will be shaped. This was borne out in the Gulf War. In that conflict the earlier "high-low" mix of combat aircraft, the F-15s and F-16s, found themselves operating in a way that put them both at the "low end" of a force mix with stealthy F-117As taking on the "high-end" role. But, in the Gulf War, the number of stealthy F-117As was quite limited, and even that "high-end" role was extremely constrained. The F-117As were dedicated to limited categories of enabling "must kill" targets, and they were the only aircraft employed within Baghdad. All other targets were consigned to less stealthy aircraft. All the aircraft involved, stealthy or not, performed well against Iraq. It is clear that targets destroyed by the stealthy F-117As and the confusion and frustration they generated on the part of Iraqi air defense forces had some role in enhancing the effectiveness of non-stealthy aircraft, but to attempt to quantify this role would be presumptuous. Absent an energetic defense by the Iraqi Air Force, the result of Saddam Hussein's particular strategic concept, detailed lessons about the employment of air power from the Gulf War will always be suspect. Yet, hindsight does illuminate the survival of sites associated with the development of weapons of mass destruction as a shortcoming of the bombing campaign, at least for the post-war comfort of the region [278]. One can assume that had more stealthy assets existed, they might have been targeted against such targets. Similarly, it is more than coincidental that the least stealthy attack aircraft employed by the Coalition, by virtue of their size, were the B-52s. They clearly operated as the lowest of the "low" end aircraft against troops in the field, well away from Iraq's central air defenses. The absence of a "high-end," long-range, land-based bomber in the Gulf War was a fact of life, one that was dealt with effectively in pursuit of immediate combat goals. This absence, however, may be seen to have had telling significance in terms of some of the crucial targets sets that survived the war with moderate or low damage. Had a modern long-range, land-based bomber been available in significant numbers in the Gulf, it is entirely plausible that a much more effective campaign to carry out the nuclear, chemical, and biological disarmament of Iraq would have been undertaken.

As it was, the United States had in the Gulf War an exceptionally proficient and potent force. But, it was one that, particularly at long ranges and heavy payloads, showed itself as not having enough stealthy "high-end" capability. A better balance between stealthy "high-end" F-117As and B-2s at longer ranges and against targets requiring greater firepower, and "low-end" non-stealthy aircraft at both theater and longer ranges might next time effect more strategically enduring damage to enemy assets that may ultimately be more threatening to the United States and its allies than the targets one is obliged to attack to make a DESERT STORM air campaign work.

5. Persistence in the target area. One of the greatest challenges for the effective employment of modern combat air power is maintaining a continual air-power presence. The history of aerial bombardment taught early on that much of the aircraft's advantage against surface forces was lost when the aerial tactics applied included keeping the attacking aircraft in the target area for a prolonged period of time or having the same aircraft return to the target for multiple bomb runs. In the era of non-stealthy aircraft this meant that the impact of combat air power tended to be a discontinuous one. In many contexts this is of little significance; however, in some it is a critical weakness. In order to provide persistence to attacks by non-stealthy aircraft, the numbers of aircraft available needed to be expanded. Aircraft were sequenced across the target so that the effect on the surface was one of continual, or at least recurring, attack. This was indeed one of the attributes of the Desert Storm air campaign, a campaign involving some 2,000 aircraft.

But, perhaps the best known example of an air campaign where persistence over the target was important was the battle for Khe Sanh in Vietnam. From January 14 to March 31, 1968, three Marine regiments and South Vietnamese Rangers were protected from two or more North Vietnamese Army divisions by long-range, land-based air power operations that involved 2,707 sorties and the delivery of 75,631 tons of ordnance [279]. In testimony before the SASC, then-Secretary of the Air Force Donald Rice applied the lessons of Khe Sanh to future bomber force structure in these terms:

Chapter 7

> ...during the 2-month battle for Khe Sanh in Vietnam, in order to insure six B-52's were on target every 3 hours around the clock, SAC required a committed force of 106 B-52's. To achieve the same target coverage with the B-2, our studies show that a force of at least 75 would be required in theater. A substantial inventory is an absolute necessity to be able to perform the sustained and/or multi-front campaign requirements that may confront future combatant commanders [280].

While this statement reflects a direct equivalence between the tonnage of bombs delivered by six B-52s across the target every three hours during the siege of Khe Sanh and the bombing capacity of a similar force of B-2s, other factors play in comparing the conventional capabilities of the two aircraft. The B-52s were flown in a series of three-ship cells stacked up at 1,000 foot intervals. Each cell was targeted against a single target "box" that the three aircrafts' "strings" of bombs would essentially cover. The "boxes" had been selected to include the most likely position of the enemy forces or facilities targeted. This approach made up for the relatively imprecise bombing accuracy of B-52s at that point in history. The cell tactics also accommodated the mediocre avionics reliability of the day by permitting the aircraft with the best bombing system to cue the others in a coordinated release. Perhaps most fundamentally, cell tactics were intended to enhance defensive capability by multiplying the effect of electronic countermeasures and combining the effectiveness of defensive gunnery.

In applying the lessons of Khe Sanh to the potential utility of a B-2-quality force of modern long-range, land-based bombers, the factors that led to the requirement for six B-52s across the target every three hours now reduce themselves to one: the nature of the target and the resulting type and tonnage of munitions needed to destroy it. The B-2's greater accuracy means that one or a few weapons can do what several B-52 loads were needed to do in 1968. Multiple cells for reliability backup should not be required. To the degree that the purpose of multiple strikes is to "keep the enemy's head down, " so he could not mass for an attack, as few as one bomber every few hours might accomplish the mission. This is particularly true if low-observable characteristics allow the bomber that makes up a given wave to loiter in the area and make multiple attacks, each with a partial weapons load, rather than dropping all weapons on a single pass. This discussion leads to the observation that B-2 forces even smaller than Donald Rice's 75 could still have considerable utility in specific bombing campaigns.

This tactic could make one approach to employing stealthy bombers for persistent presence look more like the operations of AC-130 gunships and their predecessors. Given the night-dependent stealth of the gunships, they provide a worthy precedent. Add stand-off precision weaponry and one adds the potential for continuous 24-hour-a-day, all-weather effectiveness on the part of B-2-class aircraft. With the orientational capability of systems such as JSTARS and the general availability of precision navigation equipment such as GPS, stealthy, long-range attack aircraft have the potential to provide a responsive enduring "loaded gun" presence over the battlefield rather than just a more or less frequent passing influence. This tactic might be especially effective in Bosnian-type conflicts.

6. Enhanced basing autonomy. The point has been made earlier that the range of the modern long-range, land-based bomber is a crucial factor as the location of future conflicts becomes less predictable, and regular U.S. access to overseas bases declines. Stealth adds to the effect of the long-range, land-based bomber's range in opening up broader basing options than would otherwise be possible. It should be expected that regional conflict, indeed any category of conflict, will place before the governments of neighboring states difficult decisions, sure to be opposed by some portion of their own populations. While governments may be predisposed to participating in future coalitions and according the United States and other partners basing rights or overflight permission, it may be critically important that the visibility of U.S. military activity be kept as low as possible. Indeed, low visibility could well be a condition of U.S. access. There have been numerous such cases in the recent past. During the war in Vietnam, B-52s regularly overflew the Philippines enroute to targets in Vietnam, yet they were prohibited from operating from air bases in the Philippines. The April 1986 U.S. raid on Libya was evidently refused overflight clearance from France and Spain, and visible overflight clearly would not have been acceptable to the Maghrebian countries, but the transparent artifice of flying out of sight down the middle of the Strait of Gibraltar was acceptable to the adjacent states. U.S. operations around Israel have been subject to similar restrictions with aircraft and ships limited to visits to Israel or to adjacent countries, but never in unconcealable sequence to one and then the other. The Gulf War saw U.S. operations from several countries which required that the visibility of U.S. operations be managed: Spain with bomber operations from isolated Moron AB; Turkey with operations from Incirlik AB, the one air base where U.S. force operations normally take place in peacetime, but no other bases; and even France. Stealth facilitates such political devices, and even opens up new possibilities for invited but unacknowledged operations through sovereign national airspace.

The utility of stealthy systems in achieving the low political notice requested by some potential hosts of U.S. combat operations is important. The lessons of the Gulf War include the importance of a concentration of air bases, ports, and the associated land transportation sufficient to sustain high-tempo operations. There is literally no other region of potential conflict with comparable basing. The result in any other conflict setting would imply counting on long-range systems and reaching much further afield for suitable basing. It is extremely likely that any such basing would be made available subject to tight restrictions on the visibility of the associated military operations.

7. **Low attrition over a prolonged conventional campaign.** Recent wars have characteristically resulted in historically low aircraft attrition rates. The Vietnam-era employment of heavy bombers yields the best post-World War II attrition experience. The Vietnam conflict pitted aircraft still in today's inventory against the variety of defenses that, in modernized form, were used by the Iraqis in the Gulf, and are likely to be present in future wars. In Vietnam bombers were employed against a range of targets, from those that were undefended to some of the densest concentrations of anti-air defenses ever assembled.

126,615 B-52 sorties were flown over Southeast Asia between June 1965 and August 1973. Of these 125,479 reached the target area, and 124,532 actually released their bombs [281]. Losses in these operations totaled 31 aircraft [282]. 18 of these losses were due to combat causes—all over North Vietnam [283]. These 31 represent per-mission attrition of 0.02% over the 126,615 sorties launched and a cumulative loss rate of 6.7% of the then-existing B-52 fleet. Attrition figures for the much shorter Gulf War fell quite close to the Vietnam rate, with one non-combat loss for a 0.06% per-mission attrition over some 1,600 sorties.

While these overall attrition figures appear to communicate some degree of consistency, they mask the element of the unanticipated and the enormous uncertainty of short-term losses. Fifteen B-52s were lost in the eleven-day Linebacker II campaign. Two bombers were lost in a collision on the very first B-52 mission in Vietnam.

Looking back to the more distant historical experience of World War II, there is another example of a category of bomber losses that has particular relevance for today's uncertain world. In November 1941, recognizing the gravity of Japan's build-up in the Pacific, the War Department secretly started moving its new B-17s to the Philippines. Communications intercepts indicated that secrecy had been preserved, and the Japanese thought U.S. bomber forces were limited to a few twin-engined B-18s. Actually 35 B-17s were already there, the largest concentration of such aircraft anywhere in the world [284]. Still, on

December 8, the first day of the war in the Philippines, the Japanese air attack on Clark Field destroyed 18 of the 35 B-17s deployed there, and with them the ability to interdict effectively Japanese offensive operations across the region [285].

The Gulf War emphasized a new level of sensitivity of U.S. public opinion to casualties in combat. This sensitivity is reinforced by a successful war which saw an unprecedentedly low number of U.S. casualties. There is no reason to think that this concern will not exist in the future. In such an environment, the role of stealth in decreasing aircraft losses will be important. And, the role of stealth combined with long range in reducing the vulnerability of deployed forces to unanticipated surprise might be even more significant. Even more important in day-to-day planning is the fact that the force structure now envisioned for the B-2 is so small that even peacetime attrition has clearly not been considered in sizing aircraft procurement.

8. New baseline for future technology enhancements. The central message of this chapter is that, just as stealth is not absolute in its effect, neither does stealth act in isolation to contribute value to a weapon system. It acts in combination with the systems other attributes. And it interacts over time with new technological advances. The core of the synergism of the B-2 as the modern long-range land-based bomber is the relationship between the flexibility inherent in the range and payload capability of the bomber and the fundamental advantages the stealthy vehicle has in penetrating any defensive array. Together the two constitute a basis for arguing that the B-2 is uniquely suited for future adaptation to new missions or new standards of performance of its present missions by the addition of new technologies. Those who argue most strongly and effectively in support of procuring more stealthy weapons systems are the last to suggest that stealth provides an enduring, absolute, or static advantage over any conceivable air defenses. Truth is that stealth provides an enormous lead in a dynamic and ever-changing contest between offensive and defensive capabilities. Understanding that lead will enable realization of the strategic dividend that the national investment in stealthy, long-range, land-based bombers merits.

For some period of time it should be expected that stealthy aircraft, operated knowledgeably, with appropriate attention to their limitations, should be able to penetrate the densest and most modern defenses with a high degree of success, as did the F-117A's over Baghdad. At some time in the future a motivated competitor will develop tactics or technology capable of coping with some aspect or aspects of stealth technology. This will not mean that stealth will no longer be useful, but only that it must be augmented by an evolution in tactics or technology capable of maintaining the current lead. Such an evolution may be quite subtle, a selection of optimum altitudes or flight paths. It could include an adaptation of active radar countermeasures, far more effective in hiding a stealthy platform than one with a large radar cross-section. Off-board countermeasures, jamming transmissions from space-based assets, and active, non-lethal measures against enemy air defense systems could far more easily defeat air defenses to allow a stealthy vehicle to pass than they could protect a non-stealthy one.

These same considerations favor focusing investment in weapons delivery accuracy, weapons lethality, and new approaches to locating and striking particularly difficult target categories on stealthy long-range, land-based aircraft. Implicit in assuming eventual need for such technological developments is the recognition that potential enemies of the United States themselves will be striving for some form of military advantage capable of compensating for U.S. long-range, land-based air power advantages. If the United States fails to focus its development and production efforts where it has its most significant advantages—its stealthy aircraft—the nation risks being overtaken by the quality of forces fielded by competitors with a more focussed sense of purpose.

9. Maximum weapon system service life. The unit cost of systems based on cutting edge military technologies is high; the combat advantage gained by such systems is similarly great. Making decisions over the allocation of scarce resources to such programs based only on estimates of near-term value is a highly subjective exercise that turns on the assumptions of individual Congressmen and administration officials about what the future holds. Absent a clear and present danger, considering only threats foreseeable with clarity, defense investment in major programs will continue to decline.

The modern long-range, land-based bomber, however, holds the promise of a service life of several decades. This stems from the enduring advantage that stealth technology yields regardless of the nature of the defensive systems it may be called upon to penetrate: the best now envisioned, or evolutionary advances intended expressly to contest stealthy vehicles. Stealthy vehicles will remain the weapons of choice in either case. This means that supporters of stealthy weapons programs can argue convincingly that weapons such as the B-2 are highly likely to have several decades of advantage over enemy counters and a service life of at least three decades. Indeed the B-2, purchased in the 1990's for its present conventional direct attack role, should be assumed to be its own successor as it is in some distant future re-roled into a stand-off missile delivery role. The B-2 is also the best "B-3." Investment should thus be amortized over a similar period.

156   The B-2 Bomber: Air Power for the 21st Century

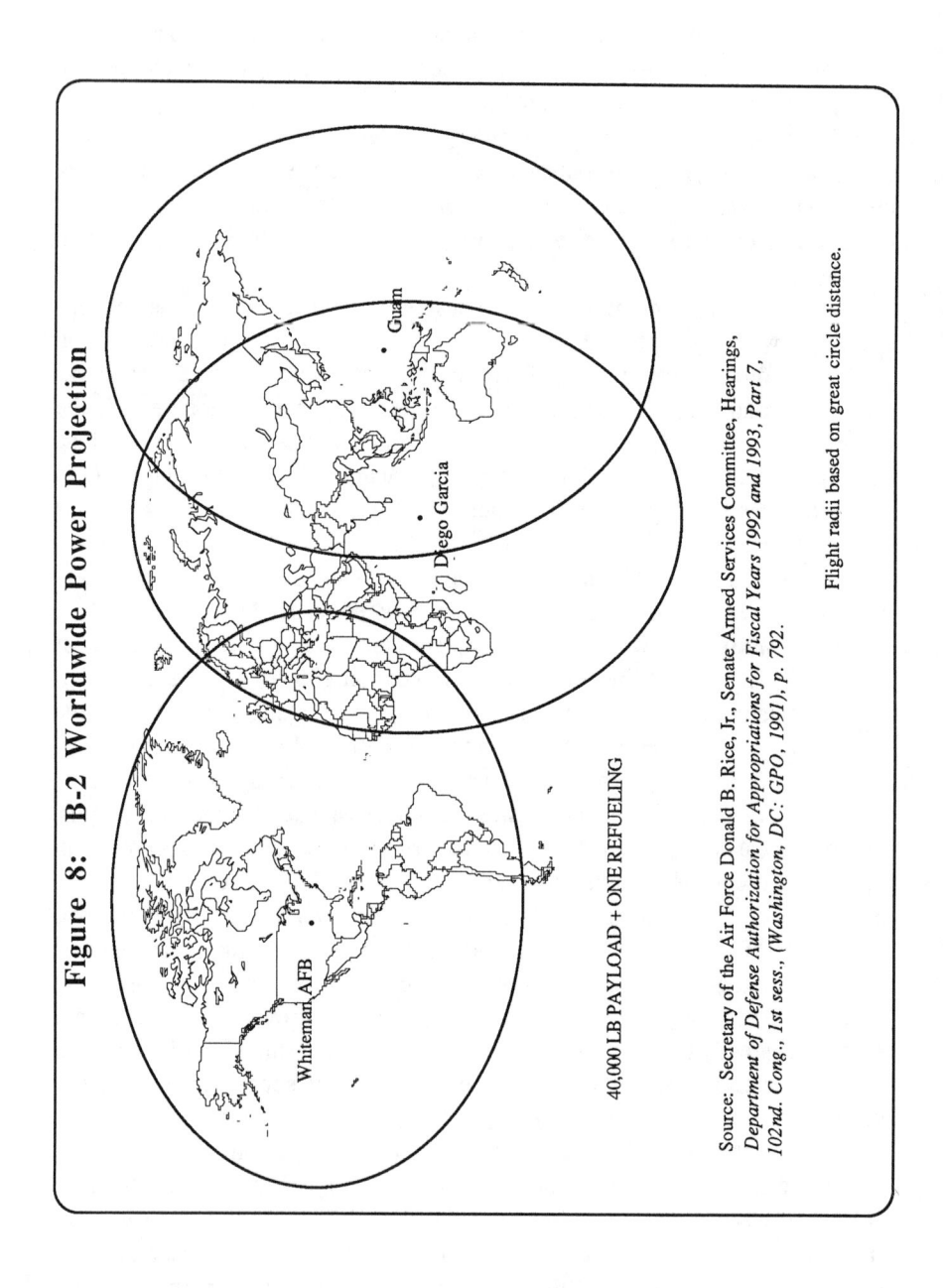

Figure 8: B-2 Worldwide Power Projection

40,000 LB PAYLOAD + ONE REFUELING

Flight radii based on great circle distance.

Source: Secretary of the Air Force Donald B. Rice, Jr., Senate Armed Services Committee, Hearings, *Department of Defense Authorization for Appropriations for Fiscal Years 1992 and 1993, Part 7, 102nd. Cong., 1st sess.* (Washington, DC: GPO, 1991), p. 792.

It is important to note that the B-52, which a large force of B-2s would be replacing, has served effectively longer than any other combat aircraft. It is reaching the limits of its useful service, not because it can no longer perform its combat role but because it is not stealthy and thus may be subject to excessive attrition by today's standards in conventional combat, and requires too much support, too much manpower, and too much fuel. The advocacy argument that B-2s are being purchased for several decades of utility is an important one. It spreads the payoffs from B-2 spending over a three-, four-, or more-decade time frame where historical experience argues eloquently for the high likelihood or near certainty that the B-2 will find combat employment, a point that cannot be convincingly argued in terms only of near-term clear and present danger.

10. Improved ability to reconstitute nuclear/nuclear equivalent capability in the face of a great- or super-power nuclear threat. A "Bottom-Up Review" of the dangers faced by the United States and the force structure required to meet them, was conducted by then-Secretary of Defense Aspin in 1993. Secretary Aspin announced in September. 1993 that the United States faces four dangers in the post-Cold War world. The first is proliferation of weapons of mass destruction; the second is regional threats; the third is threats to democracy in the former Soviet Empire; and the fourth is the danger of a weak U.S. economy [286].

Aspin and then-Chairman of the Joint Chiefs of Staff General Colin Powell cited Iraq and North Korea as examples of regional threats. Russia, with whom the United States currently enjoys good relations, is not considered a near-term military threat. But Aspin acknowledged the potential for renewed political-military rivalry with Russia if its fragile, nascent democratic system is subverted [287]. The revolt of "hard-liners" in the Russian Parliament of September-October 1993 demonstrates the political instability of the post-Soviet Russian Republic. Any new threat from Russia would be an order of magnitude greater than that currently posed by such regional powers as North Korea and could include a renewed nuclear standoff. DoD thinking reflects this understanding. According to Aspin, two principal guidelines for establishing the future requirements for strategic forces are: that they provide an effective deterrent under START I/II limits; and "allow for additional forces to be reconstituted, in the event of a threatening reversal of events" [288].

Whether arising from the ashes of the former Soviet Union, or from some other quarter, the ultimate challenge for future military forces of the United States would be the appearance of a superpower-class adversary. Today's dominant conventional wisdom holds that the reappearance on the political horizon of such a growing challenge will occur early enough to provide ample warning for an orderly rebuilding of the defense establishment before the threat becomes acute. History provides no evidence that such an assumption is realistic. History teaches the lesson that national leaders can have an infinite ability to delude themselves before a nascent threat, explaining away the clearest of evidence in order to avoid taking warning and thereby accepting the responsibility to act. The democracies have characteristically given away the first move by failing to be warned. Whether it was the Sudetenland, Pearl Harbor, the Falklands, or Kuwait, the signals of impending crisis and war do not attract the attention that Monday-morning quarterbacks invariably see as merited. In preparing for the most likely form of surprise by a new superpower threat, it should be assumed that there will be at first languid unconcern followed by enormous pressure for accelerated mobilization and the reestablishment of the highest order of deterrent threat.

Under such circumstances, existing forces will have to be the nucleus of such a "reconstitution." This was the case during the last "reconstitution " at the beginning of the Cold War. It was the case for the first years of the build-up for World War II, a five-year war during which the United States did not reach full stride until late 1942, almost half way through.

The next "reconstitution," as the last, will demand that the United States seek superpower deterrent capability from conventional forces largely postured for regional conflict. This will probably occur in a world where anti-ballistic missile defenses are commonplace, by virtue of evident near-term proliferation problems. It will occur in a world where the United States no longer has a global net of bases and established alliances. Much of the initial effectiveness of such "reconstituting" power will have to come from a reemphasis of nuclear weapons, or their operational equivalents, precision conventional weapons that can reliably destroy targets at the enemy's center of gravity. This context emphasizes the importance of stealth technology, first developed as one of the final "coffin nails" set at the demise of the Soviet threat, and certainly important to anchoring a reconstituted deterrence next time it is needed.

The future offensive potential of U.S. air power, with stealth technology at its center, can be demonstrated by published views of Russian military observers. As early as December 1990, with reductions in U.S. defense spending already well underway, General of the Army I. V. Tretyak, Commander in Chief, Air Defense and USSR Deputy Defense Minister expressed his view of U.S. potential in *Voyennaya Mysl*:

> The United States essentially has not cut back a single program for creating new offensive air-space weapons (SVKN) and modernizing existing ones.

As a result of their fulfillment, the attack potential not only will not be reduced by the late 1990's after the planned reduction in conventional arms in Europe, but may even rise compared with today's situation. We of course cannot ignore all this [289].

Russian analysis of the Gulf War further manifested respect and concern over the capabilities of U.S. offensive air power in combat. Although Russian officers were unwilling to cite stealth and the F-117A as unique in their effect, they documented their belief that this technology was central to an integrated ability to overwhelm defenses. The other aspects of this system were precision munitions and advanced active electronic warfare techniques applied against classical radar-based defenses [290]. Rare articles did break out stealth as a distinct factor, albeit not the greatest, in the defeat of Iraqi air defenses [291]. This treatment clearly shows that the ability of the United States to mount future air offensive action with a high likelihood of being able to defeat defenses that can now be conceived, has the enduring attention of at least one potential future superpower competitor.

The essential precondition for the employment of the modern long-range, land-based bomber, the stealthy B-2, as a central support of a new reconstitution will be the existence of a force of B-2s sufficient in number to reliably fulfill the bomber requirements for conventional conflicts of the regional scope that should be anticipated over the next two or three decades. An adequate conventional B-2 force should be the essential core of a nuclear B-2 force adequate to confront a new superpower threat. This is admittedly an other-than-scientific approach to relating the B-2 to specific force structure requirements of a new superpower confrontation, but reflects the proven logic of the last "reconstitution" and should have core applicability to an eventual future "reconstitution." It is only by virtue of the capabilities inherent in stealth technology that a given weapon system can be portrayed as retaining its utility far enough into the future to permit such a prediction. In the case of non-stealthy systems, service life and combat advantage are far too short to represent other than a passing influence in strategic terms.

Chapter 8
The Cost-Effectiveness of the B-2 Bomber

STEVEN J. LAMBAKIS AND JOHN J. KOHOUT III

"...*the bottom line is not dollars per [B-2] aircraft, but overall capability per dollar*" [292].

The operational advantages and strategic potential of the B-2 described qualitatively in preceding chapters are measured by defense decision-makers in terms of cost-effectiveness. Discussions about the B-2 bomber characteristically focus on its cost; they rarely are successful in linking that cost to operational payoff. Critics contend the price of the B-2 is too high. But "too high" for what? Considered in isolation, the cost of any multimillion-dollar weapon system seems excessive. In the case of the B-2 program, the price tag includes the ground-breaking scientific basic research that made B-2s superior stealth characteristics possible. It also built a production and testing capacity sized to a Cold War-era production rate of three aircraft per month. The initial B-2 program is proving out the B-2 weapon system from the production line all the way through to operational service. It is placing the nation in a uniquely well-informed position to evaluate the B-2's marginal dollar cost against measures of its military utility.

The preceding chapters presented largely qualitative insights into the domestic, international security, and military contexts within which the B-2 must be evaluated. Examined below are some more quantitative considerations of the military returns the United States stands to gain from substantial investment in the B-2. The primary mission characteristics of the B-2 first are described. Then these characteristics are explored in comparison with alternative approaches to accomplishing the same missions. Finally, program status relevant to the decision to manufacture additional B-2s is addressed.

Key Attributes of the B-2

Long range (base-to-target distances covering several thousands of miles) and large payload (bomb loads weighing tens of thousands of pounds) distinguish heavy bombers, like the B-52, B-1B, and B-2, from other strike aircraft. "Stealth" sets the B-2 apart from the older heavy bombers, as well as other aircraft, except the F-117A Stealth fighter [293]. The ability of the B-2 to deliver up to 16 highly accurate precision-guided munitions (PGMs) in a single sortie, eight times the maximum load of the F-117A, highlights the destructive potential in its large payload. Like all modern jet combat aircraft, the B-2 has the inherent speed that enables it to reach a distant theater or battle area more rapidly than armies or naval fleets. Each of these characteristics—long range, large payload, high speed, low observability, and high lethality—is intrinsic to the B-2. Each offers particular advantages in accomplishing strategic attack, air interdiction, and offensive counterair missions. Combined in the B-2, they yield an effective and efficient military instrument with broadly valuable capabilities that represent a significant advance beyond existing weapon systems, correspond to real strategic needs of the United States, and are not duplicated by any credible future weapon design concepts.

Long Range

The B-2 has an unrefueled range of 6,000 nautical miles (nm). With one aerial refueling, range extends to 10,000 nm. Intercontinental range enables B-2 bombers to strike targets anywhere on the globe from as few as three points: Whiteman Air Force Base, Missouri (the home base for the B-2 force); Andersen AFB on the Pacific island of Guam; and the airfield on Diego Garcia, a British-owned island in the Indian Ocean from which B-52G bombers operated in the Gulf War. Although operations from within a theater would have clear benefits (shorter time to target, shorter sortie duration, less crew fatigue, higher sortie rate, and lower tanker demand), long range would permit B-2 strikes from distant locations if in-theater bases were lacking, unavailable due to political constraints, or highly vulnerable to attack.

Long range provides a number of operational benefits besides global reach. Range (along with speed) gives "strategic agility," the ability to "swing" between widely separated theaters. Unlike forward-deployed U.S. forces stationed in particular geographic areas in peacetime, a strategically agile B-2 force based in the continental United States (CONUS) would exert an omnidirectional, rather than a region-specific deterrent threat. Were U.S. forces involved in two conflicts simultaneously (e.g., one in the Middle East and another in Korea), B-2s and other heavy bombers could be shifted between theaters in ways that responded to military exigencies and served overarching strategic objectives.

With its long range, the B-2 has less need for tanker support, an important consideration in regional conflicts like the Gulf War, where 60 percent of all combat missions required aerial refueling [294]. Moreover, the B-2 could fly unaccompanied far into enemy territory to eliminate targets that were beyond the reach of shorter-range strike aircraft. In Operation Desert Storm, for example, aerial tankers (and supporting fighters and electronic-warfare aircraft) had to penetrate deep into Iraqi airspace to refuel F-117As that then flew on against targets in northern Iraq, targets longer-range B-2s could have struck without refuelings [295]. If necessary, the large fuel load of the B-2 (over 160,000 pounds) could be used not for extended range, but for more loiter time in a target area, during which the bomber crew could assess target damage, carry out additional strikes, or potentially find and attack mobile or imprecisely located targets (e.g., mobile missile launchers).

Large Payload

The two bomb bays of the B-2 can carry more than 40,000 pounds of munitions. Large payload reduces the number of sorties required to deliver a given quantity of weapons. The efficiency of the heavy bomber in delivering sizable amounts of ordnance was demonstrated during the 43 days of Desert Storm, when 75 B-52Gs (3 percent of the Coalition combat aircraft) flew more than 1,600 sorties (3 percent of all attack sorties) and dropped more than 72,000 weapons weighing over 27,000 tons (30 percent of total bomb tonnage) [296]. It should be noted that one postwar analysis found that a B-2 force half the size (approximately 40 aircraft) operating from the same bases over the same period could have dropped the same bomb tonnage [297]. Large weapon loads of general purpose bombs and cluster bomb units are particularly suited for attacks on large and relatively homogenous area targets (e.g., military supply complexes, troop concentrations).

Large payload allows the B-2 to carry not only a considerable tonnage of bombs, but a useful variety of weapons. The following table lists the unguided and guided conventional munitions the B-2 will be capable of carrying. (The aircraft also could be loaded with 16 B61 or B83 unguided nuclear bombs.) The ability to vary the type and number of weapons means a more efficient matching of munitions against targets, which, besides increasing strike effectiveness, may save time, sorties, aircraft, and lives. Because of their large capacity, the bomb bays of the B-2 also should be able to accommodate new weapons developed in the future. When the first B-52s became operational in the mid-1950s, they were loaded solely with nuclear gravity (free-fall) bombs. Since that time, B-52 bomb bays also have carried Quail decoy missiles, various nonnuclear bombs, short-range attack missiles (SRAMs), and air-launched cruise missiles (ALCMs). The Quail, SRAM, and ALCM all were nonexistent when the B-52 entered service. Over its comparable service life, the B-2 likewise will have a similar potential to carry munitions not yet in the U.S. arsenal (perhaps including so-called nonlethal weapons). Indeed, the JDAM guided bombs and TSSAM cruise missile in the preceding table were not even in development when the B-2 was designed [298]. A decade later, they are to be key weapons for the bomber.

Table 3:   B-2 Conventional Weapons [299]

Weapon	Type	Weight (lbs.)	Load
Unguided Munitions			
MK-82	General Purpose Bomb	500	80
MK-117	General Purpose Bomb	750	36
MK-84	General Purpose Bomb	2,000	16
CBU-87/B, -89/B, -97/B	Cluster Munitions	1,000	36
MK-36	Sea Mine	500	80
MK-62	Sea Mine	500	80
Guided Munitions			
GPS-Aided Targeting System/GPS-Aided Munition (GATS/GAM) Weapon	Guided Bomb	2,000	16
Joint Direct Attack Munition I (JDAM I)	Guided Bomb	2,000	16
JDAM III	Guided Bomb (terminal seeker)	2,000	16
AGM-137/Tri-Service Standoff Attack Missile (TSSAM)	Cruise Missile (100 nm+ range)	2,300	8

High Speed

The B-2 has a cruising speed of nearly 500 knots (more than 550 miles per hour) [300]. Though it can fly at a high subsonic speed, the B-2 is not notably fast when compared with other combat aircraft (e.g., the supersonic F-111 strike aircraft). The B-2 relies on stealth rather than speed for survivability. It does, however, share the characteristic power projection speed advantage air power holds over all surface forces. Like other combat aircraft, the B-2 can cover distances at a rate an order of magnitude faster than ships or ground units. CONUS-based or forward-deployed heavy bombers can reach a theater quickly. For example, just 15 hours after their takeoff from Barksdale AFB, Louisiana, shortly before the start of Desert Storm, seven B-52Gs launched nearly three dozen conventional ALCMs against military communications sites and electric power facilities in Iraq. The bombers then returned to Barksdale, completing the 14,000-mile round-trip in just over 35 hours [301]. By contrast, during the buildup to Desert Storm, one carrier battle group (with the USS Saratoga) took more than two weeks to deploy from East coast ports to the Red Sea, while another (with the USS Midway) took nearly a month to deploy from Yokosuka, Japan to the Persian Gulf [302]. As the following figure shows, B-2s at Whiteman AFB can fly to all likely conflict areas within 24 hours, with forward deployment to Guam or Diego Garcia significantly reducing flight time to Korea or the Middle East, respectively.

The capability of the B-2 force to strike rapidly has several advantages. Speed (combined with intercontinental range) allows B-2s in CONUS to project a "distant presence" that may help deter would-be aggressors overseas. To the extent these aggressors find the prospect of swift retaliation more daunting than a slow response, speed would strengthen deterrence. Speed aids strike operations requiring surprise. Speed is valuable in responding to attacks that occur with little or no warning and compensates for delays in responding to warning that is received. Speed (again with range) permits prompt military action to counter aggression in regions where U.S. forces are absent or insufficient. B-2s armed with weapons that dispensed antiarmor and antipersonnel submunitions could be used to hinder an enemy offensive while U.S. and allied ground forces, as well as additional strike aircraft, were brought to the battle area. Timely air interdiction sorties that disrupted a fast-moving offensive could thwart enemy plans to seize territory from a neighboring country and present the grab as a *fait accompli* before the United States and its allies could react militarily. Speed makes it possible for long-range bombers to swing quickly between theaters and concentrate firepower within a theater. And speed enables the B-2 to take out time-critical targets (e.g., missile launchers ready to fire, weapons of mass destruction facilities with removable equipment, ground units in garrisons or assembly areas, command posts temporarily occupied by top enemy leaders, warships in port). Despite these advantages, standard cost-effectiveness analyses often ignore or undervalue the responsiveness heavy bombers gain from their speed. The Defense Department Bottom-Up Review of 1993 places heavy reliance on long-range bombers among forces aimed at destroying such high-value, time-critical targets [303].

Low Observability

Because of its low-observable characteristics, the B-2 is highly capable of evading opposing air defenses. As described in Chapter 7, the design of the aircraft minimizes the radar, infrared, acoustic, electromagnetic-emission, and visual signatures it presents to air defense sensors. Reducing radar cross section, a measure of radar signature expressed in square meters, reduces the vulnerability of aircraft to radar-based defenses. The low-observable B-2 has a radar cross section many times smaller than those of the representative nonstealthy aircraft found in the following table. In terms of radar cross section, the B-52 is similar to a large transport aircraft, the B-1B is like a fighter, the ALCM is akin to other nonstealthy winged missiles, and the B-2 is smaller than a bird. Low observability gives the B-2 a major qualitative edge over nonstealthy combat aircraft in avoiding detection and engagement by air defense systems on the ground and in the air.

Table 4: Radar Cross Sections [304]

Aircraft	Radar Cross Section (square meters)
Jumbo Jet	100
DC-9	20
Medium Fighter	10
Small Fighter	4
Small Aircraft	1
Conventional Winged Missile	0.5
B-2	**<0.001**

Note: These radar cross sections are generally representative and do not capture variations due to changes in aspects, radar frequencies, or other factors that determine RCS.

Stealth contributes to the cost-effectiveness of the B-2 in at least five ways. Because of low observability, the B-2 force is likely to suffer less combat attrition than a fleet of nonstealthy heavy bombers. Although attrition was remarkably low for all aircraft types used by the Coalition in the Gulf War, none of the 42 stealthy F-117As were lost, even though they flew nearly 1,300

Figure 9: B-2 Range and Responsiveness

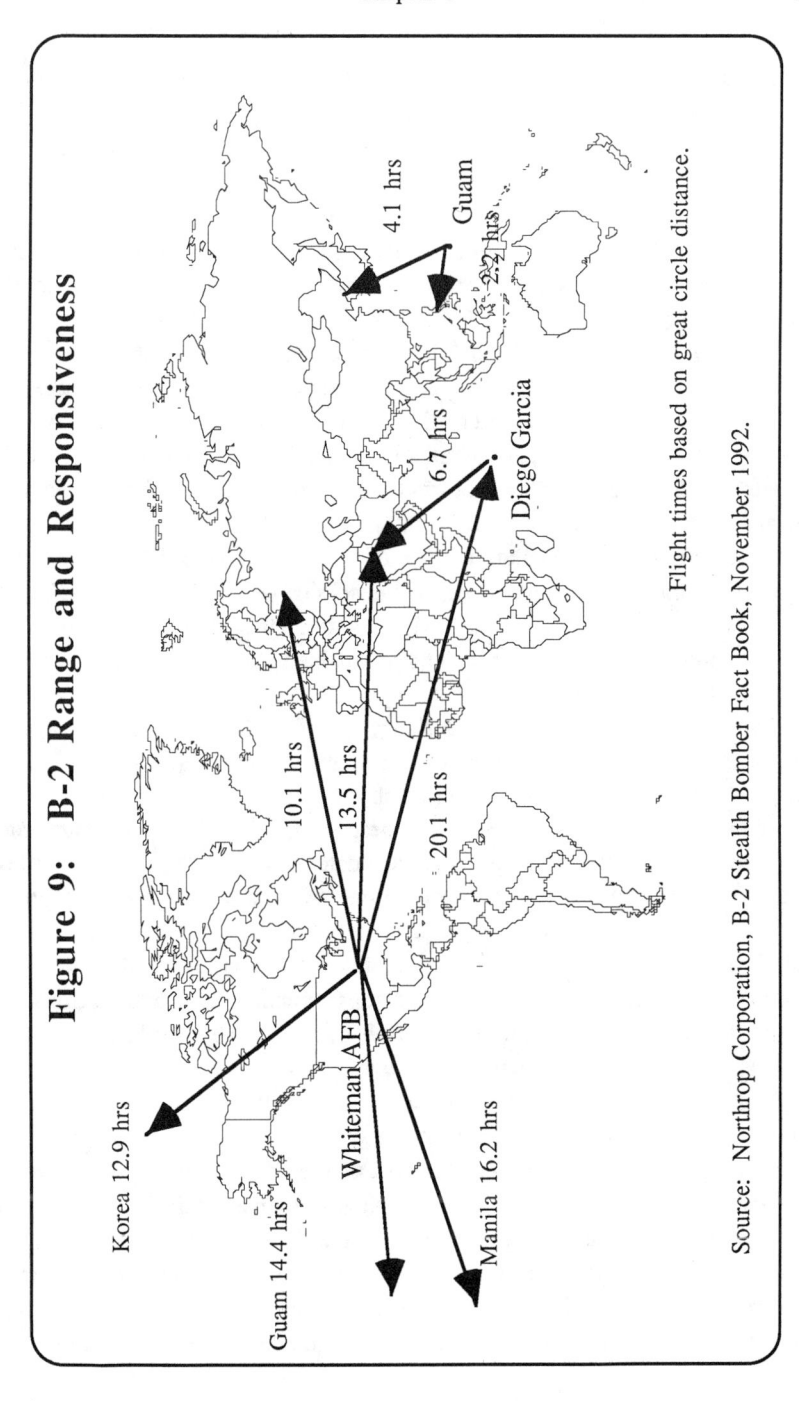

Korea 12.9 hrs
Guam 14.4 hrs
Whiteman AFB
Manila 16.2 hrs
10.1 hrs
13.5 hrs
20.1 hrs
4.1 hrs
Guam
2.2 hrs
6.7 hrs
Diego Garcia

Flight times based on great circle distance.

Source: Northrop Corporation, B-2 Stealth Bomber Fact Book, November 1992.

sorties, many against the most heavily defended targets [305]. Indeed, the low attrition experienced by Coalition air forces can be attributed, in part, to F-117A strikes that shut down elements of the Iraqi air defense system. A more survivable force loses fewer aircraft and aircrews, generates more sorties over a given period of time, and thus makes for a better return on investment. The survivability stealth affords would be critical for a prolonged, high-intensity campaign, where even a low per-sortie attrition rate eventually inflicts a prohibitive toll on a finite bomber force required to fly numerous sorties.

Unlike other strike aircraft, the B-2 can defeat air defenses without the aid of various support aircraft (fighter escorts to fend off interceptors, defense-suppression aircraft to attack radar-directed ground defenses, and electronic-countermeasures aircraft to jam radars and communications equipment). As in the Vietnam War, B-52s in Desert Storm typically required large force protection packages for attacks against defended targets [306]. Before B-52Gs could pound a huge military-industrial installation north of Baghdad, a target filled with many production, storage, and maintenance facilities, PGM-armed F-117As first had to destroy the surface-to-air missile (SAM) sites defending the complex. B-2s, in contrast, could have attacked this area target unaided [307]. The stealth of the B-2 saves the high cost of protection from support aircraft.

Stealth also can increase the effective range of the B-2, reinforcing the long reach of the aircraft. Nonstealthy bombers incur range penalties to overcome enemy defenses. To circumvent defenses, they fly indirect and thus longer routes to their targets. They penetrate hostile airspace fast and low, increasing fuel consumption and decreasing range, to escape detection and interception by radar-based defenses. And to jam or deceive enemy radars, they have on-board electronic countermeasures (ECM) equipment that displaces fuel (or payload) [308]. The low-observable B-2 flies more direct routes, at higher altitudes, with no or minimal ECM, thereby avoiding these penalties. Wider latitude in planning attack routes and altitudes, as well as attack axes and tactics, further improves the effectiveness of strike operations.

Greater payload efficiency is yet another benefit the B-2 gains from stealth. Because the B-2 can operate in defended target areas, it can deliver unguided or guided bombs that are a fraction of the cost of standoff missiles, each of which has its own airframe, power plant, and guidance system, in addition to a warhead. Moreover, the B-2 bomb bays can be loaded with more bombs than missiles (e.g., 16 JDAM weapons versus 8 TSSAMs). Stealth supports the accurate delivery of weapons by allowing strikes from higher altitudes where the field of view is better, by freeing aircrews to concentrate on attacking targets rather than evading defenses, and by giving B-2 strikes the element of surprise, which limits enemy actions to reduce target vulnerability [309].

Finally, stealth will help assure the operational longevity of the B-2. The low-observable requirements for the B-2 were derived chiefly from the need to penetrate the extensive and advanced air defense system of the Soviet Union rather than the lesser defenses of Third World countries. Now war with Russia (the core of the old Soviet empire) is much less likely than armed conflict with Third World adversaries. This does not mean, however, that the high degree of stealth incorporated in the B-2 is superfluous. The proliferation of advanced military technologies to Third World countries includes the most modern air defenses. Russian efforts to gain hard currency through arms exports are accelerating this flow. The stealth of the F-117A proved its utility against Iraqi air defenses, particularly the Baghdad defense network, which has been described as "more dense than that surrounding most East European cities during the Cold War and several orders of magnitude greater than that which had defended Hanoi during the later stages of the Vietnam War" [310]. Air defenses in other developing countries will undergo major improvements over the three decades or more the B-2 will be in service. A recent intelligence assessment predicted that, as in Desert Storm, "future U.S. crisis and contingency operations may be conducted against countries possessing formidable integrated air defense systems (IADS). Continued arms proliferation and technology transfer from Western and former Warsaw Pact countries ensure that this will be the case for most regions of strategic interest to the United States and/or its allies" [311]. The inherent stealth of the B-2 is a hedge against upgrades to air defenses wherever they may be encountered. It is one of the reasons the aircraft will remain militarily effective throughout a long service life. And the longer the service life, the greater the return on the B-2 investment.

High Lethality

Large payload allows the size and composition of B-2 weapon loads to be tailored for particular target types. High speed permits quick responses to enemy actions and places time-critical targets at risk. Stealth greatly diminishes the effectiveness of defenses interposed between B-2s and their targets and, by making bomb runs at optimum altitudes less dangerous, enhances the ability of bomber crews to detect targets.

For target search, acquisition, identification, and attack, the B-2 has a high-resolution synthetic aperture radar (SAR) effective at night and in all weather conditions. One source reports that with very high-speed processing, this radar "should be capable of acquiring near-photographic imagery at a range of almost

100 miles from the B-2's cruising altitude" [312]. (To preserve the stealth of the B-2, the radar is a unique "low probability of intercept" system that is difficult to detect by air-defense sensors designed to pick up and track radar emissions.) [313] In addition to its on-board capabilities, the B-2 could use cues from other systems (e.g., E-8 Joint Surveillance and Target Attack Radar System aircraft) to find targets.

As noted above, the B-2 can carry both unguided and guided munitions. With their high accuracy, guided munitions significantly increase the lethality of bomber strikes against point targets (e.g., command bunkers, bridges, missile sites, radars). Under current plans, the B-2 will be certified for four types of guided munitions: JDAM I, JDAM III, GATS/GAM, and the TSSAM. All four weapons now are in development and, with the possible exception of the TSSAM, which was recently cancelled by Secretary Perry [314], should be available around the turn of the century.

The JDAM I is a 2,000-pound bomb (or a 1,000-pound submunition dispenser) equipped with a guidance kit consisting of an inertial navigation system (INS) and a Global Positioning System (GPS) receiver. This "launch and leave" weapon can be used day or night, in adverse weather, and should be accurate to within 45 feet of a target. The JDAM III is similar, a 2,000-pound bomb with an INS/GPS kit, but also has terminal guidance (a radar or imaging infrared seeker) that gives an improved CEP of 10 feet or less. Loaded with JDAM weapons, a B-2 could attack a target with multiple aimpoints (e.g., an air base) on a single pass [315]. Under another weapon concept, the B-2 would use GPS-aided navigation and SAR targeting to deliver an inertially-guided, GPS-assisted bomb. The GPS-aided targeting system/GPS-aided munition (or "GATS/GAM") combination could yield a circular error probable (CEP) of less than 20 feet [316]. (CEP is the radius of a circle, centered on the target, within which half the weapons would be expected to fall.)

A TSSAM-class weapon would be a low-observable, subsonic cruise missile. It would have a range of over 100 nm and a payload of roughly 1,000 pounds. The missile could be armed with either a unitary warhead or combined-effects submunitions. Its autonomous guidance system would be good for "pinpoint accuracy," in all weather, day or night. Potential TSSAM targets include air-defense sites, airfields, parked aircraft, aircraft shelters, command-and-control bunkers, and ships [317]. A TSSAM-class weapon not only offers the capability for precision bombing, but expands the target coverage of a B-2. With TSSAMs, a single B-2 could strike as many as eight scattered targets, at ranges up to 100+ nm, from the same general launch area. The TSSAM also provides a means of further diminishing the vulnerability of the B-2 to opposing air defenses. If necessary, TSSAMs would let B-2s attack well-protected targets from points outside terminal defenses. The standoff range of the TSSAM would limit exposure of the B-2; the small size and stealth of the missile would limit its own risk of detection and interception. And standoff attack with TSSAMs might make B-2s less visually observable by enemy defenses, thereby facilitating round-the-clock bombing, during daylight as well as at night.

Guided munitions like the JDAM bombs and, eventually, a TSSAM-class cruise missile give the hefty payload of the B-2 still greater punch. With their higher accuracy, guided weapons are more likely than free-fall bombs to hit their targets and hit aimpoints chosen to cause optimal damage to those targets (e.g., the air shaft of a multistory headquarters, the generator hall or switching yard of an electric power plant, the door of a military shelter, the abutment of a bridge). Consequently, fewer guided weapons are needed to inflict a specified level of damage against a given target. If fewer weapons are needed, the target can be knocked out with fewer sorties and bomb runs. Fewer aircraft and aircrews are jeopardized. Sorties and weapons can be allocated to other targets. Autonomously guided weapons thus boost the "combat productivity" of the B-2 through multiple hits per pass and fewer weapons per target.

Production of TSSAM-class weapons is closely linked to the rationale for producing additional B-2s in the near term and to future utility of B-2s in the long term. Deputy Defense Secretary Deutch testified before the SASC that delays in the production of TSSAM would make the question of producing more B-2's "more urgent" [318].

Before ending this discussion of the B-2's lethality, it should be pointed out that at the same time precision weapon delivery increases the ability of the bomber to kill targets, it also limits unintended damage to nontargets (e.g., noncombatants, hospitals, places of worship, cultural sites). Minimizing collateral damage was one of the objectives—and successes—of the air campaign against Iraq. Accounts of conditions in Baghdad immediately after the war contain many descriptions of damaged government and military-related buildings surrounded by other buildings that were unscathed [319]. Significantly, only F-117As (with laser-guided bombs) and cruise missiles were employed against targets in the downtown area of the city [320]. As a result of the use of PGMs, along with the careful selection of strike aircraft, aimpoints, attack axes, attack timing, and rules of engagement, there probably were no more than 1,000 civilian fatalities during the air campaign [321]. Although Desert Storm set a new and more exacting standard, all previous U.S. bombing campaigns and operations also have been subject to limits on collateral damage [322]. For the same moral and political reasons, these limits will apply in the future. With its precision-strike capability, the B-2 is entirely compatible with policy guidance to keep noncombatant losses to a minimum.

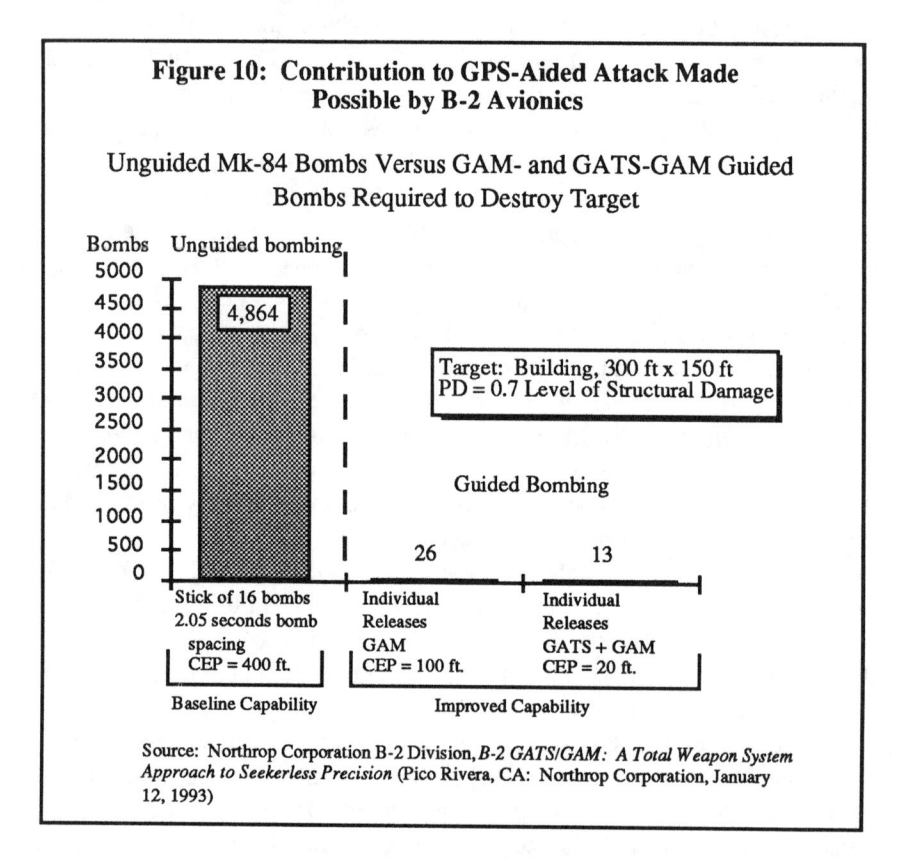

Figure 10: Contribution to GPS-Aided Attack Made Possible by B-2 Avionics

Unguided Mk-84 Bombs Versus GAM- and GATS-GAM Guided Bombs Required to Destroy Target

Bombs	Unguided bombing		
4,864		26	13
Stick of 16 bombs 2.05 seconds bomb spacing CEP = 400 ft.	Individual Releases GAM CEP = 100 ft.	Individual Releases GATS + GAM CEP = 20 ft.	
Baseline Capability	Improved Capability		

Target: Building, 300 ft x 150 ft
PD = 0.7 Level of Structural Damage

Guided Bombing

Source: Northrop Corporation B-2 Division, *B-2 GATS/GAM: A Total Weapon System Approach to Seekerless Precision* (Pico Rivera, CA: Northrop Corporation, January 12, 1993).

The cost of the B-2, in sum, buys a combat aircraft with a singular combination of range, payload, speed, stealth, and lethality. Quantitative insights into the cost-effectiveness of the B-2 can be obtained through comparison of the B-2 with alternative systems in terms of these traits. While the B-2 is impressive in each dimension that defines a heavy bomber, the true military value of the aircraft depends on the missions it can perform, missions that capitalize on its key attributes. Historical experience and contemporary operational doctrine provide an even more complete basis for cost-effectiveness analysis.

Chapter 8   173

Potential Applications of the B-2

Raids to Punish or Disarm Adversaries

The April 1986 U.S. attack on Libya and the January and June 1993 U.S. and allied strikes against Iraq exemplify the kind of punitive raid a B-2 force might mount. In the operation against Libya (code-named "El Dorado Canyon"), Air Force and Navy strike aircraft hit a set of five targets in retaliation for a series of terrorist acts supported by Libya's ruler, Col. Muammar Qaddafi [323]. Three targets were located in the Tripoli area: an army barracks that was both a command center for terrorist activities and one of Qaddafi's residences; a complex for training naval commandos; and a military airfield with transports used to aid terrorists. Benghazi, a city further to the east, was the location of the other targets: another airfield with air defense forces, and a barracks with both a terrorist training school and an alternate command center. The raid damaged all five targets and "may have helped break the cycle of accelerating Middle Eastern terrorism" [324].

One hundred and nineteen aircraft participated in the operation against Libya [325]. Eighteen F-111F strike aircraft, three EF-111A electronic-warfare aircraft, and 28 KC-10 and KC-135 tankers flew 5,000-nm, 14-hour round-trip missions from bases in Britain. Air wings from two carrier battle groups in the Mediterranean provided 14 A-6E attack aircraft, along with other aircraft that supported the A-6 as well as the F-111 strikes. These support aircraft included EA-6Bs for jamming air defense radars and communications, A-7Es and F/A-18s for attacking SAM sites, F-14s and other F/A-18s for shooting down enemy interceptors, and E-2Cs for warning and command and control. In contrast to the strike packages actually used, just six B-2s based in CONUS, supported by the same number of tankers, could have carried out the El Dorado Canyon raid [326].

The potential advantage of a CONUS-based force of intercontinental-range B-2s is indicated by the unwillingness of some U.S. allies (France, Spain, Italy, and Greece) to grant base access or overflight rights to aid the attack on Libya. France's denial of overflight rights forced the aircraft launched from Britain to fly a route around the Iberian peninsula that doubled their transit distance. Spanish officials said U.S. aircraft could overfly their territory, provided Washington did not request permission, "their theory being that if anything untoward happened they could deny participation" [327]. Receiving this response, the United States decided to avoid Spanish airspace. Hard to detect by friendly as well hostile radars, the stealthy B-2 might offer both the U.S. government and wary allies a better cloak of plausible deniability, easing overflight problems. In many cases, the long range of the B-2 might eliminate them altogether.

Stealth also is a factor that accounts for the significantly smaller number of aircraft needed for a Libya-type raid by B-2s. The targets in Libya were protected by radar-based defenses with SAMs, antiaircraft artillery (AAA), and fighter aircraft. Post-strike analyses pointed out that only three targets in the Warsaw Pact countries had thicker defenses than Tripoli and Benghazi [328]. A large percentage of the aircraft that took part in the attack struck enemy air defenses, not the five primary targets. The Air Force estimates that stealthy B-2s could have conducted the raid without the assistance of defense suppression aircraft or fighter escorts [329].

Lacking the benefits of stealth, the architects of El Dorado Canyon hoped to reduce the exposure of U.S. combat aircraft to Libyan air defenses by planning a "single-pass raid" in which all primary targets would be hit at the same time and at night. Attacking in successive waves would have been running the gauntlet more than once and flying against alerted air defenses. The firepower of the night-capable A-6Es in the two carrier air wings was judged insufficient to strike all targets simultaneously and inflict the requisite levels of damage. This was one of the reasons the F-111Fs from Britain were added to the attack [330].

Six low-observable B-2s, each with a 40,000-pound payload, in a single-wave night raid could have delivered an aggregate bomb tonnage similar to that carried by all 32 A-6Es and F-111Fs [331]. And like these aircraft, B-2s could have carried the mix of precision-guided weapons, unguided bombs, and cluster munitions most capable of producing the required target damage. Use of the F-111Fs also was intended to increase the likelihood of surprise. As Admiral William Crowe, then Chairman of the Joint Chiefs of Staff, has explained, "We knew the Libyans would expect an attack to come from the carriers, and the fleet was deployed too far to the east easily to strike at Tripoli. Undoubtedly they would have early warning of any carrier strike. But we did not believe they would be expecting us to fly through the Strait of Gibraltar" (the flight path of the F-111Fs and EF-111s) [332]. The range (and speed) of a B-2 force likewise would have given it the ability to strike suddenly, from CONUS or remote bases, along an unexpected attack axis.

El Dorado Canyon was designed to cause "maximum visible damage," while minimizing both U.S. losses and collateral damage [333]. Although only one F-111F with two airmen was lost, 84 combat aircraft and 134 crew members were at risk. A comparable raid by six B-2s, refueled by six tankers, would have risked 90 percent fewer personnel, due to the stealth and large payload of the bomber [334]. The availability of B-2s also might have made it possible to attack some potential targets (e.g., oil facilities) that planners had rejected because their destruction would entail repeated strikes [335]. The strikes on

Tripoli and Benghazi unintentionally damaged several civilian structures and killed fewer than 30 civilians. Targets were difficult to hit cleanly because of their location in or near populated areas [336]. The precision-strike capabilities of the B-2 would have been valuable for bombing these targets and limiting collateral damage. In addition, B-2s, with their low observability and capacity to loiter in target areas, might have been assigned "military and intelligence targets in the center of Tripoli" that were not struck because pinpointing them would have required the nonstealthy F-111Fs to "linger for more time than [was] deemed wise" [337].

More recently, strikes against Iraq, almost seven years after El Dorado Canyon and nearly two years after Desert Storm, were prompted by Baghdad's flouting of various resolutions of the United Nations (U.N.) [338]. Iraqi violations included disregard for no-fly zones, attempts to ban flights by U.N. weapons inspectors, and incursions into Kuwait. Coalition air power still deployed in the theater was used to enforce U.N. mandates. In January 1993, nearly 40 U.S. and allied strike aircraft, supported by some 70 other aircraft, delivered guided and unguided weapons against four hardened air defense command-and-control centers and four mobile SAM batteries in the no-fly zone covering southern Iraq. A few days later, some of these targets were restruck and additional strikes were launched against air defense sites in the no-fly zone in northern Iraq. In between these raids, four Navy ships stationed in the region fired 45 Tomahawk cruise missiles against seven buildings in an industrial complex that had played a part in the Iraqi nuclear weapons program. Overall, the air strikes and cruise missile attacks resulted in significant damage to a number of targets and encouraged Iraqi acquiescence to some U.N. demands.

Given its advantages in stealth, payload, and lethality, a B-2 force could have executed comparable attacks with fewer aircraft and fewer sorties. A B-2 raid could have been launched from CONUS. The low observability of the B-2 combined with the accuracy of JDAM or eventually the range, stealth, and accuracy of a TSSAM class munition would have been valuable in destroying the air defense targets. And the several buildings within the nuclear weapons-related facility would have been appropriate targets for B-2-delivered JDAM bombs.

A preventive raid would be a means of defanging belligerent, unstable, and outlaw regimes with nuclear, biological, or chemical (NBC) weapon capabilities. More than two dozen countries have or are working to acquire weapons of mass destruction and their means of delivery. Many of them (e.g., Iraq, Iran, North Korea, Libya) are hostile to the United States or its friends. Their NBC capabilities are potential threats to U.S. overseas interests, forces, and allies, and eventually may endanger the United States itself [339]. Under certain circumstances, one of these threats may prove intolerable. Diplomacy, sanctions, and defenses may not adequately lessen the danger. Air strikes against research centers, production facilities, storage sites, air bases, or missile launchers then might be the preferred or only option for stopping a determined antagonist from acquiring, brandishing, or using weapons of mass destruction.

The model for a preventive raid is the June 1981 Israeli attack on the Baghdad Nuclear Research Center, an operation in which eight F-16s escorted by six F-15 fighters bombed the Osirak reactor and set the Iraqi nuclear weapons program back several years [340]. Although the United States has never taken similar action, preventive attack to deny an enemy weapons of mass destruction has been contemplated in the past. During the late 1940s and early 1950s, government officials considered the possibility of an aerial first strike (really a preventive war) that would rob the Soviet Union of its nuclear potential [341]. In the early 1960s, members of the Kennedy and Johnson Administrations thought of taking military steps to keep Mao's China from getting nuclear weapons [342]. In the late 1980s, U.S. officials refused to exclude the use of force to shut down the Libyan chemical weapons plant at Rabta [343]. More recently, there were suggestions that air strikes against North Korean nuclear facilities might be necessary to stop Pyongyang from becoming a nuclear power [344]. Thus, it is quite plausible that in the future, U.S. air power, even in the absence of broader hostilities, could be called on to destroy the NBC capabilities of an opponent.

The key attributes of the B-2 would meet the likely requirements of a preventive attack to roll back the spread of weapons of mass destruction. The "distant presence" projected by B-2s standing ready at CONUS bases might lend muscle to diplomatic efforts to convince dangerous states to abandon their most menacing NBC-related activities. Were time critical, the speed and range of the B-2 would enable quick military action. (Recall that in the Cuban missile crisis, advisers to President Kennedy urged prompt air strikes to eliminate the Soviet missiles before they became operational.) It is also possible that a sudden attack would thwart countermeasures by the opposing party (e.g., schemes to relocate critical equipment from targeted facilities before they were hit) [345].

In many, if not most, cases, U.S. plans for a preventive raid would generate controversy, perhaps including opposition from allied governments. Any resulting denial of base access or overflight rights would have little or no impact on the global reach of CONUS-based B-2s. The stealth of the B-2 might allow some countries to wink at flights through their airspace. Stealth also would lessen the need for a large complement of defense suppression aircraft and reduce the number of airmen that might be killed or captured.

As with its stealthiness, the large payload of the B-2 would permit designated target sets to be attacked with fewer aircraft. PGMs in the B-2 bomb bays would be essential for destroying NBC targets efficiently and without causing excessive collateral damage. In the Gulf War, NBC and ballistic missile facilities were prominent among the scores of targets struck by laser-guided bombs from F-117As [346]. To take out eight well-defended and very hard chemical weapon bunkers near Baghdad, more than 50 F-117A sorties were necessary. Destruction of each bunker required the delivery of two case-hardened, laser-guided, 2,000-pound bombs: one to breach the structure, with a second following right behind to finish the job. Just two B-2s, each with eight large penetrating weapons, could have accomplished the same task [347]. Precise delivery of appropriate munitions, and careful timing of attacks, also were important to prevent the widespread dispersal of lethal substances (e.g., anthrax bacteria) [348]. With their on-board sensors, loiter ability, and PGMs, B-2s could strike aimpoints at NBC sites with great accuracy. (Further reduction in the risk of collateral damage from dispersed agents or radioactive material would call for new, specialized munitions.)

Against some adversaries with large-scale and partially concealed NBC and missile programs, an air operation larger and longer than a raid would be needed to wipe out threatening weapon facilities and delivery vehicles. Between the first and last days of the six-week air campaign against Iraq, several hundred sorties were allocated to the destruction of NBC targets [349]. Despite this level of effort, some production equipment and stockpiles of weapons were not attacked, due, in part, to inadequate intelligence, rather than poorly planned or executed strikes [350]. Iraqi mobile Scud missiles, once dispersed, also proved elusive targets. Over 2,500 sorties were devoted to the "Great Scud Hunt." Yet few, if any, mobile launchers were destroyed, partly because of difficulties in acquiring intelligence and distributing targeting data. In the future, if current research and development efforts yield improved targeting capabilities, B-2 on-board sensors would be supported by off-board, near-real-time data from a network integrating multiple surveillance sensors (satellites, aerial drones, manned aircraft, and ground-based systems) with intelligence processing and strike planning centers for quickly detecting and locating mobile missiles [351]. The long range, loiter time, high-altitude survivability (for good field of view), stealth (for tactical surprise), and large payload of the B-2 all would be advantageous in hunting mobile missiles.

Air Interdiction Attacks to Halt a Ground Offensive

Capabilities for rapidly projecting substantial military power over long distances to overseas flash points and war zones are essential for the defense of U.S. security interests in Southwest Asia, the Far East, Europe, and elsewhere. The end of the half-century Cold War and the increased importance of assorted ongoing and potential regional conflicts add new uncertainties to U.S. defense planning. As in the case of Iraq's seizure of Kuwait, the place, time, and circumstances of armed regional aggression demanding a U.S. military response will be difficult to predict much in advance or with great accuracy. Even with warning, the United States and its allies may be slow to react. Evidence of attack preparations may appear ambiguous, there may be an early reluctance to get involved, some may hope the crisis will pass, and too much faith may be placed in diplomatic solutions. These problems are compounded by the post-Cold War drawdown and pullback of U.S. military power.

Because of reductions in force structure and a retraction of forces from forward deployments, fewer ground force divisions, carrier battle groups, and land-based air wings will be available to cover a wider range of contingencies. Hostile forces consequently may have geographic and local numerical advantages that give them the initiative. U.S. land-based fighters and attack aircraft would take days to deploy to a distant theater. Light ground forces (e.g., elements of the 82nd Airborne Division) also could be deployed in a matter of days. The transit time for carriers and other warships would be measured in days to weeks. Heavy armored and mechanized units would not arrive in force for weeks or months. The ground forces and tactical air forces, furthermore, would depend on an in-theater infrastructure (e.g., bases, airfields, supply depots) that, at least at first, might be absent, inadequate, or at risk. Unlike other forces, heavy bombers could reach the theater within a day, and from CONUS bases.

In light of the above, there will be wars in which air power initially is the principal or only means of countering a ground offensive against a weaker U.S. ally. During the first several weeks of Desert Shield (the buildup of Coalition forces prior to Desert Storm), there was a "window of vulnerability" in which U.S. and allied ground forces would have been insufficient to defeat an Iraqi invasion of Saudi Arabia. In this initial phase of the confrontation, the U.S. theater commander "considered air power crucial to [his plans for] delaying an Iraqi attack" until adequate reinforcements of heavy armored and mechanized forces arrived by sea [352]. Similarly, in the early stages of a future conflict, heavy bombers could attack an advancing army to stop it from quickly capturing valuable allied territory or airfields and ports slated to receive subsequent deployments of combat aircraft, troops, armored vehicles, and warships.

The "distant presence" of the bomber force would be a factor in inhibiting military moves against U.S. allies. Were deterrence to fail, the ability of bombers to strike at long, even intercontinental, range would diminish the disadvantage of distance in operations against a far-off adversary on the march. The speed and range of bombers, joined with their striking power, would allow them to help in defending footholds for slower-moving surface forces and shorter-range, land-based attack aviation. Heavy bombers are well suited to the demands of the U.S. two-war strategy, which calls for military forces "sufficient to fight and win two nearly simultaneous major regional conflicts," Depending on the overall military situation, bombers could be allocated to one or both conflicts, or shifted between theaters as wartime needs or priorities changed. Employed in a strategic holding action, bombers, along with other combat aircraft and a limited ground force, might be used to contain one of these conflicts, while the bulk of U.S. forces secured victory in the other. Forces then could be shifted to finish the first fight [353].

As Table 5 shows, a future force of approximately 175 B-52H, B-1B, and B-2 bombers could deliver thousands of tons of ordnance in the first days of an enemy offensive. The 16 B-2s (primary aircraft authorized) currently programmed would make up only one-eleventh of this force and carry roughly the same proportion of its total bomb tonnage. If circumstances required, the bombers could operate from bases in the United States. Daily sortie rates would be relatively low, however, because of the long distances and flight times involved. Each bomber might fly no more than one sortie every other day. Though B-2s would provide only a small share of all sorties, the stealth of the aircraft would help make each sortie count. Repeated intercontinental missions by such a large force would stretch aerial refueling capabilities. The duration of these sorties would exhaust aircrews. Mission duration would directly reduce sortie rate. Consequently, an operation that relied exclusively on CONUS bases would be hard to sustain for more than a few days, unless an even lower sortie rate were adopted [354].

Deploying some or all of the bombers to bases nearer the theater would cut sortie length, lower tanker demand, decrease crew fatigue, increase sortie rate, and multiply the number of bombs delivered. It also would improve the ability of the aircraft to react to sudden changes on the battlefield. Part of the force might deploy as other bombers were conducting the initial strikes of the campaign. Even if bases were no closer than 2,000 nm from the target area, forward-deployed units could achieve a rate of one sortie per bomber per day. The value

Table 5: Conventional Firepower of the Future U.S. Bomber Force [355]

	CONUS Bases	Intermediate Bases	Regional Bases
Number of Bombers [1]	176	176	176
Range (nautical miles)	6,000	4,000	2,000
Sortie Duration (hours)	29	19	10
Sortie Rate Per Day	.41	.45	1.0
Bombers Across Target Per Day [2]	70	79	176
Bombs Delivered Per Day			
500-lb. Bombs [3]	4,800	5,420	12,080
2,000-lb. Bombs [4]	1,440	1,624	3,616

Notes: [1] The force of 176 aircraft assumes a total active inventory of 95 B-52Hs, 96 B-1Bs, and 20 B-2s. Of this total, a maximum of about 80 B-52Hs, 80 B-1Bs, and 16 B-2s would be available to theater commanders. These figures are drawn from the Air Force's 1992 Bomber Roadmap. [2] The number of each type of bomber was multiplied by the sortie rate per day. The products were rounded down to "whole aircraft" and totaled. [3] Bomb loads of 500-pound bombs—B-52H: 51; B-1B: 84; B-2: 80. [4] Bomb loads of 2,000-pound bombs—B-52H: 18; B-1B: 24; B-2: 16.

of forward bases was apparent in the Gulf War. As mentioned earlier, a handful of CONUS-based B-52Gs on the first night of the war flew 7,000 nm and back to launch conventional cruise missiles against Iraq. These were the only B-52G combat sorties flown from the United States. All other sorties originated from bases at four overseas locations: Diego Garcia; Moron, Spain; Fairford, England; and Jiddah, Saudi Arabia. Diego Garcia, Moron, and Fairford all were roughly 3,000 nm from targets in the theater. Round-trip missions lasted around 14 hours. B-52Gs at these bases had a daily sortie rate of .5. Bombers at Jiddah were approximately 1,000 nm from their targets. A round-trip took some five hours. With shorter flight distances and times, the B-52Gs in Saudi Arabia approached a rate of 1.3, nearly three times that for the bases located between the United States and the theater [356].

A variety of targets could be attacked to brake—or break—an offensive. Forces could be bombed in assembly areas, while moving, or in bivouac. Transportation chokepoints (e.g., bridges, tunnels) on avenues of approach also could be targeted to impede the enemy advance. Supply centers, convoys, and arteries could be struck to constrict the flow of combat essentials fueling the drive. B-2s would be fully capable of attacking all these targets with appropriate weapons (e.g., antiarmor submunitions against tank formations, PGMs against bridges, unguided bombs against large supply depots). In conflicts where the enemy was moving rapidly and friendly ground forces could not mount a strong defense, attacking maneuver units directly might be the only way to halt an offensive before it was too late. The effects from hitting chokepoints and interdicting supply lines probably would be temporary or delayed. Strikes on armored and mechanized columns would have an immediate payoff.

Analyses by the RAND Corporation indicate that B-2s operating from distant bases and loaded with antiarmor submunitions (e.g., Sensor Fuzed Weapons) could be effective in disrupting an armored advance [357]. Along with its high lethality, the low observability of the B-2 would be important to the success of air operations to prevent enemy forces from achieving quick victory at the outset of a conflict. As the leading edge of the U.S. military response, bombers would not require support from shorter-range defense-suppression aircraft. The stealthy B-2 would be much less vulnerable than other bombers to the mobile antiaircraft defenses accompanying hostile ground forces. In addition, stealth would make tactical surprise more likely. Denied warning of an air attack, an advancing unit would not be able to take steps to protect itself, without compromising its advance. As a result, "the unit would be in plain view on the road, aiding detection and identification, and easing the requirements on intelligence assets to predict the unit's exact location"; its "organic short-range defenses would not be alerted and would probably be ineffective"; and its "physical and psychological vulnerability would be increased, thus increasing the effectiveness of any ordnance delivered" [358]. In short, long range and high speed would bring B-2s to a far-off battle quickly; low observability would protect them against undamaged air defenses; large payload and high lethality would enable a relatively limited number to wreak havoc on an invading army; and the resulting disruption would buy time for later-arriving U.S. forces to deploy, reinforce friendly defenses, and eventually launch a counterattack.

B-2 Versus Aircraft Carrier Cost-Effectiveness

While the comparison between long-range, land-based bombers and carrier-borne attack aircraft imposes itself in several contexts, cost-effectiveness is an area in which it must be addressed directly. The B-2 program is often criticized as being an unreasonably expensive approach to fielding power projection capability. By comparing the B-2 with the far more expensive, yet far more popularly accepted, large-deck aircraft carrier programs of the Navy, one introduces a rational standard of comparison. One also addresses a very real political question about the appropriate direction of defense investment, because even as advocates of long-range air power are building a rationale for greater numbers of B-2s, students of sea power are questioning the future utility of large-deck aircraft carriers as the basis for extending the reach of U.S. power to land targets.

> Although some scenarios may make it necessary or desirable to use carrier aircraft to strike targets ashore—as in the case of lightly defended, mobile objectives for which precise targeting is unavailable—today's carriers and aircraft far exceed the size, complexity, and cost needed or justified by this mission. And ultimately, the risk of taking a carrier battle group or any other group of ships without support of land-based aircraft within launch range of a significant land mass occupied by a power in possession of a large, modern military must be considered carefully and cautiously [359].

While comparing a B-2 to an aircraft carrier may on the surface appear to be stretching a point, the Gulf War illustrated how close B-2 operational capability may, on any given day, come to that of a carrier battle group. Navy testimony to the HASC on April 10, 1991, stressed the importance of carrier-based aviation by describing the air strike launched jointly from the Kennedy and the Saratoga on January 17, 1991, the first day of the air war. The two carriers launched a combined strike package of 60 aircraft on a 1,341-mile mission to bomb an airfield 40 miles west of Baghdad. Of these aircraft, only eight A-6s actually delivered bombs, a total of 32 2,000 lb. laser-guided bombs [360]. This is precisely the payload of two B-2s; one B-2 could have delivered the bombs on target of each carrier. On a day-to-day basis a B-2 would not necessarily match the bombing productivity of a carrier air wing within range of its targets, but, assuming B-2 basing in or near the theater, the ratio is close, and, even with B-2s operating from the United States, it has been maintained that eight B-2s could deliver the bombs on target of an entire deployed carrier air wing [361]. Assuming logical forward basing—within or near the theater but well beyond range of enemy action—a quantitative analyst should be able to build a convincing argument that five B-2s would yield superior power projection effectiveness in future conflicts to one Carrier Battle Group.

A Navy critic of carrier aviation's contribution in the Gulf war corroborated the general tenor of these observations in these words:

> Despite the use of six aircraft carriers—with crews totaling more than 30,000 men—accompanied by extensive cruiser, destroyer, and frigate escorts, postwar analysis in Riyadh confirmed that the carrier aviation contribution to the air campaign was minor compared to that of land-based air forces [362].

Aggregating the costs of military capabilities into coherent weapons-system-like programs is not easy or necessarily precise. This is particularly true in the case of the Navy's Carrier Battle Group (CVBG). Yet, because of the scale of costs and benefits involved, this is a particularly useful cost-benefit comparison to make with the B-2 program. Each carrier and the aircraft it can launch are bought separately, as are the escorts and support ships that protect it and ensure its logistic sustenance. There is even a proportional share of an Underway Replenishment Group of ships that shuttle from the carrier's tactical location to distant supply points. The fact that advocacy for these assets can be spread across a relatively large number of individually small (in the defense authorization and appropriations context) programs skews budgetary judgments in their favor. A conservative cost estimate for a Carrier Battle Group was assembled a few years ago by the Congressional Research Service. It began with a single nuclear carrier procured for $3.2 billion (today close to $5 billion) [363], added to it the $5 billion cost of the embarked carrier air wing, then added the cost of the nine ships (of five different types) making up the Carrier Battle Group, and the logistic helicopters to link the ships for a sub-total of $14.8 billion. A two-thirds share of helicopters and seven more ships in the Underway Replenishment Group brought the procurement total for one carrier battle group to $16.5 billion. 30-year life-cycle costs for the CVBG were estimated then to approach $40.8 billion [364]. Inflated to FY93 dollars the 30-year life cycle cost of a single CVBG is around $57 billion [365]. This is very close to Northrop's estimate of 30-year life cycle costs of the initial 20-aircraft B-2 program, $62.1 billion [366]. Northrop Grumman's estimate of the 30-year cost of 20 additional B-2s is about $20 billion in FY 1995 dollars. Considering that the "Bottom-Up Review" calls for maintaining 11 active carriers plus a training carrier for the foreseeable future [367], this comparison clearly favors the B-2 program as a cost-effective approach to projecting power.

More recently the GAO undertook its own cost study of the costs of U.S. Navy carrier battle groups. This GAO study calculated costs in terms of annualized total costs based on a 50-year service life for the carrier and 30 years for the aircraft involved. The GAO concluded that the annualized cost of a notional carrier battle group was $1,485 (FY1990) millions [368]. Applying the same GAO direct cost accounting technique, Northrop calculates the average cost of each B-2 aircraft per year to be $96 (FY1993) millions [369]. Applying a deflator approximating DoD guidance to correct FY1990 figures to FY1993, one finds that the life cycle cost of one CVBG equals about the cost of 17 B-2's of the original 20-aircraft program [370]. The B-2's advantage increases when one considers expanding B-2 production beyond twenty aircraft. If one were to anticipate continued B-2 production to a total force of 60 aircraft, the B-2 costs per aircraft would decrease raising this ratio to over 26 bombers per CVBG.

Comparing the cost-effectiveness of complex, multi-role weapon systems is an inexact science. Yet, for attacking the full range of ground targets, it is apparent that a relatively small number of B-2's—somewhere in the range of one to eight—should be able to put the firepower on target of a CVBG. At the same time it is clear that many B-2's—as many as 17 to 26—could be bought and operated for the cost of a CVBG. As imprecise as they may be, these observations go far toward validating the B-2 as a cost-effective power projection system when compared to perhaps the most generally accepted power projection alternative of recent decades.

B-2 Production Cost-Effectiveness

While comparative combat effectiveness with alternative combat systems is an important part of understanding the utility of producing additional B-2s, the other side of the issue is the feasibility of extending B-2 and what it is likely to cost. The $44 billion cost of the pilot production run of 20 B-2 aircraft represents far more than the cost of production of 20 aircraft. It includes the scientific work that brought the nation's understanding of stealth technology, composite structures, production techniques for composite structures, and other associated technologies to the level where they could support the design of an operational aircraft. It includes the design and construction of production and ground testing facilities sufficiently capable to produce a large number of aircraft (at least the 132 originally specified) at a Cold War rate of three per month. It includes flight and static testing to prove the operational suitability and integrity of the B-2 design. It further includes the development of maintenance and operational procedures, tools and equipment, training sequences and aids, and the design of support facilities. Many alternative weapon system designs often compared with the B-2 in terms of overall program costs do not include these cost elements but inherit their benefit from earlier programs or count on the customer accomplishing them after aircraft delivery. For example, the F-117A is a product of technology developed under a project called Have Blue. Have Blue prototypes flew and completed their stealth testing under a program kept fiscally separate from the F-117A. The costs of that program were thus never attributed to the operational aircraft. Full B-2 program costs, however are integrally associated with the first twenty operational aircraft.

Production Decision Context

The usual business logic would say that sunk costs should be written off and not enter into a business decision. This may well be true, unless that decision implies that similar or greater start-up costs will be required for some alternative system down stream [371]. This exception is much the case with the B-2. If the nation decides that it will never again require a strike vehicle with global range, the sunk costs of B-2 can be written off. If, as is much more likely, there is a high probability that the nation will at some time in the future require a long-range conventional attack vehicle with range to match the nation's globe-spanning interests, then the investment already made in the nation's B-2 production capacity becomes an important basis for building whatever bomber force structure the Administration and Congress determine necessary in the long run.

Insuring that the United States protects the opportunity to profit from the investment associated with the initial twenty B-2s is critically important. Even though the last of the initial twenty B-2s will not be completed for several years, the capability to produce more B-2s is beginning to decline long before. Some subcontractors have completed their B-2 work and are already having to turn to other endeavors. Skills and production techniques necessary for the most efficient production of additional B-2s will progressively disperse. Boeing, for example, employed roughly 8,000 people to work on the B-2. As early as 1992 Boeing announced plans to eliminate 6,500 jobs, many a result of B-2 cutbacks [372]. Determining the dollar costs of a future decision to build additional B-2s would essentially be in terms of a dollar cost per aircraft to produce each additional bomber, if it were not for the question of the relationship between the timing of a new production decision and the stage of decline then existing in Northrop's production capacity. With the passage of time, restarting production becomes more expensive. This factor becomes increasingly significant to the unit price of additional B-2 production.

Maturity of Production Capability

Whenever the Administration and Congress decide that additional B-2 production is needed, pricing will reflect Government and Northrop Grumman decisions about rate of production, continuity of production; estimates of the costs of production factors during the period of production; and the return Northrop Grumman and its suppliers need to stay in business. A major contributor to a decision to produce more B-2s will be the maturity shown by the program to date, maturity being an indicator of the reliability with which the contractor team can produce the requisite quality and quantity of aircraft at an agreed upon price.

Several measures of manufacturing maturity are available. The percentage of major subcomponents that arrive at final assembly without requiring further work is one. In Air Vehicle 1, the first B-2, fully 50% of the components arriving at the final assembly facility required additional work. By Air Vehicle 11, 99% of components were arriving with no further work required [373]. Hands-on "touch" labor efficiency, the efficiency of direct assembly workers, is another measure. In calendar year 1991, "touch" labor efficiency increased 350%. Air Vehicle 11 will be assembled in less than half the hours required for Air Vehicle 1 [374].

The B-2 testing program is also manifesting a level of maturity unusual for complex combat aircraft. The structural ground test program was completed in December 1992 when a full-scale airframe finally "broke" at 1.6 times the maximum stress that should ever be sustained in flight. The test airframe had previously been subjected to three "ultimate load" tests to the design target of 150% of maximum design flight loads before the final planned structural failure test [375]. Refining the B-2's stealth characteristics has also progressed with singular efficiency. Radar signature anomalies detected in testing in the summer of 1991 were the subject of an intense review which resulted in an announcement by the Secretary of the Air Force that refinements in edge and surface treatments had brought the B-2's radar signature within design goals. Intense monitoring of low-observable characteristics required for successful mission performance under B-2 System Maturity Matrix milestones has shown B-2 to be as stealthy as it is required to be in all respects [376]. Indeed FY 1993 System Maturity Matrix Milestones were met well ahead of schedule [377]. These indicators of design and manufacturing maturity indicate a high likelihood that additional B-2s beyond the initial twenty would be both effective and would be reliably producible at the agreed upon price. Indeed, Northrop Grumman company officials have said in 1994 that they were willing to take a fixed-price production contract.

B-2 Operational Efficiencies

Beyond "sticker price" a decision to produce additional B-2's should reflect confidence that the B-2 is an operationally efficient system. In the past technologically advanced systems have often survived initial testing only to manifest operations and maintenance complexities that added so much to the cost of the system that it compromised long-term utility. Inefficiently small production runs have tended to magnify such problems. The four operational long-range bomber and reconnaissance types of aircraft produced in the smallest quantities (B-58 [116], B-1B [100], FB-111A [76], and the SR-71 [32]) were particularly affected by operations and maintenance costs. Most recently the SR-71 was retired long before its operational utility was exhausted because it cost so much to operate. (Congress directed in 1994 that the SR-71 Blackbird be reactivated to resume its high-level reconnaissance missions until the time that the high-endurance unmanned aerial vehicles are proven and in inventory.) Then-Major General Stephen B. Croker, former Director of Strategic, Special Operations, and Airlift Systems, Office of the Secretary of the Air Force, and then-Provisional Commander of Air Force Air Combat Command, expressed his perception of the relevance of the linkage between force numbers and service life when, in reference to a hypothetical fifteen-aircraft fleet of B-2's, he predicted that "...the aircraft surviving from a fleet that size would be in museums after 'five, six, seven years—only a portion of its designed 40-year service life—because it would prove too expensive to operate in small numbers" [378].

The currently authorized B-2 fleet is larger, and the issue being addressed here is increased production that would gradually result in a B-2 fleet that matches the strategic demand of a United States preparing for defense challenges of the next century. Yet, operational costs need to be addressed if such additional production is to be successfully advocated.

Early in the design of the B-2, the Air Force and Northrop focused considerable effort on reliability and maintainability of the B-2 aircraft. The results of this effort are already apparent. As early as last fall B-2s, in the flight testing program were exceeding Air Force "mean flying hours between unscheduled maintenance" standards by 80%. Progress in the test cycle to date indicated that by the time the B-2 fleet had logged 100,000 cumulative flying hours, only 32 hours of maintenance time would be required per aircraft flight hour. This exceeds the Air Force standard for the mature aircraft of 50 hours, and Northrop's own design goal of 44.7 hours [379]. As a result of ease of maintenance, reliability of electronic components, low fuel consumption, long engine life, and the unexpected ease with which the low-observable characteristics of the B-2's exterior surfaces can be maintained [380], B-2 operations are going to be far less costly than expected for a large modern aircraft.

Lessons learned from earlier large bomber aircraft are being applied in other support areas. Facilities being built for the B-2 at its operational base, Whiteman AFB, Missouri, are designed to further increase maintenance manpower efficiency as well as the safety of B-2 operations. A "Single Integrated Aircrew and Maintenance Training System" systematically integrates advanced simulators, training mock-ups, and carefully planned academics into a training program which ensures that personnel make the most of B-2 training flight hours. These and other components of the B-2 program manifest an advanced state of maturity indicative both of early operational utility for the twenty B-2s now being produced and cost-effective operations for any follow-on aircraft that are eventually authorized.

Chapter 9
Conclusion: The Question of Numbers

Regardless of how one approaches the question of the strategic utility of the B-2 weapon system, the issue comes down to one of force numbers. Buy enough B-2s to constitute a broadly operational force, and the system becomes strategically significant; stop the program at twenty, and it remains a highly successful demonstration of national technological prowess, but of limited strategic relevance. Nor is the strategic utility of the B-2 a question of alternative weapons systems; the B-2 is becoming the only U.S. long-range, conventional strike asset, as older bombers are retired and aircraft carriers and the medium-range attack aircraft aboard them decline in number and are rededicated to shorter-range littoral missions. Other shorter-range U.S. weapons systems are increasingly constrained in their effective employment by ever-more-restrictive host nation preconditions for U.S. access and basing. There is no new aircraft design that could perform the long-range strike mission better, and no more capable design concept is on the horizon. Yet, whatever qualitative advantages the B-2 possesses, as the only modern long-range, land-based bomber likely to exist beyond the immediate future, the B-2's strategic utility is extremely sensitive to decisions about force size. In the case of the B-2, quantity clearly does have a quality all its own.

Because the future strategic utility of the B-2 is intimately linked to force size, addressing the question of the B-2s strategic utility is only relevant if there is a powerful rationale for building more B-2s, and the Administration and Congress decide that it is time to address this issue. What can this study offer in the way of insights into why this issue is likely to be addressed, particularly now? Why should B-2 production be extended? And how many should be produced?

Reopen the B-2 Production Issue?

Congressional Views

Congressional reluctance to fund the original full B-2 program, and the decision to complete only twenty aircraft, reflected the perception that, with the end of the Cold War, defense spending and forces should be reduced drastically and restructured to reflect new defense needs. The original B-2 program was a high-cost program quite rightly targeted as a part of the post-Cold War defense drawdown. Now, though, the defense drawdown is well underway. In fact it has developed such momentum that, as the anything-but-peaceful nature of the new international security environment makes itself more apparent, the absence of agreed minimum acceptable force levels risks becoming a decided political liability for those responsible. The administration and more and more members of the Congress are increasingly attentive to where the drawdown should level-off and what the new U.S. armed forces should look like. With this new focus, both those Congressmen most concerned about maintaining a strong national defense, and those most insistent on attaining new standards of efficiency in defense-related investment should begin to see the B-2 program in a new, more favorable light. The B-2's technical uncertainties and development costs are in the past; the ability of the Air Force and the manufacturer to control production and operations and maintenance costs have been demonstrated; testing of the B-2 has proceeded with almost unprecedented smoothness; operational effectiveness of stealthy attack has been proven in combat; and no effective counters to the B-2 are evident on the horizon. These observations make an increased buy of B-2s a highly competitive alternative as the Congress and the administration work to shape a force structure for tomorrow which is potent enough to match the challenges that lie ahead and efficient enough to conform to, indeed to help enable, low defense budget levels.

The International Security Environment

The Congress and Clinton Administration are confronted by an international security environment that is far from settled. Making specific predictions of conflicts and roles the United States may choose to play in them is futile. But, making prudent observations about this environment, the leadership that the United States will insist on exerting (and that the international community increasingly insists that the United States exert), and the implications these have for U.S. military force structure needs is entirely possible. There is a remarkable continuity in goals and methods of statecraft. Absent the bipolar discipline imposed by the Cold War, regional and local instability is increasing, even in once-stable Europe. The potential for violence on the part of those who seek to overturn the established order is vastly increased by the Cold War legacy of weapons technologies which are now proliferating among developing countries. The spread of ballistic missile technology coupled with nuclear, chemical, and biological capabilities makes even distant conflicts dangerous and widens the range of their influence.

At the same time that the United States is reducing its military presence abroad, it is determined to protect interests that span the globe and play a world leadership role as the sole remaining superpower. While much U.S. influence can be exerted through economic, diplomatic, and cultural instruments of national power, the likelihood that the United States will be required to back up its leadership with military power is as great as it has ever been. Since the Berlin wall fell, the United States: has felt itself obliged to forge a broadly-based coalition and fight for Kuwait; has been torn by uncertainty over the proper course of action with respect to Bosnia; and has had to confront a presumably nuclear-armed North Korea. Classes of "trigger" events likely to convince the United States to fight, far from being in remission, appear as likely as ever.

Whether conflicts eventually materialize at the great or superpower level, or whether they are presented by regional aggressors or only involve providing a military cover for humanitarian assistance amid political turmoil, they suggest that the United States possess sufficient long-range strike capability to undergird national aims in a dangerous world. The 1993 DoD "Bottom-Up Review" appeared to recognize this problem. It neatly laid out the problems of the new security environment—including: dangers from proliferation of weapons of mass destruction; threats of aggression by major regional powers; and risks of a return to authoritarian government in the former Soviet Union. It also called for the capability to win two nearly simultaneous major regional conflicts. However, it did not call for more than 20 B-2s to contend with these threats, claiming that the capable though tiny force could be "dual-tasked" to fight both wars. [381] Senator Kent Conrad (D-ND) has given voice to this concern about the failure of the "Bottom-Up Review" to deal with its inconsistency between bomber requirements and proposed force structure. Senator Conrad diagrammed a shortage of 58 bombers in FY 95 to meet the Bottom-Up Review's own 184 bomber requirement [382]. The continuing requirement for long-range bombers will gradually force itself on the Congress and administration as patterns of U.S. success and failure in this new security environment emerge as lessons which cannot be ignored. Renewed interest in determining appropriate B-2 force structure cannot help but be fueled by such lessons. The central question remaining with respect to the B-2 program and the international security environment involves whether the U.S. Government has learned enough from post-Cold War strife already to recognize the future need for B-2-class long-range strike systems. Otherwise, it will have to subject itself to further painful lessons as future conflicts are confrontational with less than adequate modern long-range bomber forces.

American Attitudes toward the Long-Range Bomber

As the intensely political decisions are made about focusing national resources on alternative defense investments, the Congress and the Clinton Administration cannot avoid keeping an eye on popular attitudes about the alternatives under consideration. It is easy to go back to World War II and the beginning of the Cold War to document the broad support of the American people for the selection of a strategy and the building of force structure heavily reliant on the long-range, land-based bomber. The bomber has been characteristically supported as the chosen vehicle for marshaling the best of American talents and industry and directing them along a vector uniquely capable of carrying the war to the enemy homeland.

This preference for the bomber option is reflected just as strongly in the post-Cold War period. Exceptional consensus over the appropriateness of a sustained bombing campaign, whether in isolation or as a preparation for a land campaign, was a consistent theme in the policy debates preceding and accompanying DESERT SHIELD and preceding DESERT STORM. The strength of this support for bombing was all the more impressive since it predated the combat demonstration of bombing accuracies and effectiveness claimed for the new generation of U.S. air power, which included stealth for the first time. When the Gulf War bombing campaign achieved its objectives, even meeting air power advocates' most enthusiastic claims, and then was able to document its effectiveness in terms of the low casualty rate among Coalition ground forces and the brevity of the 100-hour land campaign that followed, the utility and acceptability of modern American air power received an impetus of historic proportions.

Debates surrounding alternative actions suitable for U.S. involvement in Bosnia and other parts of the former Yugoslavia demonstrate that this enthusiasm about aerial bombardment as a tactic of choice is alive and well among the American people. Defense decision-makers are obliged to enter this public enthusiasm into their calculus of appropriate force structures in response to future U.S. defense needs. As the current technological leading edge of U.S. attack aviation, the most stealthy aircraft ever designed, and the only contemporary aircraft design capable of ensuring that the United States has any long-range bombing capability beyond retirement of the B-52 and B-1, extension of the B-2 program is a compelling alternative. For the American public to awake one morning to a new, perhaps unanticipated conflict and find that it no longer has a modern, long-range, land-based bomber option would be a disturbing day indeed for the nation.

Combat Effectiveness of the Modern Long-Range, Land-Based Bomber

While policy and political acceptability of alternative defense investments are important, the ultimate standard is combat. Given the range of conflicts deemed possible, how does a particular force structure stack up in terms of being able to accomplish that which the nation demands of it? Consideration of the modern long-range, land-based bomber across a series of important principles serves to order judgments about the contribution the B-2 will provide, to make the United States capable of deterring those wars it can deter, and to permit to win those wars it must win. Being sufficient in number is near the top of this list of principles [383]. Despite being "maneuver forces" *par excellence*, airplanes achieve operational and strategic success by attrition, target by target and airplane by airplane.

Other principles are similarly important to creating combat potential. Diversity sufficient to respond to a wide range of conflicts ensures that the nation will not be out-flanked because the dimensions of a conflict were not accurately anticipated. Modern forces, particularly for the United States, apply the nation's technological advantages to enhance material investment in building effective military forces. The ability to apply power quickly generates the potential for parrying the *fait accompli*. It has added value in a functioning democracy to compensate for a lengthy decision process by providing the military ability to move quickly and effectively once the political decision to go to war is made. Adaptability to any threat geography is essential for a nation with global interests and the vocation of superpower. Given the value of the investment represented by modern weapon systems, it is important that they be logistically supportable for peak operational tempos. Surprise being a recurring theme in warfare, it is important that forces be able to generate, cope with, and dampen surprise effect. In order to achieve decision it is important that weapons be capable of focusing a maximum potential of military power in order to produce an intense military effect, and that such power be able to reach the enemy's "center of gravity." Another condition for success is flexibility sufficient both to accomplish missions at the selected level of violence and to be adaptable to missions and levels of conflict selected by an enemy in an attempt to avoid areas of U.S. advantage. Finally, force structure must be worthy of respect in the eyes of would-be foes in order to extend force effectiveness beyond the battlefield to the periods of crisis or tension in which decisions leading toward or away from war are made.

The modern long-range, land-based bomber in general, and the B-2 in particular, has shown itself to have a high degree of suitability in each of these areas. Collectively, these principles translate into the basis for great strategic utility, subject to the ever-significant condition of adequate numbers. This relationship goes far to explain the persistence of professional military advocacy for this program and the support for the B-2 that has survived within the Congress.

Access, Basing and U.S. Global Reach

The United States shares both the benefits and burdens of a unique strategic geography: the benefits of a rich continent-sized resource base and centuries of protection against potential threats by two broad oceans, and the burdens of needing to cross those broad oceans to extend global power to match U.S. global interests. At the height of the Cold War the United States found its reach enhanced by easy access to a system of overseas bases born in the wake of the Spanish-American War, enlarged as a byproduct of World War II endeavor and victory, and carried to its ultimate development by the alliance discipline imposed by the Cold War. This basing system is now collapsing as friends see the need to host U.S. bases fading and the opportunity costs growing. Only a few of the bases that once supported U.S. power projection in Korea survive. Of the massive system of bases that once blanketed Southeast Asia in support of U.S. operations in Vietnam, only Okinawa and Guam remain. U.S. bases in North Africa and South Asia are all closed with the singular exception of remote Diego Garcia. Even U.S. basing structure in the Caribbean has declined. Numbers of European bases and forward-stationed forces manifest an accelerating pattern of decline.

The Gulf War was the exception that proves the rule. U.S. intervention to aid Kuwait was almost totally dependent on the Saudi decision to host the Coalition effort and to provide their uniquely modern, capable and underutilized national complex of bases, the densest in the world, bought by decades of methodical petrodollar investment. The Gulf War air campaign was a remarkable air power victory, but one that should ring alarm bells in the minds of thoughtful defense observers. It furnished a case study of the degree of U.S. dependence on host-nation policy concurrence that now confronts U.S. decisions regarding deployments of shorter-range theater forces. Limited availability of basing is the case in every region of the world where the United States may be called upon to fight. Where bases exist, few are well endowed with modern facilities and sufficient surface logistics to support an intense campaign. Where supportable bases exist they are often remote from likely scenes of conflict. These factors act to compromise the utility of shorter-range attack assets. They even combine to stress the unique U.S. aerial refueling capability.

But, this basing situation highlights the particular qualities of modern long-range, land-based bomber forces. Such weapon systems are capable of initial attacks from the United States itself and conducting subsequent sustained bombing campaigns from forward bases far enough from the crisis location to minimize political sensitivities and to maximize the selection of logistically advantageous bases for the optimum application of firepower. These geopolitical trends are likely to continue, adding to the rationale for greater U.S. reliance on modern long-range, land-based bomber forces and encouraging greater interest in producing more B-2s.

The B-2 and the Defense Industrial Base

The defense industrial base of the United States is at a vortex of political attention and will be linked closely to future B-2 production decisions. On the broadest plane the relationship between the U.S. industrial base decisions and weapon systems choices needs to reflect an awareness of the most efficient sectors of the U.S. industrial base for converting resources into combat power. If judgment relates to the world-wide commercial competitiveness of the U.S. aerospace industry as compared with, say, U.S. automotive or maritime industries, the advantage clearly lies with aerospace. The U.S. aerospace industry is delivering a world-class commercial product competitive in any market. The B-2 represents a leading edge of that aerospace industry output, and combines general aerostructural and engine superiority with unique U.S. advantages in the niche of stealth technology.

The defense conversion issue is a focus of broad Congressional and administration interest. The potential for U.S. Government action in this area has generated a rapidly coalescing industry position that the Government can best assure a smooth conversion of unneeded defense production capacity to civil purposes by focusing on the "...fundamental and pressing need, which is deciding proper force structure required by the U.S. in the post-Cold War era" [384]. Industry leaders express confidence that, with a clear projection of future force-structure-generated demand, aerospace corporations will be able to make business decisions needed to ensure corporate survival whatever the remaining defense market. Innovations such as lean, low-rate production are offered as manageable options. These would restructure traditional high volume production to meet recent low Government-demand. Current industry ideas appear remarkably similar to aspects of resource policies suggested by Les Aspin. The B-2 program is at a stage where it is uniquely suited for further lean, low-rate production as the pilot program for the new relationship between government demand and defense industry production. Technical uncertainties have been overcome, stealth's operational effectiveness is proven, cost control has been demonstrated, and the long-term strategic utility of a larger force of these aircraft is evident.

The Relative Advantage of Stealth Technology

While the underlying rationale for any force of long-range bombers reposes on range, payload, speed, flexibility and the ability to penetrate enemy defenses, stealth is what makes the B-2 weapon system the bomber that the United States will need for the future. Stealth provides the B-2 an enduring tactical advantage with respect to any adversary for the foreseeable future. The stealthy B-2 minimizes dependence on specific foreign bases, large force-packages, complex logistical arrays, and operations under the gun of the enemy. The B-2 also minimizes vulnerability to attrition at the hands of the enemy. As a "silver bullet" penetrator it adds to the effectiveness of non-stealthy forces. Stealth holds the promise for an entirely new concept of surprise in warfare. Stealth is not invulnerable to the efforts of a determined enemy that eventually comes up with technology or tactics able to reduce stealth's effectiveness, but whatever an enemy does, stealth acts to keep U.S. air power at least one jump ahead. The military advantages of stealth technology and the degree to which the B-2 represents stealth's highest development cannot avoid being a recurring focus of Congressional and administration attention as they direct defense investment.

Costs and B-2's Comparative Efficiency Advantages

While it is self-evident that no one weapon or class of weapons can do everything required to maintain U.S. national security, the modern long-range, land-based bomber—the B-2—clearly has broad effectiveness across many missions and applicability well-tailored to the full range of possible conflicts the United States should expect to face. The B-2 is particularly competitive in efficiency terms. Whatever number of B-2s is eventually obtained, the B-2 fleet will remain small in comparison with alternative approaches to accomplishing comparable military effectiveness. At the cutting edge of military technology, it is designed for reliability and maintainability. Air and ground crews are small.

This reduces long-term personnel costs. The B-2's range permits a wide selection of operating locations thereby reducing logistical infrastructure required. Stealth and range combine to reduce attack support package and ground security needs. Overall concept integration promises long service life, therefore an extended period of amortization of costs against strategic return on investment. There is literally no other weapon system that can offer a higher likelihood of placing more accurate firepower on target, at lower cost and risk, regardless of the specific conflict environment than the B-2. As U.S. military forces continue to shrink, and concern over the adequacy of those that remain climbs, these considerations become telling arguments for extending B-2 production beyond the first twenty aircraft.

How Many B-2s Should the United States Produce?

How many B-2s should be built per year is a question with three dimensions: strategic need, economic affordability, and the preservation of U.S. military-industrial potential. It is a political issue that needs to be worked out between the Congress and the administration after consulting with professional military and industry experts.

One need only look to past employment patterns, when the United States possessed a large Cold War bomber force (approximately 2,000 aircraft at its peak) to get a sense of scale for the bomber needs generated by regional conflicts. In the Korean War three wings of about 45 B-29s each for a total of 135 bomber and reconnaissance aircraft were dedicated to destroying strategic and tactical objectives. During the Vietnam War 205 B-52s were operated from Guam and U Tapao, Thailand, against Southeast Asian targets. Approximately 75 B-52s conducted bombing operations in the Gulf War, dropping almost one third of the total weight of firepower delivered. In each of these three cases, deployed aircraft and crews were beneficiaries of a much larger pool of assets from which trained crews and replacement aircraft could be drawn. In the Korean and Vietnam wars, the deployed assets were drawn sparingly from forces already stressed by the overarching Cold War nuclear deterrence mission.

In response to then-Secretary Aspin's "Bottom-Up Review" of force structure requirements, then-JCS Chairman General Colin Powell produced a series of strategic assumptions. The first option posited fighting two regional wars at once; the second assumed fighting one regional war and holding the line in a second until victory in the first permits swinging all forces to the second—the "win-hold-win" approach; the third envisioned being able to fight no more than one war at a time. The first alternative reflected the strategy justification for current force levels. The third was widely regarded as involving unacceptable risk. The Joint Staff saw the "win-hold-win" force as requiring "100 'deployable' bombers that are used for nonnuclear attacks. The actual number of bombers would be higher because of maintenance and training requirements" [385]. Within a week of public notice of this "win-hold-win" strategy option, Secretary Aspin reconsidered his interest in "win-hold-win" and reasserted support for the more robust two-war position [386]. In long-range bomber terms this would appear to reflect Secretary Aspin's continued support for the logic behind then-HASC Chairman Aspin's preference for two 70-aircraft "Desert Storm Equivalents" of long-range bombers.

In his June 1993 congressional testimony, General John M. Loh, Commander of Air Combat Command, addressed the question of the size of U.S. bomber forces in the following terms:

> As the Commander of Air Combat Command, the organization responsible for melding our heavy bomber force into our overall combat Air Force, I believe we need about 180-200 operational bombers. In order to have that number of bombers on hand and ready for action, we would need a total bomber force of between 210-230. The difference in these two sets of numbers allows us to account for aircraft dedicated to training and for losses to periodic maintenance and upgrades.
>
> As a point of reference, we currently anticipate having a force structure that will give us 184 operational bombers. This figure is based on the 20 B-2s which you authorized last year, providing us with 16 operational bombers—the 95 B-1s we have today, yielding 84 operational bombers, and the 95 B-52Hs we will have after the currently announced B-52 force drawdown, also yielding 84 operational bombers.
>
> With such a force we can provide the quantity of sorties we will need to deal with two major regional contingencies [387].

There is also the issue of an eventual future need for the United States to respond to the resurgence of a great or superpower threat. Such development is certainly possible, and, given the pace of proliferation of modern weapons technology, such a threat could hardly fail to involve weapons of mass destruction. If a sufficient modern long-range, land-based U.S. bomber force is not extant at that time, the United States might have to seek initial reestablishment of deterrence through a premature return to nuclear-equipped forces rather than counting on high-quality conventional weaponry. The prospects of having to return to nuclear deterrence earlier than otherwise necessary because the United States had foregone its conventional bombardment advantage would appear to justify at least 132 aircraft. This bomber-force number was established earlier by exhaustive analysis as the appropriate number for nuclear-armed B-2s deployed alongside the full panoply of other bombers, ICBMs, and SLBMs arrayed against the then-well-understood Soviet threat. It is only logical that a force conceived to accomplish long-range attack missions, against as of yet unidentified future adversaries, primarily by means of delivering conventional weapons, should be larger than a force sized for nuclear attack.

Rapidly it becomes apparent that there is no single bomber force number, or B-2 force number, that can stand unassailably as the authoritative verdict of definitive analysis. One can project a convincing range of numbers drawn from recent experience that falls somewhere in the low hundreds. But, whether it is the 75 B-2s accompanied by 620 A-12 medium stealth bombers envisioned by the 1990 DoD Major Aircraft Review [388], the 100 deployable bombers of the "win-hold-win" strategy, the original 132 aircraft B-2 program, 135 bombers from the Korean War, 184 bombers from the current "Bomber Roadmap," 205 from Vietnam, or General Loh's 210-230, there is no one all-powerful number to revere. Secretary of Defense Perry's deterrence to the results of a forthcoming study, rather than defending the decision to drop to a 100 bomber force highlights the difficulty of justifying any particular number of bombers, particularly a low number [389]. While it would certainly be possible to deploy the analytical richness of operations research to derive such a number, the resulting calculus would quickly be unraveled by the weakness of underlying assumptions too dependent on an incompletely understood and fast-changing international security environment.

The appropriate philosophy around which to structure the extension of B-2 production should be to reflect on the cycles of stop-and-go defense spending that have so wastefully characterized U.S. defense budgets through the past four decades, and then to select an even, maintainable, low rate of B-2 production that is sustainable through at least the end of the next decade (2010). This steady, low rate of production should gradually assemble a substantial force of B-2s, maintain the ability to expand production should a clear and immediate need arise, and cover retirement of the remaining B-52s and eventually the B-1Bs as the ends of their service lives are reached.

What can be said about total numbers is that a decade and a half of low-rate production will not produce more B-2s than the nation needs. The current bomber force is decreasing to the target level of 184 [390]. If B-2 low-rate production were begun in 1997 at three aircraft per year, with initial funding in fiscal year 1996, the 21st deployable aircraft would become available about the year 2001–2002 [391]. Assuming delivery of about three aircraft per year to the

Air Force, the entire B-2 force would not total 40 aircraft until about 2008. By then the last remaining B-52 should be either retired or close to retirement—all B-52 airframes would be at least 46 years old in 2008. Assuming B-52 retirement, producing B-2s at three per year would result in a bomber force of B-2 and B-1B bombers, totaling about 120 in 2010. The B-1Bs would average 23 years of age in 2010 and would be candidates for retirement over the following decade, depending on how reliably they exceed their design lifetime and the level of strategic need for extending their service lives perceived at that time [392]. Anticipating retirement of the B-1B, the B-2 would then be the only long-range, land-based bomber, indeed the only long-range strike aircraft, in the U.S. inventory.

However effective and efficient the B-2 should prove to be in comparison to predecessor bomber aircraft, continued low-rate production through 2018 by which point the B-1Bs will be over 30-years old, to an eventual total force of some 70 aircraft would certainly not be excessive, for even the most sanguine assumptions about the nation's security future. This force structure vision preserves future options to accelerate or further prolong B-2 production in response to events that signal more realistic development of international security challenges to U.S. interests. This logic is reinforced by: the context of retirement of current operational bomber aircraft and the longest range attack fighter systems such as the F-111s now underway; accelerated retirement of the Navy's only medium range carrier-based attack aircraft, the A-6; cancellation or delays to projects aimed at defining any follow-on medium range attack systems; and reductions in the Navy's aircraft carrier fleet. These events point to the B-2 as being the only practical long-term long-range attack aircraft option for the United States through the foreseeable future.

The findings of this analysis are less that some specific end-strength of B-2s is required for the future strategic success of U.S. policy than that some level of continued B-2 production is crucial. The current twenty aircraft production run represents competent prototyping and makes a limited high-tech contribution within a larger bomber force. But, without a concerted effort to replace today's shrinking and aging bomber force with substantial numbers of B-2s, the United States will soon have no conventional long-range strike capability beyond token numbers of superannuated products of early to mid-Cold War technology long overdue for retirement. Indeed, without a decision to produce more B-2s, the United States is committed upon a nearly irreversible course toward that day, only a few decades away, when it will no longer have any long-range strike capability whatsoever, or will have to spend now-inconceivable sums of money on some new "B-3" bomber. A United States without a full-service fleet of B-2s will, in the future, find itself unprepared to cope with the fundamentals of its own strategic geography. Without modern long-range, land-based bombers, U.S. military forces will be unable to influence most of the world without depending on the active support of regional allies, allies increasingly likely to have their own agendas. Continued low-rate production of the B-2 offers a sound replacement strategy that will ensure the United States the military reach to match its global interests, and it will do so at reasonable and predictable cost. Such a decision would meet the policy criteria of the Congress and administration as well as the long-term strategic needs of the United States of America.

Endnotes

1. Office of the Historian, Strategic Air Command, *The Development of the Strategic Air Command 1946–1981: A Chronological History* (Omaha, NE: Office of the Historian, Headquarters, Strategic Air Command, 1982), p. 131.
2. See John Robert Ferris, *Men, Money, and Diplomacy: The Evolution of British Strategic Policy, 1919–26* (Ithaca, NY: Cornell University Press, 1989), esp. ch. 2.
3. See Robert W. Tucker and David C. Hendrickson, *The Imperial Temptation: The New World Order and America's Purpose* (New York: Council on Foreign Relations, 1992).
4. For reasons well explored in Samuel P. Huntington, "Playing to Win," *The National Interest*, No. 3 (Spring 1986), pp. 8–16.
5. Kathleen C. Bailey, *Doomsday Weapons in the Hands of Many: The Arms Control Challenge of the '90s* (Urbana, Ill.: University of Illinois Press, 1991); and Janne E. Nolan, *Trappings of Power: Ballistic Missiles in the Third World* (Washington, D.C.: Brookings Institution, 1991), are useful in explaining these problems.
6. For further development of five stages of the strategic value of airpower (experimental/marginal adjunct to terrestrial forces, useful adjunct, important adjunct, indispensable adjunct, and war-winner) see Colin S. Gray, *Benefit Studies in Support of Space Asset Planning* (Fairfax, VA: National Security Research, Inc., February 1993). An annotated briefing prepared for Headquarters, U.S. Air Force Space Command.
7. Geoffrey Perret, *A Country Made By War: From the Revolution to Vietnam—the Story of America's Rise to Power* (New York: Vintage Books, 1989), p. 328.
8. Wesley Frank Craven and James Lea Cate, eds., *The Army Air Forces In World War II*, vol. 1, *Plans and Early Operations: January 1939 to August 1942* (Chicago: University of Chicago Press, 1964), pp. 12, 13.
9. Cited in Craven and Cate, pp. 70, 71. See also pp. 64–71.
10. The United States supported the Nicaraguan government in its 1927–1933 war against the rebel Augusto César Sandino. The Army Air Service believed

that dive-bombing could be used effectively in guerrilla warfare. This proposition was tested in July 1927 when a Marine outpost was attacked by some 800 rebels. The besieged outpost was in Ocotal, 125 miles from Managua, and Marine ground reinforcements were not in a position to accomplish a rescue. Field commanders recognized that the only way to counter Sandino's superior numbers was to deliver a timely counterstroke in this critical situation by employing a number of DH-4B bombers against the assaulting forces. These primitive bi-planes carried gunners and a very small bomb load. But, unfamiliar with air attacks, the rebels suffered between 100 and 200 casualties and were forced to halt their attack against the Marine garrison. Richard P. Hallion, *Strike from the Sky: The History of Battlefield Air Attack; 1911–1945* (Washington, D.C.: Smithsonian Institution Press, 1989), pp. 71–73.

11. Craven and Cate, p. 61. The authors point out that during the 1930s, the War Department led an effort to construct a bomber that could fly 5,000 miles at a speed of 200 miles per hour. The B-17 grew out of what was known as Project A, parent also to the B-24 and B-29 (see pp. 65, 66).

12. See interviews with General Curtis E. Lemay and General Leon W. Johnson in Richard H. Kohn and Joseph P. Hanrahan, eds., *Strategic Air Warfare* (Washington, D.C.: Office of Air Force History, 1988), pp. 19, 20.

13. James C. Gaston, *Planning the American Air War: Four Men and Nine Days in 1941* (Washington, D.C.: NDU Press, 1982), p. 65.

14. Robin Cross, *The Bombers: The Illustrated Story of Offensive Strategy and Tactics in the Twentieth Century* (New York: Macmillan Publishing Company, 1987), p. 126.

15. Gaston, p. 67.
16. Perret, p. 404; Craven and Cate, p. 238.
17. Craven and Cate, pp. 559, 562, 563.
18. *Congressional Record*, December 30, 1941, p. 10134.
19. *Congressional Record*, December 26, 1941, p. A5714.

20. Remarks of Mr. Rankin in *Congressional Record*, May 28, 1941, pp. A2546 and A2571. De Seversky, a WWI Russian military ace and aeronautical engineer, emigrated to the United States during the Russian revolution. He was a test pilot for the U.S. Air Service and later founded a small aircraft manufacturing company. He argued that "the moment when air power can reach across oceans as easily as it now bridges narrower waters will mark the final elimination of sea power as a primary element of warfare." He predicted in his June 1941 article that "the Atlantic will be wide open to the full fury of aerial assaults from one shore to the other within 2 or 3 years." (Article reprinted in *Congressional Record*, May 28, 1941, pp. A2546–48).

21. *Congressional Record*, July 2, 1942, pp. A2601, 2602.

22. *Congressional Record*, February 4, 1942, p. 1021, 1022. See also remarks of Congressman Carl Hinshaw in *Congressional Record*, December 7, 1942,

p. A4211, 4212; Congressman William S. Hill in *Congressional Record*, May 24, 1943, p. A2587.

23. Remarks of Harry Flood Byrd in *Congressional Record: Proceedings and Debates of the 78th Congress, First Session*, vol. 88, part 11 (Washington, D.C.: GPO, 1943), May 24, 1943, pp. A2990, 2991.

24. See remarks of Congressman Patman in *Congressional Record*, February 18, 1943, p. 1107.

25. Cited by Mr. Jennings Randolph in *Congressional Record*, December 15, 1942, p. A4311.

26. *Congressional Record*, June 26, 1942, p. 5623.

27. For some postwar remarks by U.S. legislators on the value of bombers, see Rep. Jennings Randolph in *Congressional Record*, June 30, 1945, pp. A3170–3172; Rep. Carl Hinshaw, *Congressional Record*, May 17, 1945, p. A2348; and Senator Elbert Thomas, *Congressional Record*, December 10, 1945, p. A5369.

28. *Congressional Record*, March 1, 1947, pp. 1823, A1527–28; March 2, 1949, p. 1733.

29. *Congressional Record*, March 16, 1942, p. A1528; March 18, 1942, pp. A1560–A1562; and March 28, 1942, p. A1839.

30. Harry S. Truman, *Years of Trial and Hope: 1946–1952* (Garden City, NY: Doubleday & Company, 1956), pp. 337, 341; and Robert Frank Futrell, Brig. Gen. Lawson S. Moseley, and Albert F. Simpson, *The United States Air Force in Korea, 1950–1953* (New York: Duell, Sloan and Pearce, 1983), pp. 4, 440.

31. Futrell, et. al., p. 27.

32. William S. White, "Senator Demands U.S. Call Up Guard," *New York Times*, July 13, 1950, p. 6.

33. Futrell, et. al., pp. 41, 42.

34. Futrell, et. al., pp. 179–184; Cross, *The Bombers*, pp. 186, 187.

35. Truman, pp. 395, 396; Perret, pp. 462, 463.

36. Anthony Leviero, "Truman Rules Out China Bombing Now," *New York Times*, January 5, 1951, pp. 1, 3.

37. Futrell, et. al., pp. 439, 440.

38. *Congressional Record*, May 14, 1951, pp. A2753–2756.

39. Earl H. Tilford, Jr., "Setup: Why and How the U.S. Air Force Lost in Vietnam," *Armed Forces & Society*, vol. 17, no. 3, 1991, p. 327.

40. Guenter Lewy, *America in Vietnam* (New York: Oxford University Press, 1978), p. 374.

41. *The Pentagon Papers* (New York: Bantam Books, 1971), p. 251. See also pp. 242–253.

42. Associated Press, "Goldwater Poses New Asian Tactic," *New York Times*, May 25, 1964, p. 1. Goldwater also called for the use of low-yield atomic weapons in order to defoliate the forests, exposing the North Vietnamese supply lines.

43. Tom Wicker, "Forces Enlarged," *New York Times*, August 5, 1964, pp. 1, 2; and UPI, "Lodge Asserts He Is Happy U.S. Met Force with Force," *New York Times*, August 5, 1964, p. 2.

44. *The Pentagon Papers*, p. 307, 308.

45. Perret, p. 520. One point of irony about the Rolling Thunder campaign was the use of the SAC's B-52s in a tactical role (to perform even close support missions like those undertaken at Khe Sanh) while tactical fighters were used to carry out strategic bombing. The B-52s were not used in a strategic role until Linebacker II in 1972.

46. Lewy, p. 379.

47. See remarks of Senators Mansfield and Church in *Congressional Record*, July 8 and July 12, 1965, pp. 15855-56, 16434-35.

48. Lewy, pp. 383-385. The subcommittee concluded that the doctrine of "gradualism" prevented the United States from bringing the full force of air power to bear against the enemy and that the tactical details of military operations ought to be given over to the military officials.

49. Henry Kissinger, *White House Years* (Boston: Little, Brown and Company, 1979), pp. 1118, 1121, 1154.

50. Lewy, p. 200.

51. Lewy, pp. 200, 410.

52. Richard Nixon, *RN: The Memoirs of Richard Nixon* (New York: Warner Books, 1979), p. 242.

53. Cited by Lewy, p. 414.

54. Kissinger, *White House Years*, p. 1461 (parenthetical remarks added).

55. Henry Kissinger, *Years of Upheaval* (Boston: Little, Brown and Company, 1982), pp. 316-318.

56. Kissinger, *Upheaval*, p. 326.

57. Dwight D. Eisenhower, *The White House Years: Waging Peace, 1956-1961* (Garden City, NY: Doubleday & Company, 1965), pp. 271, 276.

58. Office of the Historian, Headquarters, Strategic Air Command, *The Development of the Strategic Air Command, 1946-1981: A Chronological History* (Omaha, NE: Headquarters, Strategic Air Command, 1982), pp. 106, 107.

59. Nixon, pp. 476, 477.

60. Nixon, p. 498.

61. Kissinger, *Upheaval*, p. 591.

62. Kissinger, *Upheaval*, pp. 591-600; Nixon, p. 500.

63. Ronald Reagan, *An American Life*, (New York: Simon and Schuster, 1990), p. 518; and Ronald Reagan's address to the nation, "Reagan: 'We Have Done What We Had to Do'," *Washington Post*, April 15, 1986, p. A23.

64. Caspar W. Weinberger, *Fighting for Peace: Seven Critical Years in the Pentagon* (New York: Warner Books, 1990), p. 191, 192.

65. Reagan, "Reagan: 'We Have Done What We Had to Do'," p. A 23; Weinberger, pp. 192–201.

66. See the remarks of Representatives and Senators in *Congressional Record*, April 15, 1986, pp. 7439, 7472–7475, 7525–7531, 7597, 7696, 7697; Steven V. Roberts, "From Capitol Hill, Words of Support Are Mixed With Some Reservations," *New York Times*, April 15, 1986, p. A10 and "Lawmakers Say U.S. Failed to Consult Them Properly," *New York Times*, April 15, 1986, p. A17; Edward Walsh and Helen Dewar, "Retaliation Wins Bipartisan Nod From Congress," *Washington Post*, April 15, 1986, p. A21; Adam Clymer, "A Poll Finds 77% in U.S. Approve Raid on Libya," *New York Times*, April 17, 1986.

67. Jean Edward Smith, *George Bush's War* (New York: Henry Holt and Company, 1992), p. 85.

68. John M. Broder, "U.S. plans aim to 'decapitate' Iraq by strikes at key leaders," reprinted from *Los Angeles Times* in *Buffalo News*, September 16, 1990, p. A1.

69. For remarks in support of air strikes see Senator Timothy Wirth (pp. 156–158), Dr. James Schlesinger (p. 168), Adm. William Crowe (p. 196), Gen. David Jones (pp. 238, 239), Senator Sam Nunn (p. 272), Henry Kissinger (pp. 272, 280, 286, 298), Edward Luttwak (pp. 319–321, 347, 369), Senator John McCain (p. 352), LTG William Odom (p. 501), and Gen. Colin Powell, (p. 663) in U.S. Congress, Senate Committee on Armed Services, *Hearings: Crisis in the Persian Gulf Region; U.S. Policy Options and Implications* (Washington, D.C.: GPO, Doc. Nr. S. Hrg. 101–1071, 1990).

70. Ann Devroy and John Lancaster, "Bush Threatens to Send Jets To Back Up Iraq Inspections, *Washington Post*, September 19, 1991, p. A1; Helen Dewar, "Dole Seeks Vote To Allow Force Against Iraq," *Washington Post*, July 30, 1991, p. A12.

71. "Word for Word," *Defense News*, August 3–August 9, 1992, p. 18.

72. Barton Gellman and Ann Devroy, "U.S. Delivers Limited Air Strike on Iraq," *Washington Post*, January 14, 1993, p. A1; Ann Devroy and Barton Gellman, "MiG Downed As Gulf Allies Display Might," *Washington Post*, January 18, 1993, p. A1; AP, "Bush's Last Message to Hill Is About Iraq," *Washington Post*, January 21, 1993, p. A18; see also Charles Krauthammer, "Iraq: Clinton's First Crisis," *Washington Post*, January 22, 1993, p. A21; Anthony H. Cordesman, "How to Hit Iraq," *New York Times*, August 19, 1992, p. A21; Albert Wohlstetter, "High Time," *National Review*, February 15, 1993, pp. 30–33; and Albert Wohlstetter and Fred Hoffman, "The Bitter End," *New Republic*, April 29, 1991, pp. 20–24.

73. Cited by Don Oberdorfer, "U.S. Verifies Killings in Serb Camps," *Washington Post*, August 4, 1992, p. A1.

74. Paul M. Rodriguez, "Bosnia 'Desert Storm' ruled out," *Washington Times*, August 7, 1992, p. A8; Carol Giacomo, "U.S. may strike Serbian military targets, aide says," *Washington Times*, August 16, 1992, p. A1.

75. Elaine Sciolino, "Clinton Urges Stronger U.S. Stand On Enforcing Bosnia Flight Ban," *New York Times*, December 12, 1992, p. A1; Unattributed, "U.S. Air Strikes on Serb Positions Urged by Indiana Rep. McClosky," *Washington Post*, November 20, 1992, p. A48; and William Drozdiak, "NATO Sets Plans To Enforce Ban On Serb Flights," *Washington Post*, December 16, 1992, p. A29.

76. John M. Goshko and Don Oberdorfer, "U.S. to Study Wider Options on Balkans," *Washington Post*, January 28, 1993, p. A16; see also Leslie H. Gelb, "Balkan Strategy Part I," *New York Times*, February 25, 1993, p. A19.

77. The plan drawn up near the end of 1992 by UN special envoy Cyrus Vance and European Community negotiator David Owen called for the creation of ten semiautonomous provinces within the former state of Bosnia-Hercegovina. The provinces would be dominated by local communal majorities, with the Serbs likely controlling three. The Bosnian Serbs resisted the plan on the grounds that it would compel them to return previously conquered territories back to Croatian and Muslim forces.

78. Helen Dewar, "Congress Torn Over Balkan Role," *Washington Post*, April 29, 1993, p. A1; Michael R. Gordon, "NATO General Is Reticent About Air Strikes in Bosnia," *New York Times*, April 21, 1993, p. A10; Bill Gertz, "Admiral: Air Strikes in Bosnia would fail and cost U.S. lives," *Washington Times*, April 28, 1993, p. A1.

79. Daniel Williams, "'No Good Options' on Balkans," *Washington Post*, April 20, 1993, p. A16; R.W. Apple, Jr., "Clinton Says U.S. Must Harden Line Toward the Serbs," *New York Times*, April 27, 1993, p. A1; and Daniel Williams, "U.S. Studies 2-Point Strategy on Balkans," *Washington Post*, April 29, 1993, p. A35.

80. Neil A. Lewis, "Shultz's Advice to Clinton: Attack the Serbs at Once," *New York Times*, April 27, 1993, p. A7.

81. The analytical method for addressing the value of a class of military capability in terms of thirteen "principles" for successful defense planning, applied to the modern long-range, land-based bomber in this chapter, was first prototyped by NSR in 1991 for the Defense Posture Analytical Model project undertaken under contract to the Computer Sciences Corporation for Headquarters, Strategic Air Command. It was subsequently applied to mission areas as diverse as Special Operations Forces in work done for the Office of the Assistant Secretary of Defense, Special Operations and Low Intensity Conflict, and Space Operations done for Headquarters, Air Force Space Command.

82. James P. Coyne, *Airpower in the Gulf* (Arlington, VA: Air Force Association, 1992), p. 79.

83. GATS uses the B-2's computational capability to specify a target's position with great accuracy relative to the GPS location of the bomber. This is accomplished by using a series of radar range arcs to define the target's precise position relative to the bomber. The B-2's computers then resolve this relative

location into GPS coordinates in terms of the bomber's best GPS position. Any errors in the bomber's GPS position apply equally to bomber and target. The GAM part of the program is a relatively straightforward GPS-guided bomb. GATS will update the bomb's guidance system position with that of the B-2 and then program to follow a trajectory to the coordinates of the target. Accuracy of GATS/GAM weapons delivery is currently projected to be within 20 feet under all weather conditions. *B-2 GATS/GAM: A Total Weapon System Approach to Seekerless Precision, A Status Report (*Pico Rivera, CA: Northrop, January 12, 1993).

84. It is significant in highlighting the diversity of function of the long-range, land-based bomber that for most of the Cold War years the second largest fleet of such aircraft, and in recent years the largest, has been maintained by the U.S. Navy. These are the Lockheed P-3 "Orion" patrol bombers which have anchored and covered the Navy's sea control and ASW operations around the world. At the end of FY 1992, 247 of these aircraft which were first delivered to the Navy in 1958 were still in service. Since then modifications have kept this force effective, and the production line was recently reopened for foreign purchases. "Facts and Figures," *Sea Power* 36, no. 1 (January 1993), pp. 192, 193.

85. A piece of folklore associated with the British retaking of the Falklands gives some perspective on the importance of long-range strike aircraft to such an endeavor. In accordance with the cited restatement of British defense policy, the Vulcan bombers had been deemed to have adequate unrefueled range for all conceivable missions. Their refueling probes and plumbing were removed and all aerial refueling training discontinued. When the invasion took place, the RAF found itself in the position of sending mechanics with tool kits to each of the USAF museums to which the British had donated older air refueling-capable Vulcans in order to remove the air refueling probes and plumbing and repatriate them to England for reinstallation on operational Vulcans. This contributed to successful Vulcan raids on Argentine installations in the Falklands. There was one exception where the pilot, reportedly a bit "rusty" on refueling technique, was forced to recover in Brazil, where the aircraft and crew were interned for the duration.

86. Les Aspin, "Remarks by Secretary of Defense Les Aspin and General Colin L. Powell, Chairman, JCS, Armed Forces Welcoming Ceremony, Fort Myer, VA, February 1, 1993," Office of the Assistant Secretary of Defense, Public Affairs, fax, February 10, 1993, p. 4.

87. This chapter summarizes findings of a global survey of access and basing accomplished by NSR for the Northrop Corporation, entitled *Worldwide Access to Air Bases for Contingency Operations* (Fairfax, VA: National Security Research, Inc., June 1991), 95 pp.

88. Major Mark Adkin, *Urgent Fury: The Battle for Grenada*, (Lexington, MA: D.C. Heath and Company, 1989), pp. 143–144.

89. "Indivisible Airpower," *Air Force Magazine,* March 1984, p. 49.

90. Adkin, p. 141.

91. Frank Uhlig, Jr., "Amphibious Aspects of the Grenada Episode," *American Intervention in Grenada: The Implications of Urgent Fury* (Boulder, CO: Westview Press, 1985), p. 89.

92. Uhlig, p. 89.

93. Uhlig, p. 92.

94. The OECS sent a token force of 300 troops. See *New York Times*, October 26, 1983.

95. Robert S. Greenberger, "US Invades Grenada in Warning to Russia and Cuba About Expansion in Caribbean," *Wall Street Journal*, October 26, 1983.

96. Adkin, p. 318.

97. Philip Shabecoff, "Most O.A.S. Members Assail Action," *New York Times*, October 27, 1983.

98. Robert R. Ropelewski, "How Panama Worked: Planning, Precision, and Surprise," *Armed Forces Journal International*, February 1990, p. 27.

99. Lorenzo Crowell, "The Anatomy of Just Cause: The Forces Involved, the Adequacy of the Intelligence, and Its Success as a Joint Operation," in Bruce W. Watson and Peter G. Tsouras, eds., *Operation Just Cause: The U.S. Intervention in Panama* (Boulder, CO: Westview Press, 1991), pp. 76, 77.

100. *Ibid.*, p. 78.

101. *Ibid.*, p. 77.

102. Noris Lyn McCall, "Assessing the Role of Air Power," in Watson and Tsouras, p. 117.

103. Peter Almond, "Stealth Steals Some Applause for Panama Debut," *Washington Times*, January 8, 1990, p. 3. Almond quotes Bill Sweetman of Jane's Publications regarding the F–117A: "This is a plane very much designed to support Special Operations forces. This was a fairly good example of what it can do. Its stealth characteristics...mean in Third World situations the pilot doesn't really have to worry about being detected. He can focus on navigation and aiming."

104. McCall, p. 119.

105. "SAC Tankers Heavily Used in Panama Operation," *Aerospace Daily*, January 2, 1990, p. 3.

106. "World Criticism of U.S. Intervention Mounts," *Washington Post*, December 22, 1990, p. 29.

107. Alan R. Goldman and E. Maria Biggers, "The International Implications," in Watson and Tsouras, p. 182.

108. Abraham F. Lowenthal, "Rediscovering Latin America," *Foreign Affairs*, Fall 1990, p. 36.

109. Secretary of Defense Dick Cheney, *Annual Report to the President and the Congress* (Washington, D.C.: GPO, January 1993), pp. 84, 85.

110. Everett G. Martin, "Peru-Ecuador Border Clash Dies Down, But Oil May Ignite More Latin Conflicts," *Wall Street Journal*, February 4, 1981, p. 30.

111. Office of the Historian, Headquarters, Strategic Air Command, *The Development of the Strategic Air Command 1946–1981: A Chronological History* (Offutt AFB, NE: Office of the Historian, Headquarters, Strategic Air Command, 1982), p. 73.

112. William H. Lewis, "War in the Western Sahara," in Robert E. Harkavy and Stephanie G. Neuman, *The Lessons of Recent Wars in the Third World: Approaches and Case Studies, Vol. I* (Lexington, Mass.: D.C. Heath & Co., 1985), p. 117.

113. It has even been suggested that the principal reason for staging from Britain was political rather than military; that is, the United States wanted to prove that its controversial attack enjoyed the support of at least one European power. See David Gates "American Strategic Bases in Britain: The Agreements Governing Their Use," *Comparative Strategy*, No. 1, 1989, p. 116.

114. Richard F. Grimmett, "US Military Installations in NATO's Southern Region," *Report prepared for the Subcommittee on Europe and the Middle East of the House Foreign Affairs Committee by the Congressional Research Service, The Library of Congress* (Washington, D.C.: CRS, 7 October 1986), p. 19.

115. Distances manually extracted from Department of Defense, Defense Mapping Agency, *DoD Flight Information Publication (Enroute) Charts and Supplement, Africa*, (St. Louis, MO: Defense Mapping Agency Aerospace Center, February 7, 1991).

116. The French force had its headquarters in the same compound as Chadian Air Force Headquarters, and most of its aircraft were deployed on the Chadian military apron of N'Djamena International Airport. At its peak level, the French force normally consisted of approximately eleven Mirage F-1 interceptors, one rotational C-135FR tanker, two Transall transports, several Puma helicopters, and periodically deployed additional support aircraft. The French resurfaced the runway at Abeché in eastern Chad where a number of the F-1's stood air defense alert. Small contingents of ground forces were stationed north of N'Djamena to help provide early warning. French air defense of their assets in N'Djamena, as well as Chadian assets close to them, included Crotale and I-Hawk surface to air missiles. Fuel for this force and heavy supplies, along with what was required by Chadian military and civil flight operations, was shipped overland from Douala, Cameroun, approximately 1,100 miles by truck. Much of this route lacked paved roads. Other support for the French arrived by weekly French Air Force flights or as commercial air freight on more frequent UTA or Air Afrique flights from Paris.

117. Victor Flintham, *Air Wars and Aircraft: A Detailed Record of Air Combat, 1945 to the Present* (New York: Facts on File, 1990), p. 94.

118. *Foreign Affairs*, Chronology 1983 Issue, pp. 802, 803.

119. In the Chadian case, Hissein Habré made life difficult for the French even though he needed them. His "trusted lieutenant" Colonel Idriss Deby, thoroughly aware of these tensions between Habré and the French, then seized power while

criticizing his predecessor's closeness to the French, only to reestablish essentially the same relationship with France once he was ensconced in the Presidential palace.

120. Department of the Navy, Office of Information, *Navy Talking Points: Navy-Marine Corps Team—Desert Storm* (Washington, D.C.: Department of the Navy, Office of Information, Spring 1991), p. 2.

121. Gen George L. Butler, USAF, Commander-in-Chief, Strategic Air Command, testimony before the Senate Armed Services Committee, April 23, 1991, in U.S. Congress, Senate, Committee on *Authorization for Appropriations for Fiscal Years 1992 and 1993*, Armed Services, Department of Defense, Hearings, (S. Hrg. 102-255), Part 1 (Washington: GPO, 1991), p. 733.

122. Data from TSgt Alan Dockery, SAC Public Affairs, (402) 294-5656, by telephone on 5/14/91.

123. Michael A. Dornheim, "F-117A Pilots Conduct Precision Bombing in High Threat Environment," *Aviation Week and Space Technology*, April 22, 1991, p. 51.

124. "Marines Attribute Success to Conventional Bombing," *Aviation Week and Space Technology*, April 22, 1991, pp. 92-93.

125. Edward N. Luttwak, "Air Power in US Military Strategy," in Richard H. Schultz, Jr. and Robert L. Pfaltzgraff, Jr., *The Future of Air Power: in the Aftermath of the Gulf War* (Maxwell AFB, AL: Air University Press, July 1992), pp. 34-35.

126. U.S. Department of Defense, *Conduct of the Persian Gulf War: Final Report to Congress, Appendix T* (Washington, D.C.: Department of Defense, April 1992), p. T-150.

127. The bases are Ramat David, Tel Nof, Hatzor, Nevatime, Hatzerim, Ramon, and Ovda. W. Seth Carus, *The Threat to Israel's Air Bases*, AIPAC Papers on U.S.-Israeli Relations, No. 12 (Washington, D.C.: American Israel Public Affairs Committee, September 1985), p. vii.

128. Carus, p. 2.

129. Carus, p. 19.

130. Such a threat is posed by virtue of Saudi Arabia's purchase of Brazilian Astros II rockets and its request for the American MLRS system. W. Seth Carus, p. 31; *Military Balance, 1990-1991* (London: International Institute for Strategic Studies, 1990), p. 116; and *Strategic Survey, 1988-1989* (London: International Institute for Strategic Studies, 1989), p. 15.

131. Robert E. Harkavy, *Bases Abroad: The Global Foreign Military Presence* (Oxford University Press, 1989), p. 367.

132. Harkavy, *Bases Abroad*, p. 6.

133. Grimmett, p. 5.

134. David Gates, "American Strategic Bases in Britain: The Agreements Governing Their Use," *Comparative Strategy*, No. 1, 1989, p. 113.

135. Bases such as Tan Son Nhut, Bien Hoa, Nha Trang, Qui Nhon, Chu Lai, and Da Nang anchored U.S. military air power in Vietnam.

136. Cam Ranh Bay, Phan Rang, Tuy Hoa, and Phu Cat were four of these bases built from scratch, at great expense, and over many tedious months. Lt Col Price T. Bingham, *Operational Art and Aircraft Runway Requirements* (Maxwell AFB, AL: Air University Press, 1989), p. 5.

137. Charles K. Hopkins, *SAC Tanker Operations in the Southeast Asia War* (Offutt AFB, NE: Office of the Historian, Headquarters, Strategic Air Command, 1979), pp. 19, 24.

138. It is worth noting that US Navy vessels made a port call in China in 1989 for the first time since the Communists seized control of the country in 1949.

139. See, e.g., Harkavy, *Bases Abroad*, pp. 83, 85.

140. The Pakistanis declined to extend previous basing agreements.

141. Steve Coll, "Policy on U.S. Planes Threatens India's Leader," *Washington Post*, February 17, 1991, p. A32.

142. The two countries recently signed an agreement promising not to target the other's nuclear facilities.

143. Barbara Crossette, "India Wary of U.S. Relief Force in Bangladesh," *New York Times*, May 16, 1991, p. A13.

144. Since the end of World War II the oceans have ceased to represent an inexhaustible resource, available to any taker, and have become instead an area of intense competition for scarce goods. Barry Buzan, A Sea of Troubles? Sources of Dispute in the New Ocean Regime, *Adelphi Papers*, Number 143 (London: The International Institute for Strategic Studies, Spring 1978), p. 1.

145. Department of the Navy, *Annotated Supplement to the Commander's Handbook on the Law of Naval Operations (NWP 9 (Rev. A)/FMFM 1-10)* (Washington, D.C.: Office of the Judge Advocate General, Department of the Navy, 1989), pp. AS2-16-1, AS2-17B-1- AS2-17b-5.

146. Sheila E. Widnall, Secretary of the Air Force, "Report of the Secretary of the Air Force," in Les Aspin, Secretary of Defense, *Annual Report to the President and the Congress* (Washington, D.C.: GPO, January 1994), p. 272.

147. See testimony of Mr. Jack Welch, Air Force Assistant Secretary for Acquisition, and Lt. Gen. Ronald Yates, Military Deputy for Acquisition before the Subcommittee on Strategic Forces and Nuclear Deterrence, Committee on Armed Services, U.S. Senate, June 13, 1989, in U.S. Congress, Senate, Committee on Armed Services, *Department of Defense Authorization for Appropriations for Fiscal Year 1990 and 1991*, Hearings, Part 6, Strategic Forces and Nuclear Deterrence (Washington, D.C.: GPO, 1989, Document No. S. Hrg. 101-251, pt. 6), pp. 307-361. Included in this hearing is the USAF presentation, "The B-2 In Perspective," (pp. 329-346) which portrays B-2 first as a nuclear bomber, and secondarily as a conventional platform.

148. SASC, *DoD Authorizations for FY 1990 and 1991*, pp. 321-322. As late as April 1990, Secretary Cheney declared: "I think it is important to emphasize that we are not buying the B-2 for its conventional capability. It is being purchased

specifically as part of our SIOP capability, to deliver strategic nuclear weapons." U.S. Congress, House, Committee on Armed Services, *Hearings on Department of Defense Authorization Act for Fiscal Year 1991—H.R. 4739* (Washington, D.C.: GPO, 1991, Document No. H.A.S.C. 101–45), p. 723.

149. See Secretary of Defense Richard Cheney's testimony in U.S. Congress, House, Committee on Armed Services, *Hearings on National Defense Authorization Act for Fiscal Year 1990—H.R. 2461* (Washington, D.C.: GPO, 1989, Document No. H.A.S.C. 101–7), p. 271. The counting rule for penetrating bombers remains in the START Treaty; Russia and the other nuclear-armed former republics of the USSR (Ukraine, Kazakhstan, Belarus) have agreed to observe the START Treaty.

150. Secretary of Defense Dick Cheney, "Statement before the House Armed Services Committee in Connection with the Defense Major Aircraft Review" (mimeo), April 26, 1990, p. 6.

151. The decision to end the B-2 program at 20 was announced by then-President Bush in his January 20, 1992, State of the Union message. DoD arrived at the figure of 20 aircraft a few weeks earlier. See General Colin S. Powell's testimony, delivered January 31, 1992, in SASC, *Department of Defense Authorization for Appropriations for Fiscal Year 1993 and the Future Years Defense Program* (Washington, D.C.: GPO, 1992, Doc. No. S. Hrg. 102–833, Part 1), p. 122.

152. General Loh before the SASC, June 29, 1993, in SASC, *Department of Defense Authorization for Appropriations for Fiscal Year 1994 and the Future Years Defense Program* (Washington, D.C.: GPO, 1993, Doc. No. S.Hrg. 103–303, Part 7), p. 517.

153. HASC, *National Defense Authorization Act for Fiscal Years 1992 and 1993* (Washington, D.C.: GPO, May 13, 1991, Report 102–60), p. 12.

154. HASC, *National Defense Authorization Act for Fiscal Year 1991* (Washington, D.C.: GPO, August 3, 1990, Report 101–665), p. 344; HASC, *National Defense Authorization Act for Fiscal Years 1992 and 1993*, pp. 289–290; HASC, *National Defense Authorization Act for Fiscal Year 1993* (Washington, D.C.: GPO, May 19, 1992, Report No. 102–527), pp. 298–300; U.S. Congress, Senate, Committee on Armed Services, *National Defense Authorization Act for Fiscal Year 1991* (Washington, D.C.: GPO, July 20, 1990, Report No. 101–384), p. 29.

155. HASC, *National Defense Authorization Act for Fiscal Year 1993*, pp. 8, 169. SASC, *National Defense Authorization Act for Fiscal Year 1991*, p. 38.

156. HASC, *National Defense Authorization Act for Fiscal Years 1992 and 1993*, p. 8.

157. Jeff Cole, "Stealth Bomber Has Problems, Says House Panel Head," *Wall Street Journal*, June 29, 1992, p. B-7.

158. HASC, *National Defense Authorization Act for Fiscal Year 1993*, p.15.

159. SASC, *National Defense Authorization Act for Fiscal Year 1993*, p. 49; HASC, *National Defense Authorization Act for Fiscal Year 1993*, p. 18.

160. Northrop Corporation, *B-2 Stealth Bomber Fact Book*, (Pico Rivera, CA: Northrop, November 1992), pp. 1-3.

161. "B-2 Test Program to Meet Fiscal 1993 Milestones," *Aviation Week and Space Technology*, February 15, 1993, p. 67.

162. U.S. Air Force, Office of Public Affairs, "B-2 Congressional Restrictions Summary" (mimeo), October 18, 1993, p. 1. See also U.S. Air Force, "Background Briefing; Subject: B-2," (mimeo), October 18, 1993, and "Aspin Seeks Release of Delayed B-2 Funds," *Aviation Week & Space Technology*, October 25, 1993, p. 28.

163. See Michael E Brown, *Flying Blind: The Politics of the U. S. Strategic Bomber Program* (Ithaca: Cornell, 1992), p. 272.

164. See Nick Kotz, *Wild Blue Yonder: Money, Politics, and the B-1 Bomber* (New York: Pantheon, 1988), p. 195.

165. Brown, pp. 279-280.

166. Kotz, pp. 231.

167 All three supported the B-2 program in 1994 by voting against an amendment to strike the SASC's insertion of $150 million into the Defense Authorization bill, to maintain B-2 production capabilities in FY95 and for studies of bomber requirements. *Congressional Record*, July 1, 1994, p. S.8156.

168 Congressional Record, July 1, 1994, p. S8141.

169. John McCain, "Power Projection and Roles and Missions," *Congressional Record*, July 2, 1992, pp. S9582-S9585. SASC, *National Defense Authorization for Fiscal Year 1993*, pp. 396-407; In 1991, McCain favored moving away from the penetrating bomber. *SASC, National Defense Authorization Act for Fiscal Years 1992 and 1993*, p. 416. That year, McCain cosponsored an amendment to eliminate funding for B-2 production in 1992. *The Congressional Record*, August 1, 1991, p. 1160.

170 These members signed a letter, dated July 28, 1994, to then-HASC Chairman Ronald V. Dellums, requesting that $150 million be included in the Defense Authorization Act to maintain the B-2 supplier base and to study future bomber options.

171. HASC, *Hearings on National Defense Authorization Act for Fiscal Year 1991—H.R. 4739* (Washington, D.C.: GPO, Document No. H.A.S.C. 101-45, 1991), p. 615. See also Kasich's statement in *Congressional Record*, May 20, 1991, p. H3193, and June 5, 1992, p. H4291.

172. HASC, *Hearings on National Defense Authorization Act for Fiscal Years 1992 and 1993—H.R. 2100* (Washington, D.C.: GPO, Document No. H.A.S.C. 102-6, 1991), pp. 505-507. Rice countered Kasich with the following explanations: The concurrency problem had been obviated in the late 1980s by a programmatic move, in cooperation with the congressional committees, toward low rate initial production of just two aircraft per year, for five successive years. With regard to B-2 missions, attacking SRTs was not proclaimed as a primary B-2 mission at least as far back as

1989; for payload, the B-2 will possess a variety of conventional weapons capabilities, to include precision-guided munitions as well as iron bombs.

173. See, for example, Exon's statement at the first public B-2 hearing in June, 1989, in SASC, *DoD Authorization for Appropriations for FY1990 and 1991, Part 6* (Washington: GPO, Doc. No. S. Hrg. 101–251),p. 308, and his opposition to an amendment which would have deleted funding for the B-2 in 1992: *Congressional Record*, August 1, 1991, pp. S11669–73.

174. Letter from Sen. Daniel K. Inouye to Secretary of Defense Les Aspin, July 14, 1993, reproduced in *Inside the Air Force*, July 23, 1993, pp. 7–8.

175. Murtha ordered a CBO memorandum, which reported that a force of B-2s could replace part of the Navy's carrier-based attack aircraft, allowing the carrier force to be reduced from twelve to nine ships. See David Fulghum, "Congressional Report Says B-2 Could Absorb Part of Navy Attack Role," *Aviation Week and Space Technology*, October 14, 1991, p. 24, and CBO Staff Memorandum, *Using B-2 Bombers for Conventional Naval Missions*, September 1991.

176. See Ronald V. Dellums, "Preventive Engagement: Constructing Peace in a Post-Cold War World," *Harvard International Review*, Fall 1993, pp. 24–27.

177. See *Congressional Record*, September 18, 1990, pp. H7765–H7767; May 20, 1991, pp. H3243–H3245; June 5, 1992, pp. H4275–H4280; Sept. 8, 1993, pp. H6489–6493.

178. *Congressional Record*, September 18, 1990, p. H7762.

179. *Congressional Record*, September 18, 1990, pp. H7758–H7762.

180 *Congressional Record*, July 1, 1994, p. S8156.

181. The defense subcommittees of the House and Senate Appropriations Committees, and their chairmen, are also important in the process of building congressional consensus on defense decisions. While their power is theoretically equal to that of the Armed Services committees, these bodies historically have not taken the lead in addressing the annual defense request. Rather, these committees usually confer and bargain with the Armed Services committees in advance of release of authorization recommendations. Open disagreements between the authorizing and appropriating committees are seldom sharp.

182. Les Aspin, "Do We Need The B-2?" House floor statement, July 23, 1990 (mimeo).

183 *Congressional Record*, August 17, 1994, p. H8551.

184 *Congressional Record*, June 30, 1994, p. S8059.

185. Sam Nunn, "The Defense Department Must Thoroughly Overhaul the Services' Roles and Missions," *Congressional Record*, July 2, 1992, pp. S9559–S9565.

186. The other areas of apparent duplication listed by Nunn are: contingency or expeditionary ground forces; theater air defenses; space operations; helicopter forces; intelligence; functional organizations and activities; logistics and support

activities; administrative and management headquarters; and guard and reserve component forces. *Congressional Record*, July 2, 1992, pp. S9561.

187. Nunn in *Congressional Record*, July 2, 1992, p. S9561.
188. Nunn in *Congressional Record*, July 2, 1992, p. S9561.
189. HASC, *National Defense Authorization Act for Fiscal Year 1991*, p. 15.
190. SASC, *National Defense Authorization Act for Fiscal Year 1991*, pp. 68–69.
191. SASC, *National Authorization Act for Fiscal Years 1992 and 1993*, pp. 62–70.
192. SASC, *National Defense Authorization Act for Fiscal Years 1992 and 1993* (Washington, D.C.: GPO, 102nd Congress, 1st Session, Report 102–113), July 19, 1991, pp. 63–66.
193. *Ibid*, p. 62.
194. SASC, *National Defense Authorization Act for Fiscal Year 1993* (Washington, D.C.: GPO, 102nd Congress, 2nd Session, July 31, 1992, Report No. 102–352), p. 49. Congressman John Kasich indicated in a House floor statement that "the Senate," at the time Secretary Cheney offered to terminate the B-2 program at 20 (December 1991), wanted to procure "well over 40" B-2 bombers. *Congressional Record*, June 5, 1992, p. H4291.

195 An amendment to the FY 1994 Defense Authorization bill was introduced by Senators Pat Leahy of Vermont and James Sasser of Tennessee, capping the B-2 force at 20, was passed by the Senate with the acquiescence of Senator Nunn. Nunn did not debate the amendment, as it corresponded with the Clinton Administration's position on the issue. Nunn called for "thorough deliberation and debate" in the future on enlarging the B-2 force. *Congressional Record*, September 10, 1993, pp. S11398-S11400.

196. SASC, *National Defense Authorization Act for Fiscal Year 1994* (Washington: GPO, Document No. 103–112), pp. 33–39. With regard to the B-1B, Senator Nunn is quoted, in *Air Force Times*, as saying: "The biggest problem with the B-1 is it blocked the number of B-2s we desperately need as we try to project power in the world." Steven Watkins, "The B-1 Blunder: How the Service is Undermining its Bomber Force, February 21, 1994, p. 10; reproduced in *Current News Supplement*, February 15, 1994, pp. A1–A2.

197. *National Defense Authorization Act for Fiscal Year 1994* (Public Law 103–160, November 30, 1993 (107 Stat. 1547), Section 132.

198 See *Congressional Record*, June 22, 1994, pp. S7422-S7424; June 30, 1994, pp. S8057, S8059-S8071; July 1, 1994, pp. S8140-S8148, S8156.

199 *Congressional Record*, August 17, 1994, pp. H8548-H8549; H8553-H8554; H8557-H8558; H8561-H8563; September 26, 1994, pp. H9636-H9637; September 29, 1994, pp. H10261-H10266.

200. Aspin, "An Approach to Sizing American Conventional Forces For the Post-Soviet Era: Four Illustrative Options," February 25, 1992 (mimeo), pp. 25–26.

201. Aspin, "Force Structure Excerpts: Bottom-Up Review," September 1, 1993 (mimeo), p. 5.

202. Aspin, "Force Structure Excerpts," p. 10.

203. Also included in the MRC building block are 4-5 Army Divisions, 4-5 Marine Expeditionary Brigades, 10 Air Force fighter wings, 4-5 Navy aircraft carrier battle groups, and special operations forces. Aspin, "Force Structure Excerpts," p. 10.

204. Aspin, "Force Structure Excerpts," p. 10.

205. Aspin, "The Military Option: The Conduct and Consequences of War in the Persian Gulf," January 8, 1991 (mimeo), p. 23.

206. Les Aspin and William Dickinson, *Defense for a New Era: Lessons of the Persian Gulf War* (Washington, D.C.: GPO, 1992), p.7.

207. Aspin, "Force Structure Excerpts," pp. 7–8.

208. Aspin, "Excerpts," p. 8.

209. Aspin, "Excerpts," p. 7.

210. Aspin, "Excerpts," pp. 11, 17.

211. Les Aspin, Press Conference in connection with the Bottom-Up Review, September 1, 1993 (mimeo), p. 15. The figure for submarines in 1999 is from Les Aspin, *Annual Report to the President and the Congress, 1994* (Washington, D.C.: GPO, 1994), pp. 27, 169.

212. Les Aspin and General Colin Powell, USA, Chairman of the Joint Chiefs of Staff, "Bottom-Up Review," Briefing (mimeo), 1 September, 1993, slide (p.) 39, "Bottom-Up Review: What Does it Change?".

213. U. S. Congress, House, Committee on Appropriations, Subcommittee on Defense, *Department of Defense Appropriations Hearings*, Part 4, pp. 60, 63.

214. Aspin and Powell, "Bottom-Up Review," September 1, 1993 (mimeo), slide (p.) 19, "Bottom-Up Review: Modernization."

215. "Pentagon's Plan for Bombers, MILSTAR may be Wrong, Perry Says," *Defense Daily*, March 10, 1994, p. 363; reproduced in *Current News*, March 10, 1994, p. 6; *Inside the Air Force* and "Loh Asks Northrop for Cost Estimate of Keeping B-2 Line Open," December 24, 1993, pp. 7–8.

216. McPeak said: "We're simply trying to configure the bomber force to operate very economically for the next six or seven years. At the end of the decade...we will consider bringing [more B-1s] back in if we want to plus up the bomber force[.]" David A. Fulghum, "Lawmakers Criticize USAF Budget Priorities," *Aviation Week & Space Technology*, March 7, 1994, p. 24.

217. Steven Watkins, "The B-1 Blunder: How the Service is Undermining its Bomber Force," *Air Force Times*, February 21, 1994, p.10; reproduced in *Current News Supplement*, February 15, 1994, pp. A1–A3.

218. David Fulghum, "Lawmakers Criticize USAF Budget Priorities," *Aviation Week & Space Technology*, March 7, 1994, p. 24.

219. "Pentagon's Plan for Bombers, MILSTAR May Be Wrong," *Defense Daily*, March 10, 1994, p. 363; reproduced in *Current News*, March 10, 1994, p. 6.

220 *Congressional Record*, August 11, 1994, p. S11300.

221. SASC, Authorization for Appropriations for Fiscal Year 1994 and the future years Defense Program (Washington: GPO, S. Hrg. 103-303, Part 7), p. 499.

222. Ed Offey, "Showdown Ahead on B-2 Production," *Seattle Post-Intelligencer*, February 16, 1994, p. 3; reproduced in *Current News*, February 16, 1994, p. 4.

223. Stevens in 1994 joined Senators Thurmond and Inouye in voting against an attempt to delete the $150 million to maintain B-2 industrial capacity which had been added to the Authorization bill by Senator Nunn and the SASC (the vote was 55-45); Representatives Young and Murtha, along with 209 colleagues signed the letter orchestrated by Representative Norman Dicks, urging Rep. Dellums to allow the House-Senate conference to keep the $150 million in the Authorization Act.

224. "Perry: Higher B-2 Buy 'Not Appropriate' Unless Threat Emerges," *Inside the Air Force*, February 4, 1994, p. 1.

225 Thomas E. Ricks and Jeff Cole, "Perry Opposes Renewing Work on Stealth Jet," *Wall Street Journal*, November 4, 1994, pp. A3-A4.

226 Secretary of Defense William Perry, quoted in *Congressional Record*, July 1, 1994, p. S8146.

227 See Glenn C. Buchan and David R. Frelinger, "Providing an Effective Bomber Force for the Future," prepared statement submitted to the Senate Armed Services Committee, May 5, 1994 (mimeo), pp. 29-30.

228 Maj. Gen. jasper Welch, USAF (ret.), "Bomber Forces for 'Cold Start' Conflict," *Air Force Magazine*, December 1994, pp. 30-39, esp. pp. 37, (table 9) 39 (table 11). In fighting a single major regional contingency, the B-2-heavy force costs $11 to $24 billion less than the Administration's B-52/B-1-dominated force.

229 Statement by John Deutch in response to a question, in Deutch, "DoD News Briefing: Presidential Defense Funding Initiative" (mimeo), December 1, 1994, p. 7.

230 William Myers, memorandum to Bruce MacDonald, Staff Member, House Committee on Armed Services, August 3, 1994 (mimeo), 5 pp.

231 "What 20 More B-2 Bombers Will Really Cost," *Defense Week*, December 12, 1994, pp. 14-15.

232 "TSSAM troubles could lead to further B-2 production," *Aerospace Daily*, March 15, 1994.

233 Stephen Daggett and Keith Berner, "Items in the Department of Defense budget that may not be directly related to traditional military capabilities," memo to Congress, March 21, 1994, p. CRS-7.

234. Philip Finnegan, "Republicans Eye Conversion, Peacekeeping Cuts," *Defense News*, November 14-20, 1994, pp. 1, 18.

235   Deputy Secretary of Defense John Deutch, "News briefing on the Presidential Defense Funding Initiative" (mimeo), December 1, 1994, p. 3.
236   House Republican Conference, *Legislative Digest*, September 27, 1994, p. 27.
237   House Republican Conference, *Legislative Digest*, September 27, 1994, p. 25.
238   See *Congressional Record*, September 18, 1990, p. H7760, and May 21, 1991, p. H3291.
239   *Congressional Record*, May 21, 1991, p. H3292.
240. Air Force Secretary Donald Rice asserted that the force of 20 B-2s represented a worthwhile and useful capability. However, he did say: "Do we wish we could have more? Sure we do." and "[the decision to terminate B-2 at 20] was not pure budget. We took capabilities into account. But, certainly, the budget played very strongly in the decision." Donald Rice, testimony in U.S. Congress, Senate, Committee on Armed Services, *Department of Defense Authorization for Appropriations for Fiscal Year 1993 and the Future Years Defense Program* (Washington, D.C.: GPO, Doc. No. S. Hrg. 102-833, Part 1) p. 792.
241. See National Security Research, Inc., *Aerospace Forces and U.S. Security: The Next Quarter-Century*, draft report prepared for Directorate of Plans, Headquarters, United States Air Force (Fairfax, VA: National Security Research, Inc., June 21, 1993).
242. The views of the Russian military regarding the implications of the Desert Storm air campaign are summarized in Mary C. FitzGerald, "Russia's New Military Doctrine," *Naval War College Review*, Vol. XLVI, No. 2 (Spring 1993), pp. 24-44.
243. The two lower ratings are "weak" and "losing badly/lost." See chart produced by the Office of Sen. Jeff Bingaman, based on the National Critical Technologies Report, and critical technologies reports prepared by the Department of Defense, the Department of Commerce, and the Council on Competitiveness, in Senate Armed Services Committee, Hearings, *Department of Defense Authorization for Appropriations for Fiscal Years 1992 and 1993* (Washington, DC: GPO, 1991, Doc. No. S. Hrg. 102-255, Part 5), pp. 107-111.
244. HASC, *National Defense Authorization Act for Fiscal Year 1995* (Washington: GPO, May 10, 1994, Report 103-499), p. 52; SASC, *National Defense Authorization Act for Fiscal Year 1995* (Washington: GPO, June 14, 1994, Report 103-282), p. 38.
245. Statement of Secretary of Defense William Perry before the House Budget Committee, in connection with the Fiscal Year 1995 Budget for the Department of Defense (mimeo), February 23, 1994, Chart 13.
246. Department of Defense, Office of the Comptroller, *National Defense Budget Estimates for FY 1994*, May 1993, table 7-8, pp. 140-141.

247. Secretary of Defense William J. Perry, Keynote Address, in *Shrinking the Defense Infrastructure*, Conference Report for 1993 Center for Naval Analyses Annual Conference (Alexandria, VA: Center for Naval Analyses, 1993), p. 11.

248. Bruce A. Smith, "U.S. Firms Face Long Adjustment," *Aviation Week & Space Technology*, March 15, 1993, p. 48; Richard Hardy, Vice President, General Manager, Military Airplanes Division, Boeing Defense and Space Group, "The Industrial Base and the Future of U.S. Aerospace Power," in National Security Research, Inc., *The Role of Aerospace Power in U.S. National Security in the Next Quarter Century*, proceedings of a conference sponsored by the Directorate of Plans, Headquarters, U.S. Air Force, March 16, 1993 (Fairfax, VA: National Security Research, Inc., April 16, 1993), p. A-41.

249. Norman R. Augustine, Chairman and Chief Executive Officer, Martin Marietta Corporation, in House Armed Services Committee, Hearings, *National Defense Authorization Act for Fiscal Year 1993—H.R. 5006* (Washington, DC: GPO, 1992, Doc. No. H.A.S.C. 102-42), p. 355.

250. Perry, in *ibid.*, pp. 364-365. Note that Perry expressed these views before assuming his present position in the Department of Defense.

251. Secretary of Defense Les Aspin, "Bottom-Up Review," news briefing, The Pentagon, September 1, 1993 (transcript provided by the office of the Assistant Secretary of Defense for Public Affairs), p. 15; Deputy Secretary of Defense William J. Perry, "U.S. Military Acquisition Policy," address to the Conference on U.S. and Russian Military Technical Policy, sponsored by the Department of State and the National Defense University (mimeo), September 28, 1993.

252. Department of the Air Force, *Bomber Modernization: Deterrence at the Crossroads* (Washington, DC: Department of the Air Force, June 1990).

253. Northrop Corporation, "The B-2 Assembly Story," *B-2 Stealth Bomber 1994 Factbook*, March 28, 1994, pp. 5-6.

254. Lt Gen Stephen B. Croker, USAF, Speech to the American Institute of Aeronautics and Astronautics Annual Meeting, Washington, DC (mimeo), May 4, 1993, p. 6.

255. Department of Defense, *Critical Technologies Plan*, Report for the Committees on Armed Services of the United States Congress (Washington, DC: Department of Defense, May 1991), p. 10-3.

256. Les Aspin, "Tomorrow's Defense From Today's Industrial Base: Finding the Right Resource Strategy for a New Era," address before the American Defense Preparedness Association, February 12, 1992 (mimeo); Aspin, *Finding the Right Resource Strategy for a New Era*, report issued February 11, 1993.

257. John D. Morrocco, "'Silver Bullet' Option Eyed for F-22, SSF," *Aviation Week & Space Technology*, May 31, 1993, p. 20; Anthony L. Velocci, Jr., "Fewer Players to See Late-Decade Upturn," *Aviation Week & Space Technology*, March 15, 1993, p. 45.

258. Croker, Speech to the American Institute of Aeronautics and Astronautics Annual Meeting, pp. 3–7.

259. Some of the analysis that follows is based on National Security Research, *The Logic of Bomber Force Numbers* (Fairfax, VA: NSR, April 1992), Appendix.

260. General Accounting Office (GAO), *B-2 Bomber: Acquisition Cost Estimates*, NSIAD-93-48BR (Washington, DC: GAO, February 1993), p. 2.

261. GAO, *B-2 Bomber: Acquisition Cost Estimates*, p. 6.

262. Jeff Ethell and Joe Christy, *B-52 Stratofortress* (New York: Charles Scribner's Sons, 1981), p. 99.

263. Senate Armed Services Committee, Hearings, *Department of Defense Authorization for Appropriations for Fiscal Year 1993 and the Future Years Defense Program* (Washington, DC: GPO, Doc. No. S. Hrg. 102–833, Part 2, 1992), p. 791.

264. Remarks made by Ralph Crosby of Northrop Corporation at the naming ceremony for the B-2 bomber *Spirit of California*, March 31, 1994. This estimate is expressed in then-year, rather than constant, dollars.

265. It should be noted that prior to the end of B-52 production in 1962, 116 B-58 bombers also were built.

266. Quoted in Barbara Opall, "Loh: Industrial Base To Guide AF Weapon Plans, *Defense News*, February 8–14, 1993, p. 6.

267. Croker, p. 6; John D. Morrocco, "JSSA Surprise Entry in Pentagon Review," *Aviation Week & Space Technology*, May 10, 1993, p. 21.

268. John D. Morrocco, "USAF Aim: Lean Production," *Aviation Week & Space Technology*, May 24, 1993, pp. 23–24.

269. Bob Bott and Tom Goldwyn, McDonnell Douglas, "F-15 Lean Manufacturing Initiatives," briefing to National Security Research staff, May 5, 1993.

270. Aspin, "Tomorrow's Defense from Today's Industrial Base," p. 16.

271. Aspin, *Ibid*, pp. 15 and 16.

272. Northrop Corporation, "The B-2 Works," *B-2 Stealth Bomber Fact Book*, November 1992. See also Northrop, "B-2 Test Status," *B-2 Stealth Bomber 1994 Factbook*.

273. Secretary of Defense Dick Cheney, "Statement before the House Budget Committee in Connection with the FY 1993 Budget for the Department of Defense" (mimeo), February 5, 1992, p. 32.

274. Aspin, "The B-2 Stealth Bomber: How Many and for What," address before the Electronic Industries Association (mimeo), July 11, 1991, pp. 4–6. See also Bottom-Up Review News Briefing, p. 20.

275. National Aeronautic Association, News Release, February 27, 1992.

276. Trevor N. Dupuy, ed. *International Military and Defense Encyclopedia* (Washington, D.C.: Brassey's Inc., 1993), Vol. 5, "Stealth and Counterstealth Technology" by Jay H. Goldberg, p. 2544.

277. This reduced profile while surfaced has at times been employed to great tactical advantage. During the early years of U.S. involvement in World War II, for example, German submarines operating along the U. S. Atlantic Coast often hunted shipping at night while surfaced. They were able to see target shipping in silhouette against the lights of coastal towns and even engage them with gunfire, saving scarce torpedoes. The crews of the target vessels could not see the surfaced submarines early enough to respond effectively.

278. Rowan Scarborough, "Report on Failure Versus Scuds Sounds Warning for U.S.," *Washington Times*, May 7, 1993, p, A9.

279. Jeff Ethell and Joe Christy, *B-52 Stratofortress* (New York: Charles Scribner's Sons, 1981), p. 68.

280. Secretary of the Air Force Donald B. Rice in U.S. Congress, Senate, Committee on Armed Services, *Department of Defense Authorization for Appropriations for Fiscal Years 1992 and 1993: Strategic Forces and Nuclear Deterrence: Hearings* (Washington: GPO, 1991 Doc. No. S. Hrg. 102–255, Part 7), April 23, 1991 through June 20, 1991, p. 839.

281. Ethell and Christy, p. 92.

282. Marcelle Size Knaack, *Encyclopedia of U.S. Air Force Aircraft and Missile Systems, Vol. II: Post-World War II Bombers* (Washington, D.C.: Office of Air Force History, 1988), pp. 258, 269, 279.

283. *Ibid*.

284. Jeffrey S. Underwood, *The Wings of Democracy: The Influence of Air Power on the Roosevelt Administration, 1933-1941* (College Station, TX: Texas A&M Press, 1991), p. 180.

285. Underwood, p. 183.

286. Les Aspin, "Briefing and Press Conference on the Bottom-Up Review," (mimeo), September 1, 1993, p. 2.

287. Aspin, "Briefing on the Bottom-Up Review," p. 2.

288. Les Aspin, "Force Structure Excerpts—Bottom-Up Review," (mimeo), September 1, 1993, p. 16.

289. General of the Army Ivan Moiseyevich Tretyak interviewed by Editor Colonel V. P. Chigak, "Defense Sufficiency and Air Defense, *Voyennaya Mysl*, December 1990, pp. 2–11; reported in FBIS, JPRS-UMT-91-004-L, May 30, 1991, p. 2.

290. Candidate of Technical Services N. Novichkov and L. Galin, "Suppression of Iraqi Air Defenses in Operation 'Desert Storm'," *Zarubezhnoye Voyennoye Obozreniye*, September 1991, pp. 29–33; reported in FBIS, JPRS-UFM-92-006-L, May 14, 1992, p. 13.

291. Lieutenant Colonel A. Ya. Manachinskiy, Lieutenant Colonel V. N. Chumak, and Colonel (Ret.) Ye. K. Pronkin, "Operation Desert Storm: Results and Consequences," *Voyennaya Mysyl*, January 1992, pp. 88–92; reported in FBIS, JPRS-92-UMT-006-L, May 14, 1992, p. 49.

292. Lt. Gen. Charles A. Horner, Commander, U.S. Central Command Air Forces, and Brig. Gen. Buster C. Glosson, Director of Campaign Plans, U.S. Central Command Air Forces, prepared statement in House Appropriations Committee, Hearings, *Department of Defense Appropriations for 1992, Part 5* (Washington, DC: GPO, 1991), p. 469.

293. Although designated a "fighter," the F-117A (like the F-111) actually is a medium-range bomber.

294. Eliot A. Cohen, Director, Gulf War Air Power Survey (GWAPS), *A GWAPS Primer*, April 19, 1993, p. 6.

295. Department of the Air Force, *Reaching Globally, Reaching Powerfully: The United States Air Force in the Gulf War* (Washington, DC: Department of the Air Force, September 1991), pp. 56–57.

296. Department of Defense, *Conduct of the Persian Gulf War, Final Report to Congress* (Washington, DC: GPO, April 1992), pp. 150, 675, 676.

297. Strategic Air Command analysis, cited by Secretary of the Air Force Donald Rice in written response to question submitted by Sen. J. James Exon, in Senate Armed Services Committee, Hearings, *Department of Defense Authorization for Appropriations for Fiscal Years 1992 and 1993, Part 7* (Washington: GPO, Document No. S. Hrg. 102–255), p. 839.

298. It should be noted, however, that the original specifications for the B-2 did require the bomber to ". . .provide the capability to conduct missions across the spectrum of conflict, including general nuclear war . . . nuclear engagements less than general war, conventional conflict, and peacetime crisis situations." See B-2 Weapon System Specification, November 21, 1981. In Northrop Corporation, "The Mission of the B-2," *B-2 Stealth Bomber 1994 Factbook*, March 28, 1994.

299. Secretary of Defense Dick Cheney, written response to question submitted by Sen. Daniel Inouye, in Senate Appropriations Committee, Hearings, *Department of Defense Appropriations for Fiscal Year 1993, Part 4*, 102nd Cong., 2nd sess. (Washington, DC: GPO, 1993), p. 408; General Accounting Office, *Strategic Bombers: Adding Conventional Capabilities Will Be Complex, Time-Consuming, and Costly*, GAO/NSIAD-93-45 (Washington, DC: GPO, February 1993), p. 28; Office of Public Affairs, Office of the Secretary of the Air Force (SAF/PA), Fact Sheet: Tri-Service Standoff Attack Missile (TSSAM), June 1991; SAF/PA, information on GATS/GAM weapon, October 6, 1993.

300. Bill Sweetman, *Northrop B-2 Stealth Bomber: The Complete History, Technology, and Operational Development of the Stealth Bomber* (Osceola, WI: Motorbooks International, 1992), p. 95.

301. Pete Williams, Assistant Secretary of Defense for Public Affairs, news briefing, January 16, 1992, OSD/PA transcript, pp. 4–5; Richard P. Hallion, *Storm Over Iraq: Air Power and the Gulf War* (Washington, D.C.: Smithsonian Institution Press, 1992), p. 171.

302. Office of the Chief of Naval Operations, *The United States Navy in 'Desert Shield'/'Desert Storm'* (Washington, D.C.: Department of the Navy, May 15, 1991), pp. A-2, A-3, A-7. It should be pointed out that at the time Iraq invaded Kuwait, one carrier battle group led by the *USS Eisenhower* was forward deployed in the central Mediterranean, while another, led by the *USS Independence*, was stationed in the Indian Ocean near Diego Garcia. *Ibid.*, p. 11. When forward deployment of surface forces is possible, the speed advantage of air power is diminished.

303. Aspin, "Force Structure Excerpts—Bottom-Up Review" (mimeo), September 1, 1993, p. 8.

304. Department of the Air Force, *Bomber Modernization: Deterrence at the Crossroads* (unclassified briefing, Washington, DC: Department of the Air Force, June 1990); Gen. Larry D. Welch, Chief of Staff of the Air Force, in Senate Armed Services Committee, Hearings, *Department of Defense Authorization for Appropriations for Fiscal Year 1991, Part 7*, 101st Cong., 2nd sess. (Washington, DC: GPO, 1990), p. 404.

305. DoD, *Conduct of the Persian Gulf War*, pp. 164, 702–703.

306. *Ibid.*, p. 676. On the importance of support forces for B-52 missions in the Linebacker operations against North Vietnam, see Karl J. Eschmann, *Linebacker: The Untold Story of the Air Raids Over North Vietnam* (New York: Ballantine Books, 1989).

307. U.S. Congress, House, Committee on Appropriations (HAC), Hearings, *Department of Defense Appropriations for 1992, Part 5* (Washington: GPO, 1991), p. 473.

308. Jasper Welch, "Assessing the Value of Stealthy Aircraft and Cruise Missiles," *International Security*, Vol. 14, No. 2 (Fall 1989), p. 53.

309. With regard to the last point, another example from the Gulf War illustrates how the tactical surprise provided by stealth can increase target vulnerability. During the first week of Desert Storm, a large strike package with 56 nonstealthy F-16s attacked the Baghdad Nuclear Research Center. That daylight raid, the largest of the war, was unsuccessful. Lack of surprise was one of the reasons for the poor results. According to the commander of U.S. air forces in the conflict, "when the first airplanes rolled in, [the Iraqis] started up these smoke pots they had on the [berm] around the [facility] and within seconds the whole target was covered with smoke and that contributed to the inaccuracy of the F-16 bombing." A few days later, four F-117As returned to the target at night, caught the enemy unawares, and destroyed three out of four nuclear reactors. HAC, *Department of Defense Appropriations for 1992, Part 5*, pp. 461, 486, 490; DoD, *Conduct of the Persian Gulf War*, p. 697.

310. DoD, *Conduct of the Persian Gulf War*, p. 12.

311. Rear Adm. Edward D. Sheafer, Jr., Director of Naval Intelligence, Statement on Intelligence Issues before the Seapower, Strategic, and Critical

Materials Subcommittee of the House Armed Services Committee (mimeo), February 5, 1992, pp. 67–68.

312. Sweetman, *Northrop B-2 Stealth Bomber*, pp. 61–63, 95 (quotation is from p. 63). See also Jay Miller, *Northrop B-2 Stealth Bomber*, Aerofax Extra 4 (Stillwater, MN: Specialty Press, 1991), pp. 26, 42.

313. Oliver C. Boileau, Jr., "B-2 Stealth Bomber," The Royal Aeronautical Society's 37th R.J. Mitchell Lecture, Southhampton, England, March 1993 (transcript), p. 5.

314. Eric Smith, "Pentagon to Cut $7.7 Billion in New Weapons Programe," *The New York Times*, December 10, 1994, p. 11.

315. Information on the JDAM I and III is drawn from Department of the Air Force, *Enhancing the Nation's Conventional Bomber Force: The Bomber Roadmap* (Washington, D.C.: Department of the Air Force, June 1992), pp. 6, 12; Air Combat Command, "Air-To-Surface Munitions Requirements," briefing presented at the Air Combat Command Requirements Conference hosted by the National Security Industrial Association, November 4–6, 1992; General Accounting Office, *Strategic Bombers: Adding Conventional Capabilities Will Be Complex, Time-Consuming, and Costly*, GAO/NSIAD-93-45 (Washington, D.C.: GAO, February 1993), pp. 29–31, 38–39.

316. Northrop Corporation B-2 Division, *B-2 GATS/GAM: A Total Weapon System Approach to Seekerless Precision* (Pico Rivera, CA: Northrop Corporation, January 12, 1993).

317. This description of the TSSAM is based on information in an Office of Public Affairs, Office of the Secretary of the Air Force, Fact Sheet: "Tri-Service Standoff Attack Missile (TSSAM)," June 1991 and Memorandum for Correspondents No. 278-M, June 6, 1991; *Enhancing the Nation's Conventional Bomber Force*, pp. 6, 12; Secretary of Defense Dick Cheney, written response to question submitted by Sen. Daniel Inouye, in Senate Appropriations Committee, Hearings, *Department of Defense Appropriations for Fiscal Year 1993, Part 4* (Washington, D.C.: GPO, 1993), p. 419; Pete Williams, Assistant Secretary of Defense for Public Affairs, quoted in Barton Gellman, "Pentagon Unveils a Stealthy Cruise Missile," *Washington Post*, June 7, 1991, p. A8.

318. *Aerospace Daily*, March 15, 1994, p. 400.

319. See, for example, the reports quoted in Hallion, pp. 197–200.

320. DoD, *Conduct of the Persian Gulf War*, p. 116.

321. On Coalition measures to limit collateral damage, see ibid., pp. 98–99, 611–612. The estimate of civilian fatalities is taken from John G. Heidenrich, "The Gulf War: How Many Iraqis Died?" *Foreign Policy*, No. 90 (Spring 1993), pp. 117–119. Perhaps a third of these fatalities was due to the destruction of a military command-and-control bunker that, unknown to strike planners, also sheltered the families of Iraqi officials.

322. See Conrad C. Crane, *Bombs, Cities, and Civilians: American Airpower Strategy in World War II* (Lawrence, KS: University Press of Kansas, 1993).
323. The raid against Libya is described in Brian L. Davis, *Qaddafi, Terrorism, and the Origins of the U.S. Attack on Libya* (New York: Praeger, 1990), pp. 133–143; "Attack on Terrorism," *Aviation Week & Space Technology*, April 21, 1986, pp. 18–25; Robert E. Venkus, *Raid on Qaddafi: The Untold Story of History's Longest Fighter Mission by the Pilot Who Directed It* (New York: St. Martin's Press, 1992); John F. Lehman, Jr., *Command of the Seas* (New York: Charles Scribner's Sons, 1988), pp. 371–375; William J. Crowe, Jr. (with David Chanoff), *The Line of Fire: From Washington to the Gulf, the Politics and Battles of the New Military* (New York: Simon & Shuster, 1993), pp. 132–145; Caspar W. Weinberger, *Fighting for Peace: Seven Critical Years in the Pentagon* (New York: Warner Books, Inc., 1990), pp. 187–200.
324. Davis, p. 169.
325. Department of the Air Force, *The B-2 in Perspective* (Washington, D.C.: Department of the Air Force, July 1989), Slide 11.
326. U.S. Air Force, *Bomber Modernization: Deterrence at the Crossroads*, Slide (p.) 20.
327. Crowe, p. 137.
328. Lehman, p. 373.
329. USAF, *Bomber Modernization*.
330. Crowe, p. 137; Weinberger, p. 189; "Attack on Terrorism," p. 22.
331. USAF, *Bomber Modernization*, p. 20.
332. Crowe, pp. 136–137.
333. Davis, pp. 85, 146; Reagan, *An American Life*, p. 518; Weinberger, *Fighting For Peace*, pp. 190, 191, 196, 200; Crowe, *Line of Fire*, p. 134.
334. USAF, *The B-2 in Perspective*, Slide 11; USAF, *Bomber Modernization*, p. 20. Tanker personnel are not considered "at risk."
335. Crowe, p. 135.
336. Davis, pp. 139–143; Lehman, p. 371.
337. Crowe, p. 134.
338. For accounts of the postwar raids on Iraq, see David A. Fulghum, "Allies Strike Iraq for Defying U.N.," *Aviation Week & Space Technology*," January 18, 1993, pp. 22–25; Barton Gellman and Ann Devroy, "U.S. Delivers Limited Air Strike on Iraq," *Washington Post*, January 14, 1993, pp. A1 & A18; David A. Fulgham, "Clashes With Iraq Continue After Week of Heavy Air Strikes" and "Pentagon Criticizes Air Strike on Iraq," *Aviation Week & Space Technology*, January 25, 1993, pp. 38, 42 & 47; Ann Devroy and Barton Gellman, "U.S. Attacks Industrial Site Near Baghdad," *Washington Post*, January 18, 1993, pp. A1 & A24.
339. See R. James Woolsey, Director of Central Intelligence, Statement before the Senate Governmental Affairs Committee (mimeo), February 24, 1993; Lawrence K. Gershwin, "Threats to U.S. Interests," *Comparative Strategy*, Vol. 12, No. 1

(January–March 1993), pp. 7–13. One public opinion survey found that almost 75 percent of those polled considered Third World nuclear weapons a "very" or "extremely" serious threat to U.S. security (only international drug trafficking ranked higher). Ninety percent of the respondents believed keeping nuclear weapons out of the hands of Third World countries and terrorists was "very" or "extremely" important. (See Americans Talk Security Project, *Nuclear War and Weapons*, Report No. 3 [Winchester, MA: Americans Talk Security, April 1990]).

340. Shlomo Nakdimon, *First Strike: The Exclusive Story of How Israel Foiled Iraq's Attempt to Get the Bomb* (New York: Summit Books, 1987).

341. Marc Trachtenberg, "A 'Wasting Asset': American Strategy and the Shifting Nuclear Balance, 1949–1954," *International Security*, Vol. 13, No. 3 (Winter 1988/89), pp. 5–11, 32–44.

342. Gordon H. Chang, *Friends and Enemies: The United States, China, and the Soviet Union, 1948–1972* (Stanford, CA: Stanford University Press, 1990), pp. 228–252.

343. Thomas C. Wiegele, *The Clandestine Building of Libya's Chemical Weapons Factory: A Study in International Collusion* (Carbondale, IL: Southern Illinois University Press, 1992), pp. 31, 46, 115.

344. See, for example, the statements by Congressman John Murtha (chairman of the defense subcommittee of the House Appropriations Committee), cited in David A. Fulghum, "Congress Grows More Critical of Budget Cuts," *Aviation Week & Space Technology*, March 22, 1993, p. 26. Recently, Secretary of Defense Perry addressed option of a military strike to disarm North Korea. Remarks by William Perry, Secretary of Defense, "Meet the Press," NBC News, memo transcript, April 3, 1994, p. 6.

345. Before the start of the Desert Storm air campaign, Iraq removed and hid equipment from its chemical and biological weapons facilities and Scud production complexes. Robert M. Gates, Director of Central Intelligence, Statement on "The Proliferation of Weapons of Mass Destruction and the Intelligence Community Response" before the House Committee on Banking, Finance, and Urban Affairs (mimeo), May 8, 1992, p. 8; DoD, *Conduct of the Persian Gulf War*, p. 156.

346. Harold P. Myers and Vincent C. Breslin, *Nighthawks Over Iraq: A Chronology of the F-117A Fighter in Operations Desert Shield and Desert Storm*, Special Study 37FW/HO-91-1 (Tonopah, NV: Office of History, Headquarters 37th Fighter Wing, January 9, 1992).

347. SASC, *Department of Defense Authorization for Appropriations for Fiscal Years 1992 and 1993, Part 7*, p. 798.

348. Tony Capaccio, "Computer Runs Honed Attacks On Nuclear, Chemical Sites," *Defense Week*, August 5, 1991, p. 3; DoD, *Conduct of the Persian Gulf War*, pp. 154–155.

349. DoD, *Conduct of the Persian Gulf War*, p. 159.

350. Eliot A. Cohen, "Highlights of the Gulf War Air Power Survey," briefing, The Pentagon, May 12, 1993 (briefing slides); Woolsey, "Statement before the Senate Governmental Affairs Committee," pp. 9–10.

351. See the discussions of the Advanced Research Project Agency's "War Breaker" program in William B. Scott, "DARPA System to Find, Kill Mobile Targets Quickly," *Aviation Week & Space Technology*, February 22, 1993, pp. 59 & 61; Scott, "War Breaker Program Explores New Sensor, Targeting Systems," *Aviation Week & Space Technology*, May 31, 1993, pp. 37–38; Scott, "War Breaker I&P Project Aims to Cut Strike Cycle Times," *Aviation Week & Space Technology*, June 7, 1993, pp. 151 & 153; Director of Defense Research and Engineering, *Defense Science and Technology Strategy* (Washington, D.C.: Department of Defense, July 1992), pp. II-15–II-23.

352. DoD, *Conduct of the Persian Gulf War*, pp. 33–39 (the quotation is from p. 34). The air power available at the time included land-based attack aviation (e.g., F-15Es, A-10s) and Navy and Marine air (A-6s, F/A-18s, AV-8Bs), as well as B-52G bombers.

353. Aspin, "Force Structure Excerpts—Bottom-Up Review," p. 10. See also Secretary of Defense Les Aspin and Gen. Colin Powell, Chairman of the Joint Chiefs of Staff, "Bottom-Up Review," news briefing, The Pentagon (transcript provided by the Office of the Assistant Secretary of Defense for Public Affairs), September 1, 1993, pp. 6–7, 19–20, and accompanying briefing slides.

354. Gen. Michael P.C. Carns, Vice Chief of Staff of the Air Force, written response to question asked by Sen. Sam Nunn, in Senate Armed Services Committee, Hearings, *Department of Defense Authorization for Appropriations for Fiscal Year 1993 and the Future Years Defense Program* (Washington, D.C.: GPO, 1992 Doc No. S. Hrg. 102-833, Part 4), p. 206.

355. Department of the Air Force, *Enhancing the Nation's Conventional Bomber Force: The Bomber Roadmap* (Washington, DC: Department of the Air Force, June 1992), p. 6; Gen. Michael P.C. Carns, Vice Chief of Staff of the Air Force, written response to question asked by Sen. Sam Nunn, in Senate Armed Services Committee, Hearings, *Department of Defense Authorization for Appropriations for Fiscal Year 1993 and the Future Years Defense Program, Part 4*, 102nd Cong., 2nd sess. (Washington, DC: GPO, 1992), pp. 206-208; Department of the Air Force, written response to question submitted by Sen. Ted Stevens, in Senate Appropriations Committee, Hearings, *Department of Defense Appropriations for Fiscal Year 1992, Part 3*, 102nd Cong., 1st sess. (Washington, DC: GPO, 1991), p. 907; Air Combat Command, "Strategic Attack/Interdiction," briefing presented at the Air Combat Command Requirements Conference hosted by the National Security Industrial Association, November 4-6, 1992.

356. David A. Perin, *A Comparison of Long-Range Bombers and Naval Forces*, CIM 204.90 (Alexandria, VA: Center for Naval Analyses, December 1991), p. 40.

357. See Christopher Bowie et al., *The New Calculus: Analyzing Airpower's Changing Role in Joint Theater Campaigns*, MR-149-AF (Santa Monica, CA: RAND Corp., 1993), pp. 54–56.

358. Jasper Welch, "Assessing the Value of Stealthy Aircraft and Cruise Missiles," *International Security*, Vol. 14, No. 2 (Fall 1989) p. 52.

359. Captain Charles R. Girvin III, "Twilight of the Supercarriers," *Proceedings*, July 1993, pp. 42, 43.

360. Benjamin F. Schemmer, "Six Navy Carriers Launch Only 17% of Attack Missions in Desert Storm," *Armed Forces Journal International*, January 1992, p. 12.

361. Glenn W. Goodman, Jr., "USAF's Case for the B-2 Opens Pandora's Box for the Navy," *Armed Forces Journal International*, September 1991, p. 5.

362. Girvin, p. 44.

363. Girvin, p. 45.

364. Ronald O'Rourke, *The Cost of a U.S. Navy Aircraft Carrier Battlegroup*, (Washington, D.C.: Congressional Research Service, The Library of Congress, June 26, 1987), p. 9.

365. Deflator from FY88 to FY93 of 0.71 used to approximate guidance in Office of the Comptroller, The Department of Defense, *National Defense Budget Estimates for FY1993* (Washington, D.C.: Office of the Department of Defense, March 1992), pp. 36–41.

366. Gus Von Wolffradt, *GAO CVBG Structure & Affordability Report Reviewed for BASB* (Pico Rivera, CA: B-2 Division, Northrop Corporation, May 1993), p. 6.

367. Aspin, "Force Structure Excerpts—Bottom-Up Review," p. 16.

368. General Accounting Office, *The Structure and Affordability of USN Carrier Battle Groups* (Washington, D.C.: The General Accounting Office, February 1993).

369. Von Wolffradt, p. 8.

370. Deflator from FY90 to FY93 of 0.90 used to approximate guidance. Department of Defense, Office of The Comptroller, *National Defense Budget Estimates for FY1993* (Washington, DoD, 1993), Table 5-1, p. 33.

371. Since the invention of the airplane, the cost of each generation of aircraft has greatly outpaced inflation. This is true for fighters, bombers, commercial airliners, and helicopters. Norman Augustine, in his book, *Augustine's Laws*, demonstrates that the cost of "high technology military hardware" has increased by a factor of four every 11 years. This "law" indicates that a new bomber would be considerably more costly than the B-2. Norman R. Augustine, *Augustine's Laws* (New York: Viking Penguin, 1986), pp. 108–114.

372. The Northrop Corporation, *B-2 Stealth Bomber Fact Book* (Pico Rivera, CA: Northrop, November), 1992, p. 5.

373. Northrop, *B-2 Stealth Bomber Fact Book*, p. 2.

374. *Ibid.*, p. 4.

Endnotes

375. Michael O. Levitate, "Industry Outlook," *Aviation Week and Space Technology*, January 11, 1993, p. 13.

376. Northrop, *B-2 Stealth Bomber Fact Book*, p. 3.

377. B-2 Test Program to Meet Fiscal 1993 Milestones," *Aviation Week and Space Technology*, February 15, 1993, p. 67.

378. David A. Fulghum, "TAC Orders Studies on Uses for 15 B-2s Despite Doubts on Small Fleet's Viability," *Aviation Week and Space Technology*, December 16/23, 1991, p. 23.

379. William B. Scott, "B-2 Reliability Focus Pays Early Dividends," *Aviation Week and Space Technology*, October 12, 1992, p. 52.

380. *Ibid.*, p. 53.

381. Aspin, "Force Structure Excerpts—Bottom-Up Review," pp. 1–2, 10, 11.

382. "Pentagon's Plan for Bombers, MILSTAR May be Wrong, Perry Says," *Defense Daily*, March 10, 1994, p. 363.

383. It is instructive to recall the case of Nazi Germany, which late in World War II, developed exceptionally capable new generations of weapons including the first operational jet fighters, cruise missiles, and first armed ballistic missiles. The direct military effect of these developments proved to be hardly more than a historical footnote because the numbers of the new weapons were too small to affect the outcome of the war.

384. Anthony L. Velocci, Jr., "Executives Blast Clinton Conversion Plan," *Aviation Week and Space Technology,* May 24, 1993, p. 27.

385. Michael R. Gordon, "Cuts Force Review of War Strategies," *New York Times*, May 30, 1993, p. 16.

386. John Lancaster, "Aspin Opts for Winning 2 Wars—Not 1 1/2—at Once," *Washington Post,* June 25, 1993, p. A6.

387. General John M. Loh, "Opening Statement on the Future of the Bomber Force for presentation to the Senate Committee on Armed Services, Subcommittee on Nuclear Deterrence, Arms Control and Defense Intelligence" (mimeo), June 29, 1993, p. 4.

388. Testimony of Secretary of Defense Richard Cheney in hearing on the Major Aircraft Review by the Department of Defense, in U.S Congress, Senate, Committee on Armed Services, hearings, *Department of Defense Authorization for Appropriations for Fiscal Year 1991* (Washington, GPO, Doc. No. S. Hrg. 101–986, pt. 1), pp. 776–777, 781–782.

389. Pentagon's Plan for Bomber, MILSTAR May be Wrong, Perry Says," *Defense Daily*, March 10, 1994, p. 363.

390. Croker, p. 2.

391. From discussion with Fred King of Northrop, June 1, 1994.

392. The projected retirement timing of the remaining B-52s and B-1Bs reflects the great uncertainty involved in foreseeing mechanical problems or abrupt maintenance cost growth that could accelerate retirement of both aircraft types well in

advance of optimistic official projections. Counting on even the 38-year service life that the B-52s will have in the year 2000 requires that the B-52 remain in service 50% longer than any other jet-powered combat aircraft in U.S. military history. Except for the B-52, the longest serving U.S. combat aircraft achieved a fleet-wide average age of 23 years. These were the very last special purpose F-4s (Wild Weasel and Reconnaissance models) shortly before their retirement. "The Active Duty Fleet," *Air Force Magazine*, May 1993, p. 44. It is worth noting that the only B-52 loss of the Gulf War involved a progressive failure related to the complexity of this aging and dated design.

About the Authors

John J. Kohout III is a Senior Analyst at the National Institute for Public Policy. He served as a B-52 Aircraft Commander, Bomb Wing Deputy Commander for Operations, and as both Director for Plans and Director of Programs at Headquarters, Strategic Air Command. Col. Kohout earned the *Diplôme de l'Institut* (M.A. equivalent) from *Institut d'Études Politiques* of the University of Paris; he is a graduate of the U.S. Air Force Academy.

Dr. Steven J. Lambakis is a Policy Analyst at the National Institute for Public Policy, where he specializes in issues of strategic force modernization, arms control, space, and special operations forces. He is author of *Winston Churchill, Architect of Peace: A Study of Statesmanship and the Cold War* (Greenwood Press, 1993). Dr. Lambakis Ph.D. is from The Catholic University of America.

Dr. Keith B. Payne is President of National Institute for Public Policy, and Adjunct Professor of International Relations at Georgetown University. He is a political scientist specializing in questions of strategic deterrence and defense, and weapons proliferation. He has authored, co-authored, or edited twelve books including *Proliferation, westliche Sicherheit and begrenzte Ranketenabwehr* (Report Verlag, 1992), and frequently testifies before congressional committees. Dr. Payne is Editor of the journal, *Comparative Strategy*, and holds a Ph.D. from the University of Southern California.

Dr. Colin S. Gray is Professor of International Politics at the University of Hull, United Kingdom. An internationally-known political scientist and thinker on issues of grand strategy, national security, warfare, and arms control, he was previously President of the National Institute for Public Policy, Director of National Security Studies and the Hudson Institute, Assistant Director of the International Institute for Strategic Studies, and a professor at several U.S. and Canadian Universities. His numerous books include *Weapons Don't Make War: Policy, Strategy, and Technology* (University Press of America, 1993). Dr. Gray holds a Ph.D. from Oxford University.

Bernard C. Victory is a Research Analyst at the National Institute for Public Policy. He specializes in strategic forces, arms control, weapons proliferation, and domestic politics. Mr. Victory was previously a researcher with the Congressional Library of Congress. He earned an M.A. from Columbia University.